Governing Finance

A VOLUME IN THE SERIES

Cornell Studies in Money

edited by Eric Helleiner and Jonathan Kirshner

A list of titles in this series is available at www.cornellpress.cornell.edu.

Governing Finance

East Asia's Adoption of International Standards

Andrew Walter

Cornell University Press
Ithaca and London

First published 2008 by Cornell University Press
Printed in the United States of America

Library of Congress Cataloging-in-Publication Data

Walter, Andrew.
Governing finance : East Asia's adoption of international standards / Andrew Walter.
p. cm. — (Cornell studies in money)
Includes bibliographical references and index.
ISBN 978-0-8014-4645-0 (cloth : alk. paper)
1. International financial reporting standards. 2. Financial institutions—Southeast Asia—State supervision. 3. Financial institutions—Korea (South)—State supervision. 4. Corporate governance—Southeast Asia. 5. Corporate goverance—Korea (South) 6. Accounting—Standards—Southeast Asia. 7. Accounting—Standards—Korea (South) I. Title. II. Series.

HG187.A789W34 2008
657'.83330218—dc22

2007029235

Cornell University Press strives to use environmentally responsible suppliers and materials to the fullest extent possible in the publishing of its books. Such materials include vegetable-based, low-VOC inks and acid-free papers that are recycled, totally chlorine-free, or partly composed of nonwood fibers. For further information, visit our website at www.cornellpress.cornell.edu.

Cloth printing 10 9 8 7 6 5 4 3 2 1

Contents

Figures

Tables

Acknowledgments

Thanks are due to various individuals and institutions who assisted in the research and preparation of this study: the staff at the Institute of Defence and Strategic Studies at NTU in Singapore where I spent a very enjoyable year as a visiting fellow, and Barry Desker and Yuen Foong Khong for encouraging me to apply for a fellowship there and for supporting my research; Yeeming Chong for her friendly and efficient assistance; the LSE for granting me a year's leave to conduct initial research over 2001–2; the Korea Foundation for inviting me to Korea in summer 2000 and for arranging a series of interviews; the Japan Foundation Endowment Committee for funding a research trip to Tokyo in 2002; my former and current research students, including Yong-Ki Kim, Thitinan Pongsudhirak, Wang-Hwi Lee, and Hyoung-kyu Chey, who helped to organize interviews in some countries and who responded to various requests for information; Hogi Hyun for his assistance and hospitality in various parts of the world; Leonard Sebastian and Devi Santi for helping to arrange interviews in Jakarta; Michael Wood for introductions in Asia; Jean-François Drolet and Oskar Tetzlaff for data collection; Vanessa West for editing the bibliography; Paula Durbin-Westby for preparing the index; and finally to the many interviewees in different countries who generously provided information and often further assistance to this project. Mark Thatcher made helpful comments upon the general argument and parts of the manuscript. Thitinan Pongsudhirak and Kheamasuda Reongvan both gave helpful comments on the Thailand chapter. Two anonymous reviewers provided extensive and constructive comments on the whole manuscript, prompting a fundamental restructuring and many alterations to details. Roger Haydon and the series editors at

Cornell provided a generous mixture of advice and encouragement at crucial points. Teresa Jesionowski and Herman Rapaport both provided many helpful suggestions on how to improve the final product. None of the above is in any way responsible for remaining errors. This book is dedicated to Nina and our wonderful children, Lara and Ben, and to my parents.

A.W.

Abbreviations

ADB	Asian Development Bank
ADR	American Depository Receipt
AMF	Asian Monetary Fund
APEC	Asia-Pacific Economic Cooperation
BAFIA	Banking and Financial Institutions Act (Malaysia)
BCBS	Basle Committee on Banking Supervision
BCP	Basle Core Principles for Banking Supervision
BFSR	Bank Financial Strength Ratings (Moody's Investor Services)
BIS	Bank for International Settlements
BI	Bank Indonesia
BNM	Bank Negara Malaysia
BOK	Bank of Korea
BOT	Bank of Thailand
CAMELS	Capital adequacy, Asset quality, Management, Earnings, Liquidity, and Sensitivity
CAR	Capital Adequacy Ratio
CCL	Contingent Credit Line (IMF)
CCS	Comprehensive Consolidated Supervision
CEO	Chief Executive Officer
CPSS	Committee on Payments and Settlements Systems
CDRC	Corporate Debt Restructuring Committee (Malaysia)
DCF	Discounted Cash Flow
DPM	Deputy Prime Minister
DR	Depository Receipt
DSBB	Dissemination Standards Bulletin Board (IMF)
DTA	Deferred Tax Asset

EMEPG	Emerging Market Eminent Persons Group
EPB	Economic Planning Board (Korea)
EPF	Employees Provident Fund (Malaysia)
ESOP	Employee Share Ownership Program
FATF	Financial Action Task Force
FDI	Foreign Direct Investment
FDIC	Federal Deposit Insurance Corporation (United States)
FIDF	Financial Institutions Development Fund (Thailand)
FHC	Financial Holding Company
FLC	Forward-Looking Criteria
FSA	Financial Services Authority (United Kingdom); Financial Services/Supervisory Agency (Japan)
FSAP	Financial Sector Assessment Program
FSC	Financial Supervisory Commission (Korea)
FSF	Financial Stability Forum
FSLIC	Federal Savings and Loans Insurance Corporation (United States)
FSS	Financial Supervisory Service (Korea)
FSSA	Financial System Stability Assessment
FY	Financial Year
G7	Group of Seven
G10	Group of Ten
G20	Group of Twenty
G22	Group of Twenty Two
GAAP	Generally Accepted Accounting Principles
GATT	General Agreement on Tariffs and Trade
GDDS	General Data Dissemination Standard
GLC	Government-Linked Company
GOI	Government of Indonesia
IAIS	International Association of Insurance Supervisors
IAS	International Accounting Standards
IASB	International Accounting Standards Board
IBRA	Indonesian Bank Restructuring Agency
ICGN	International Corporate Governance Association
IFAC	International Federation of Accountants
IFIs	International Financial Institutions
IFRS	International Financial Reporting Standards
IMF	International Monetary Fund
IMFC	International Monetary and Financial Committee (IMF)
IOD	Institute of Directors
IOSCO	International Organization of Securities Commissions
KASB	Korea Accounting Standards Board
KCCG	Korean Committee on Corporate Governance
KDB	Korea Development Bank
KDIC	Korea Deposit Insurance Corporation

KFAS	Korea Financial Accounting Standards
KFTC	Korea Fair Trade Commission
KLSE	Kuala Lumpur Stock Exchange
KSE	Korean Stock Exchange
LLL	Legal Lending Limit
LOI	Letter of Intent
MAS	Monetary Authority of Singapore
MASB	Malaysian Accounting Standards Board
MEFP	Memorandum of Economic and Financial Policies
MICG	Malaysian Institute of Corporate Governance
MITI	Ministry of International Trade and Industry (Japan)
MSE	Ministry of State-Owned Enterprises (Indonesia)
MOF	Ministry of Finance
MOFE	Ministry of Finance and the Economy (Korea)
NBFI	Non-Bank Financial Institution
NEAC	National Economic Action Council (Malaysia)
NEP	New Economic Policy (Malaysia)
NGO	Non-Governmental Organization
NOP	Net Open Position
NPL	Non-Performing Loan
NTA	Net Tangible Assets
NYSE	New York Stock Exchange
OBS	Office of Banking Supervision (Korea)
OECD	Organization for Economic Cooperation and Development
OFC	Offshore Financial Center
PCA	Prompt Corrective Action
PCG	Principles of Corporate Governance (OECD)
PPP	Purchasing Power Parity
PSPD	People's Solidarity for Participatory Democracy (Korea)
ROA	Return on Assets
ROCA	Risk management, Operational control, Compliance, and Asset quality
ROSC	Report on the Observance of Standards and Codes
ROE	Return on Equity
SC	Securities Commission (Malaysia)
SDDS	Special Data Dissemination Standard
SEC	Securities and Exchange Commission
SET	Stock Exchange of Thailand
SFC	Securities and Futures Commission (Korea)
SME	Small or Medium Enterprise
SOE	State-Owned Enterprise
TRIS	Thai Rating and Information Services Co.
UMNO	United Malays National Organisation
WTO	World Trade Organization

Governing Finance

Introduction

International Standards and Financial Governance

The financial contagion that spread from Thailand in mid-1997 to the rest of Asia and then on to Brazil, Russia, and finally to the developed world's financial centers was a major shock to the global economy. It was also a shock to global political elites and a watershed in the long-running debate about the need for reform of the global financial architecture. Faced with a crisis that destabilized some of the world's most rapidly growing countries, governments in the major developed countries responded by launching one of the most ambitious governance reform projects in living memory. Its main objective was to transform domestic financial governance in emerging market countries and, in particular, to eradicate the "cronyism, corruption, and nepotism" assumed to lie at the heart of Asia's (and by extension most of the developing world's) financial vulnerability.

The envisaged transformation was consistent with a new consensus in Western policymaking and academic circles. In promoting the adoption of "international best practice" standards of regulation, the reform project advocated a transition from a relational, discretionary approach to regulation to a more arm's-length, nondiscretionary approach. Others have summarized this as a transition from a "developmental" state toward a neoliberal "regulatory" state (e.g., Jayasuriya 2005).[1] A key characteristic of "regulatory neoliberalism," best seen as an ideal type, is the delegation of regulation and enforcement to strong "independent" agencies. The act of delegation itself has become associated with international best practice as the preferred solution to time inconsistency and policy capture problems.[2] The model of regulatory neoliberalism suggests that the agencies that apply and enforce regulation should be technocratic, apolitical, and insulated from predatory vested interests. Once achieved for financial regulation, developing countries might more fully—and hopefully much more safely—participate in the global financial system.

How was such a convergence upon regulatory neoliberalism to be achieved? The governments of major countries saw the solution in the elaboration of best practice international standards of financial regulation and the promotion of developing country compliance with these standards. Compliance with international standards is different from the ideal type of regulatory neoliberalism, but it has been seen as the main means of bringing about convergence upon the latter. I argue that this approach has serious flaws. First, the international standard-setting process is inevitably politicized and often produces standards that are sometimes vague and at other times inappropriate to the circumstances of particular countries. Second, even when international standards do approach current "best practice," country compliance is often poor and the international mechanisms for promoting compliance are weak.

The focus of this book is primarily upon the latter problem. In particular, what determines the quality of compliance with international standards? And, related to this, why is poor quality compliance sustainable over time despite the apparently considerable pressure from multilateral institutions and capital markets to adopt international standards? At various points I discuss why some international standards are of poor quality or inappropriate for many developing countries, but my main focus is upon the compliance problem and the obstacle this places in the path of convergence upon regulatory neoliberalism.

The problem is not simply that regulatory neoliberalism is an ideal type that can never be fully realized in practice. Rather, I argue that the depth of the compliance problem reveals that the main sponsors of the international standards project misconstrued the politics of state transformation and so underestimated the possibility of reform failure. Behind the vision of encouraging a transition toward regulatory and institutional best practice is a strong presumption that Western rules and practices could be patched relatively easily onto developing political economies thereby de-politicizing financial regulation. In practice, however, we see a highly politicized reform process in which domestic groups that stand to lose from these reforms mobilize to block or to modify it. In some countries, and in some areas of regulation, these groups have successfully penetrated the new regulatory frameworks, with the result that the quality of compliance with international standards varies widely.

Low compliance with international standards does not always mean poor quality regulation (though it often does). In the more successful countries, political and economic elites have adapted international standards to suit local conditions. Notably, contrary to the prescriptions of regulatory neoliberalism, agency independence from government in East Asia and the transparency of political intervention are often low.[3]

I do not wish to imply that the goal of improving regulatory frameworks in developing countries is misguided. On the contrary, it is clearly in the interests of developing countries that improvements in financial governance are realized. In the East Asian context, the low priority afforded to prudential regulation in the past became very dangerous and threatened the viability of national development strategies. However, the idea that the creation of independent regulatory agencies, applying and enforcing Western-style standards, would be considered necessary and sufficient to achieve this objective was at best naive. In practice, it has sometimes simply allowed politicians and associated vested interests to pursue the form but not the substance of compliance.[4]

The argument has three general implications. First, both scholars and many proponents of international convergence have underestimated the often large gaps that can persist between formal rules and institutions, on the one hand, and actual policy and actor behavior, on the other. Second, developing countries have various ways of resisting international compliance and convergence pressures through what I call "mock compliance." In other words, there is more room for policy flexibility and divergence from regulatory neoliberalism than many assume. Third, the argument largely supports the view that domestic politics and institutions continue to be of great importance even in a policy area that is supposedly heavily constrained by financial globalization. The overall process is one of complex adaptation, not simple adoption.

The Approach of This Book

I proceed by asking three main questions. First, to what extent do Asian countries comply with international regulatory standards? Second, what explains compliance and noncompliance? Third, to what extent is noncompliance a sustainable strategy for developing countries and private sector actors?

To answer the first question, I investigate compliance with some of the most important international standards by the main crisis-hit countries of East Asia: Indonesia, Malaysia, South Korea, and Thailand. These were the prime targets of the international reform project and where regulatory failures were seen as endemic.[5] Furthermore, in the recent past these countries had enjoyed a reputation for good economic governance and successful reform (Haggard 1990; Haggard and Kaufman 1992, 1995; World Bank 1993). For these reasons, the East Asian countries are arguably the crucial test of the reform project and, perhaps, its best hope.

Indeed, for some international standards, East Asian countries have a good compliance record. The level and quality of compliance by Asian countries with the International Monetary Fund's (IMF) Special Data Dissemination Standard (SDDS), for example, is fairly high.[6] There was a delay between the onset of the crisis and East Asian compliance with SDDS, but these delays were not much worse than the G7 average (see table I.1).[7] Korea was only the tenth country to adhere to SDDS, putting it well ahead of most other OECD countries.

On the face of it, Asian countries have also done much to comply with other international standards, notably those in financial regulation and supervision, accounting, and corporate governance. However, as we will see, the quality of compliance in these areas is often less good than for SDDS, and sometimes it is quite low. To preview one example, a recent assessment of corporate governance in Asia came to the following conclusion:

> A few years ago regulators were praised for tightening up on rules and regulations; today it is apparent that many of these rules have only a limited effect on corporate behaviour. Where implemented, they are often not carried out effectively. (CLSA Emerging Markets 2005, 3)

TABLE I.1
SDDS subscription, posting, and compliance dates, selected countries and groups

	Date of subscription (1)	Date metadata were posted on the DSBB (2)	Date when subscriber met SDDS specifications (3)	3–1 (days)	3–2 (days)
Average all countries	20 April 1998	2 October 1998	30 March 2001	1,060	897
G7 average	5 July 1996	19 November 1996	3 January 2000	1,258	1,124
Indonesia	24 September 1996	21 May 1997	2 June 2000	1,328	1,091
Korea	20 September 1996	30 March 1998	1 November 1999	1,121	571
Malaysia	21 August 1996	19 September 1996	1 September 2000	1,450	1,422
Singapore	1 August 1996	19 September 1996	30 January 2001	1,619	1,571
Thailand	9 August 1996	19 September 1996	16 May 2000	1,357	1,317

Sources: IMF, DSBB: http://dsbb.imf.org/Applications/web/sddssubscriptiondates/ (accessed 22 June 2005).

Note: The average figure is for all 61 SDDS subscribers as of 22 June 2005.

If, as I argue, a similar story can be told with respect to financial supervision and accounting quality, what explains this variable compliance record with international standards (my second question)? I argue that a combination of external and domestic pressures have made it difficult for Asian governments to oppose compliance openly with these international standards. However, such compliance can be very costly for particular domestic interests that are often well organized and politically influential. Governments caught in between these contradictory pressures often opt for a strategy of mock compliance. This combines the rhetoric and outward appearance of compliance with international standards together with relatively hidden behavioral divergence from such standards.[8] The degree of mock compliance varies substantially across Asia and has been reduced over time in some areas, but its importance tends to be underestimated by those who focus on the compliance power of neoliberal ideas (Hall 2003) and of international institutions and markets (Ho 2001; Jayasuriya 2005; Pirie 2005; Simmons 2001; Soederberg 2003). This in turn suggests that some elements of developmental and predatory state behavior associated with pre-crisis East Asia persist, though now within an entirely new formal regulatory discourse. This argument is consistent with other literature that stresses the relative resilience of different varieties of capitalism.[9]

The third question asks why mock compliance might be a sustainable strategy over time. My answer is that mock compliance strategies are sustainable when it is very difficult or costly for outsiders to observe the true quality of compliance. When information about the actual behavior of regulatory agencies and of the companies they supervise is poor, mock compliance strategies can be sustainable because market actors and international institutions find it difficult to detect and to punish relatively poor quality compliance. I argue that this condition applies to the main international standards associated with financial regulation and much less to SDDS.

Methodology

The methodological approach adopted here requires some justification. As noted above, I mainly proceed via in-depth case studies in the main crisis-hit Asian countries. Since the quality of compliance with international standards varies considerably across these cases, this comparative approach should tell us much about the impact of domestic and international factors on compliance outcomes. I focus mainly on international standards for which private sector compliance costs and third party monitoring costs tend to be high: bank supervisory standards, corporate governance standards, and accounting standards. It is in these areas that I expect mock compliance strategies to be both more attractive and more sustainable. This contrasts with SDDS, for which private sector compliance costs are small or even negative and the ease of outsider monitoring is greater.

I investigate compliance in only one general policy area, financial regulation, for a number of reasons. This is primarily because, as noted above, financial regulation is the area in which post-crisis reform efforts have been concentrated. In addition, financial intervention was at the heart of the developmental state (Woo-Cumings 1991). Finance is also generally seen as central to the neoliberal model of economic governance and to the promotion of a modern capitalist economy (Mishkin 2001). Furthermore, many argue that the external forces that promote compliance with Western standards are especially strong in finance (e.g., Soederberg, Menz, and Cerny 2005). If compliance outcomes in this area diverge from international standards, it is likely that this will also be true for other areas of economic policy.

It is important to be clear about the compliance benchmark employed in the book. I argue that international financial standards have two main sources. The first source is standards issued by international standard-setting bodies, such as the Basle Committee for Banking Supervision (BCBS), the Organization for Economic Cooperation and Development (OECD), and the International Accounting Standards Board (IASB). The second source is national standard setting in the major Western countries, whose own rules and practices, as I argue in chapter 1, became strongly associated with regulatory neoliberalism and international best practice regulation from the 1990s. Using both sources as benchmarks for assessing compliance involves few difficulties for two main reasons. First, the United States and the United Kingdom have often dominated the standard-setting process in international organizations. Second, adopting countries themselves have tended to see the two sources as complementary, with international standards providing general principles and the major Western countries providing specific examples of applied rules and institutional forms.

I investigate compliance with international standards by considering compliance outcomes in the four different countries in detail. Qualitative country case studies of this kind can take advantage of the fact that for compliance, the devil is usually in the detail.[10] Rather than looking at compliance with each international standard in every country chapter, however, I adopt a graduated strategy aimed at reducing repetition and allowing greater empirical depth. Thus, in the first two empirical chapters (on Indonesia and Thailand), I assess compliance with international standards in banking regulation and corporate governance respectively. Having already introduced the issues involved, the subsequent chapter on Malaysia can more efficiently assess compliance in both areas. The final chapter on Korea widens the scope further by assessing compliance with banking regulation, corporate governance, and accounting standards.

The structure of the book is as follows. Chapter 1 outlines the origins of the international standards project in the Asian crisis of 1997–98, which helped both to define and to boost regulatory neoliberalism at a global level. Chapter 2 outlines in greater detail my theory of compliance and distinguishes it from its main competitors.

The empirical assessment of financial regulation in the crisis-hit countries begins with chapter 3, which evaluates compliance with international banking regulation and supervision standards[11] in Indonesia. Chapter 4 does the same for corporate governance standards in Thailand. In chapter 5, I evaluate compliance with international banking supervision and corporate governance standards in Malaysia. Chapter 6 extends the net wider in evaluating Korea's compliance with international banking supervision, corporate governance, and accounting standards.

Chapter 7 draws together the results of the four empirical chapters and assesses them in light of the theoretical framework offered here. I also discuss the implications of these findings for our understanding of convergence more generally, of the effects of compliance outcomes on the effectiveness of financial regulation in developing countries, and of the future of international financial reform. It is now a standard proposition that in order for countries to benefit from globalization, they must have appropriate domestic institutions (World Bank 2001). This book accepts that institutional reform is often necessary to achieve more effective financial regulation, but its findings suggest that focusing on compliance with current international standards may not always achieve this. The major Western countries have been far too confident of the superiority of their own regulatory frameworks and far too sanguine about their relevance for other countries.

1

The Asian Crisis and the International Financial Standards Project

This chapter explains the impact of the Asian crisis of 1997–98 on the international financial standards regime that emerged promptly on its heels. Although some international standards existed before 1997, the crisis played a key role in focusing international attention on financial supervision failures in major developing countries and in promoting the idea that the dissemination of and compliance with international best practice standards was the solution. Thus, the crisis was a crucial factor in the emergence of the international standards project. Part of the reason for this was that the crisis helped to entrench the intellectual dominance of a particular model of regulation, "regulatory neoliberalism," upon which many of these new international standards would be based.

The structure of the chapter is as follows. In the first section, I briefly outline what I mean by "the new international standards regime," as this term is not in standard usage in the literature. Although it is beyond the scope of this book to examine in detail the politics behind the emergence of each particular standard, I focus on the emergence of some of the international standards of most importance for this study: in the areas of banking regulation and supervision, corporate governance, and accounting. In the second section, I show how the Asian crisis helped both to promote the new international standards regime and the model of regulatory neoliberalism that underlies it. The third section concludes the discussion.

The New International Standards Regime

At the apex of the new international standards regime are the twelve "key standards for sound financial systems," a compendium of which is provided by the Financial Stability Forum (FSF).[1] Table 1.1 outlines these key standards, the international organization responsible for their issuance, and the date of promulgation.[2] As can be seen, the standards range from sectoral (e.g., banking) and functional (e.g., accounting) policy areas, to macroeconomic policy and data transparency. In many cases, the standards amount to general principles rather than detailed prescription, but sometimes these are supplemented by additional documents specifying in more detail their practical application and methodologies for assessment of compliance.

There are a number of things to note about this list. First, it reflects a general trend for key aspects of domestic economic regulation and governance to become matters of international negotiation. The key standards are intended to represent best practice principles for regulation and economic governance relevant to all countries. Second, most of the standards were issued after the Thai baht collapsed in July 1997, though some were under negotiation before the onset of the crisis. Some have since been modified and updated. Third, there is a wide range of international institutions responsible for their dissemination, including the major international financial institutions (IFIs) and other more specialized standard-setting bodies. Some, such as the International Accounting Standards Board (IASB)

TABLE 1.1
Financial stability forum: Twelve key standards for sound financial systems

Macroeconomic policy and data transparency	*Standard-setting body, date agreed*
Good practices on transparency in monetary and financial policies	IMF, 09/1999
Good practices in fiscal transparency	IMF, 04/1998
Special data dissemination standard	IMF, 03/1996
General data dissemination system	IMF, 12/1997
Institutional and market infrastructure	
Insolvency	World Bank, 01/2001
Principles of corporate governance	OECD, 05/1999; 04/2004
International accounting standards	IASB, 10/2002, ongoing
International standards on auditing	IFAC, 10/2002
Core principles for systemically important payment systems	CPSS, 01/2001
The Forty Recommendations of the Financial Action Task Force/The 8 Special Recommendations Against Terrorist Financing	FATF, 04/1990; 02/2002
Financial regulation and supervision	
Core principles for effective banking supervision	BCBS, 09/1997; 10/2006
Objectives and principles of securities regulation	IOSCO, 09/1998
Insurance core principles	IAIS, 09/1997; 10/2003

Source: http://www.fsforum.org/compendium/key_standards_for_sound_financial_system.html (accessed 23 October 2006). See the Appendix for a brief description of the standards and standard-setters.

and the International Federation of Accountants (IFAC), are private sector organizations, but in this case they have received a stamp of approval from the G7 countries. In general, as we shall see, the G7 countries dominate the process of standard setting and have taken the lead in the international standards project.

Fourth, each of the 12 key standards contains more detailed specific codes and principles. For example, there are currently 25 Basle Core Principles for Banking Supervision (BCP) and over 40 International Financial Reporting Standards (IFRS).[3] By January 2001, the FSF Compendium comprised in total 71 specific standards that were seen as important for financial stability; the list continues to grow. Many of these standards are interdependent. For example, the effective implementation and monitoring of minimum capital requirements and risk management requirements in the BCP require banks to employ sophisticated accounting standards, as well as good disclosure and corporate governance practices.

To varying degrees, the standard-setting bodies allow flexibility of implementation at the national level. This is commonly justified by the argument that varying national institutional configurations and traditions mean that the details should be left up to individual governments. However, it can also reflect the difficulty of achieving agreement between countries in some areas. Historically, for example, IAS/IFRS and U.S. GAAP have competed for international preeminence, though there has been convergence between these two over time and eventual harmonization is a possibility. The OECD's Principles of Corporate Governance (PCG) were a compromise between different traditions of corporate governance and explicitly state that there is no single best model. This contrasts with the approach of the Basle Committee's BCP, which exhibit much greater confidence about what constitutes best practice. Even so, the need to appease different national and business constituencies has meant that even the BCBS has often opted for general principles rather than specific rules.[4] Nevertheless, as I argue below, the growing intellectual dominance of regulatory neoliberalism in the late 1990s enabled regulatory agencies in a few major countries, notably the United States and the United Kingdom, to offer their national rules and practices as worthy of emulation in cases where international standards are ambiguous or too general.

In addition to the standards themselves, the regime includes mechanisms to encourage their adoption. Since May 1999, the IMF's annual Article IV consultations with member countries have included the question of observance of international standards. More importantly, the joint IMF-World Bank Financial Sector Assessment Program (FSAP) involves the assessment of countries' financial regulation and stability on a voluntary basis. To supplement Fund and Bank expertise in this area, which is limited, external experts from international agencies such as the BCBS and IOSCO,[5] and from national central banks and supervisory agencies, have been drafted into this assessment exercise. The FSAP consultations produce Financial Sector Stability Assessments (FSSAs), which include the assessment of compliance with one or more sets of standards, though the government may prevent their publication in part or in full. Typically, a country's political authorities pose more objections to draft FSSA reports than do senior officials in national regulatory agencies.[6] Summary FSSA reports are then prepared for the IMF and World Bank executive boards and, when published, have sensitive information removed, usually including the staff's quantitative assessment of compliance with each particular standard.[7] The consequence may be that key issues are sometimes avoided, including by the IFIs' executive boards. A recent review found this was true in the case of an unpublished FSSA of the Dominican Republic, which suffered a banking crisis less than a year after its FSAP review (IEO 2006, 40).

The IFIs also produce related Reports on the Observance of Standards and Codes (ROSCs). These reports, initiated in January 1999 by the IMF, provide summary assessments of countries' observance of international standards; ROSCs relevant to financial regulation are usually prepared in the context of an FSSA. As with FSSAs, participation in ROSC modules is voluntary, though the Fund and Bank initially gave consideration to making it mandatory.[8] There is an explicit expectation that ROSCs are made public, but some countries have continued to resist publication. As of 31 May 2003, 410 ROSC modules for 79 countries were completed, of which 292 (71 percent) were published. The cumulative publication rate is currently about 75 percent. Both participation and publication generally fall with levels of economic development. Publication rates for macroeconomic transparency ROSCs approach 90 percent, while those for the more sensitive areas of financial supervision, accounting, auditing, corporate governance, and insolvency have been about 65 percent (IMF 2003c, 3–5).

The FSAP process is costly in terms of time and resources and the question has been raised whether the IFIs should concentrate on "systemically important countries."[9] There is an unavoidable tension between the Fund's emphasis on systemic stability and the Bank's concern with fostering financial development. Certainly, many of the countries that have participated in the assessment program are not systemically important. Self-assessment is therefore encouraged in some areas, such as the BCP, and the IFIs and G10 countries have provided some technical assistance and training to help laggards implement core standards.

To what extent does market pressure promote FSAP participation and the publication of reports? Soederberg (2003, 13) has argued that "compliance with ROSCs is not voluntary, as noncompliance would send negative signals to the international financial community, resulting in possible capital flight and investment strike." However, there is no empirical support for this claim. Thailand, for example, was approached by the IMF in March 1999 to conduct a general ROSC review, but the Thai government refused, because the report "would surely have come out unfavourably for us."[10] This suggested that the Thai government was concerned about potential market reaction to their participation, yet it exercised a choice not to participate. Another relevant case is Turkey. As of June 2000, only months before Turkey suffered a severe financial crisis, Turkey's only published ROSC was on fiscal policy transparency. Since that time, and despite the pressures on the Turkish government that followed from the financial and economic crisis, Turkey only published one more ROSC—on Data Dissemination. Given the demonstrated vulnerability of the Thai and Turkish economies to capital flight, this hardly suggests that such countries have no choice regarding public participation in the FSAP. Moreover, even when assessments are undertaken, over one-third of the developing countries have chosen not to publish them. Perhaps unfortunately for countries that chose not to publish, the U.S. GAO (2003) publicized information on nonpublishers, though even for these countries there is no evidence that markets systematically punished them.

Published assessments were for some time in conspicuously short supply in Asia. Although the situation has improved somewhat since 2003, three of the four main crisis-hit countries have avoided participation: Indonesia, Malaysia, and Thailand. Unfortunately for this study, extensive published FSSA/ROSC reports exist only for Hong Kong, Korea, Japan, and Singapore (the latter three only appeared since 2003). Indonesia has published four ROSCs (on data dissemination, accounting/auditing, corporate governance and fiscal transparency), Thailand two (corporate governance and data dissemination), Malaysia only one (corporate governance), and China none, despite international pressure to participate (U.S. GAO 2003, 19). Consultations with Brazil and India were launched in 2001 (Huang and Wajid 2002), but neither has since published a full FSSA, even though both completed one (IEO 2006, 124). Although countries that have participated in FSAPs do often cite the positive market signal that participation can provide as a reason for participating and for publishing reports (IEO 2006, 13), such market pressure has clearly proved insufficient in important cases (table 1.2).

In fact, market actors have had limited interest in FSSAs and ROSCs. Where ROSCs were available, private sector actors have felt that ROSC publications have poor coverage, are too opaque, too infrequent, and rarely updated (FSF 2001, 29–32). Private firms sometimes complain that the IFIs need to do "naming and shaming," but the countries themselves often prevent this (IEO 2006, 41). The IFIs also fear the potential political and economic consequences of greater frankness, wishing to encourage rather than discourage FSAP publication and to avoid jeopardizing the confidential relationship with country clients. As a result, it is rare to find frank

TABLE 1.2
FSSA and ROSC modules completed (published and unpublished) as of 1 July 2004, major emerging market countries

	FSSA	Data dissemi-nation	Fiscal transpar-ency	Monetary & fiscal policy transparency	Banking supervi-sion	Insur-ance reg-ulation	Securities market regulation	Pay-ments systems	Corpo-rate gov-ernance	Account-ing & auditing	Anti–money laundering & terrorist financing	Total ROSCS pub-lished
Argentina		P	P	P	P							4
Brazil	U		P	U	U	U	U	U	U	U		1
Chile		P	P						P			3
China												0
Hong Kong, China	P	P	P	P	P	P	P	P	P		P	9
Hungary	P	P	P	P	P	P	P	P	P			8
India	U	P	P	U	U		U	U	P			3
Indonesia												0
Korea, Republic	P	P	P	P	P	P	P	P	P			8
Malaysia									P			1
Mexico	P	P	P	P	P	P	P	P	P			8
Pakistan			P									1
Philippines	U		P	U	P	U	U	U	P	P		4
Poland	P	P	P	P	P	P	P	P	P	P		9
Russian Federation		P										1
Singapore	P			P	P	P	P	P			P	6
South Africa	U	P	U	U	U	U	U	U	P	P	P	4
Thailand												0
Tunisia	P	P	P	P	P	P	P	P				7
Turkey		P	P						P			3
Venezuela												0
Total Published	7	12	13	8	9	7	7	7	11	3	3	80

Sources: IMF and World Bank websites, US GAO 2003, Appendix VIII.
Note: ROSC modules are often published as part of FSSAs. Insolvency ROSCs are not included because these standards were under negotiation.
"P" = Published FSSA/ROSC; "U" = Unpublished but completed FSSA/ROSC (from US GAO 2003, Appendix VIII).

assessments of compliance failure in published reports. Overall, therefore, the ability of the IFIs to promote convergence upon the standards regime must be in some doubt.

Explaining the New International Standards Regime

Why did this new standards regime emerge and what is its relationship to the Asian crisis of 1997–98? In this section, I show that the international standards project was under way before the Asian crisis struck, but the crisis enlarged its scope and ambition. The dominant interpretation of what caused the crisis provided the justification for the domestic institutional reforms entailed by the standards project. The crisis also reinforced the apparent preeminence of the Anglo-Saxon model and the appeal of regulatory neoliberalism in the financial sector in particular.

The Origins of the International Standards Regime

The initial steps toward a regime for international financial regulation began in the mid-1970s, with the creation of the BCBS in December 1974. This relatively unknown international institution, based at the Bank for International Settlements (BIS) in Basle, Switzerland, is at the heart of financial standard setting. Established by the G10 central bank governors after the failures of the Herstatt Bank and Franklin National Bank in West Germany and the United States, the BCBS was principally concerned with the regulatory consequences of the internationalization of the banking sector. It adopted the Basle Concordat on the sharing of supervisory responsibilities in 1983. The Latin American debt crisis of the 1980s in turn led to the Basle Capital Adequacy Accord of 1988, since dubbed "Basle I" (Kapstein 1994). These initiatives prompted subsequent related work by other international organizations with which the BCBS works closely, particularly the securities and insurance regulators, working under the auspices of IOSCO and the International Association of Insurance Supervisors (IAIS).

The Basle Committee's work was focused on regulatory coordination among the major developed countries that made up its membership. The twin objectives of Basle I were (1) to reduce the vulnerability of domestic financial systems in the developed world to the various disruptions that deregulation and internationalization could produce and (2) to level the regulatory playing field for internationally active banks, most of whom were based in developed countries. The 1990 agreement of the FATF on rules to limit money laundering in the international banking system was similarly designed to protect the interests of the major developed country governments.

Despite the activities of the BCBS and similar bodies, there was much complacency about financial regulation in developing countries in the early 1990s, the heyday of the "Washington Consensus" (Naim 1999; Williamson 1990). By then, an earlier economic literature advocating the importance of gradualism and "sequencing" of liberalization was largely ignored (McKinnon 1973; Shaw 1973). This literature argued that domestic financial deregulation should come very late in the reform process, and capital account opening last of all. Nevertheless, even this literature was largely silent about the need for strengthened financial regulation in the sequencing process.[11]

The triumph of market liberalism at the end of the Cold War swept aside arguments about optimal sequencing. Poland's "big bang" liberalization of 1990 effectively liberalized everything at once, well in advance of the construction of robust regulatory institutions. There was little attention given to the institutional requirements of financial sector deregulation and capital account openness, possibly excepting the now standard recommendation of central bank independence in monetary policy.[12] Before and after the Asian crisis, the U.S. government also pushed financial liberalization on behalf of its private financial sector (U.S. Treasury 2000). The IMF itself, with its limited institutional knowledge of financial sector regulation, was also guilty of complacency and myopia (IMF 1999a).

In late 1994, the Mexican crisis exposed the dangers of rapid financial liberalization for developing countries. The crisis of this star pupil of the Washington Consensus focused the attention of the G7 countries on the "international financial architecture," discussed first at the Halifax summit of June 1995.[13] Particular emphasis was placed upon the lack of timely and reliable publicly available data relating to Mexico's financial and general economic position in the lead-up to the crisis. Possibly because Mexico had already adopted the Basle capital adequacy standard, prudential regulation was not yet the focus of concern; nor was the wisdom of capital account openness questioned. Rather, "data transparency" became the new mantra. The G7 argued that "well-informed and well-functioning financial markets are the best line of defence against financial crises."[14]

The G7 ministers asked the IMF to take the lead in establishing benchmarks for the public provision of timely and reliable economic data. The eventual result was the establishment of the Special Data Dissemination Standard (SDDS) in 1996.[15] Within little more than two years, however, it became clear that transparency alone would not solve the problem. Thailand, notably, had posted data to the SDDS since 19 September 1996 (as had Malaysia, the Philippines, and Singapore), well before the Baht crisis broke. Indonesia had posted its data on 21 May 1997.[16] When East Asia succumbed to financial crisis only a few years after Mexico, the financial reform debate was reignited and for a time ranged more broadly than at any time since the Bretton Woods conference of 1944.

The Asia Crisis, Regulatory Failures, and International Standards

Despite Japan's mounting economic difficulties, in the mid-1990s the developing countries of East Asia appeared to be in a much stronger position to resist the kinds of endemic financial crisis that periodically enveloped Latin American countries. East Asia's rapidly expanding exports, high savings, and resilient growth fostered the general belief that Latin-style financial crises were highly unlikely in the region. East Asian states, combining a varying mixture of outward orientation and market interventionism, had apparently produced a sustainable economic miracle (Haggard 1990; Wade 1990; World Bank 1993). Even those who argued that this miracle had its limits (Krugman 1994) did not foresee the kind of crisis that hit the region in 1997. This general optimism was shared by IMF surveillance teams, who concentrated on the broadly strong macroeconomic positions of the East Asian countries (IEO 2003, 23).

When the Thai, Indonesian, and South Korean crises occurred in the second half of 1997, this view was shattered. Some initially placed part of the blame on the premature liberalization of capital flows (Radelet and Sachs 1998; Wade and Veneroso 1998). In this view, volatile international capital flows had destabilized and undermined a hitherto successful developmental model. The appropriate solution was to re-regulate international capital flows and the banks, securities firms, hedge funds, and institutional investors that had engaged in destabilizing herd behavior. However, the argument that financial liberalization was largely to blame did not explain why other relatively open economies such as Hong Kong and Singapore were much less affected. Lower leverage and larger foreign exchange reserves seemed part of the explanation for these countries' greater resilience (Kaminsky 1999; Lindgren et al. 1999). They also had stronger prudential supervision than did Indonesia, Korea, and Thailand.[17]

An alternative view blamed the East Asian model itself, generalizing the emerging critique of the faltering Japanese system to the region as a whole. In this view, the legacy of industrial policy and state-directed credit to favored industries, and, at least in some cases, of political and corporate corruption, resulted in substantial over-investment and excessive leverage (Corsetti, Pesenti, and Roubini 1998; Krugman 1998). A dramatic deterioration of the private sector balance sheet in these economies had been masked by apparently prudent macroeconomic policies,[18] and facilitated by weak financial and corporate regulation. From this perspective, moral hazard was endemic in East Asian government intervention or, more pejoratively, "crony capitalism." In other words, the causes of the crisis lay firmly at home.

This interpretation suggested an obvious solution: "Any country active in international financial markets must meet internationally accepted standards [of financial regulation]" (Eichengreen 2000, 184). It was a solution that appealed to policymakers in G7 and IFI circles, with the partial exception of Japan and France. The U.S. Treasury under Robert Rubin and Laurence Summers, and Alan Greenspan at the U.S. Federal Reserve Board, pushed this view especially vigorously (Blustein 2001). Michel Camdessus, IMF Managing Director, argued in March 1998:

> By now, there is broad consensus on what needs to be done to strengthen financial systems—improve supervision and prudential standards, ensure that banks meet capital requirements, provide for bad loans, limit connected lending, publish informative financial information, and ensure that insolvent institutions are dealt with promptly.[19]

This view also proved popular in other countries. For example, in May 1998 the APEC finance ministers' meeting in Kananaskis, Canada, endorsed efforts to enhance the surveillance of financial sector supervisory systems, particularly in emerging market countries, in part by peer review. The 1999 report of the APEC Economic Committee, "APEC Economies Beyond the Asian Crisis," argued that "the crisis has shed light on under-regulated financial sectors and weak corporate governance as important weaknesses in the crisis-hit economies" (APEC Economic Committee 1999, part 1, 3). It also emphasized domestic institutional reforms rather than radical reforms to the international financial architecture.

In East Asia itself, technocratic, reformist circles often accepted the domestic interpretation of the crisis, as did opposition political parties in countries like Korea and Thailand (Blustein 2001, 101; Haggard 2000, 100–107; Hall 2003, 89–92; Siamwalla 1998, 11; Yoon 2000). Korea's Kim Dae-Jung subsequently won political office on a platform that pledged to bring regulatory policies and institutions up to international best practice standards (Hall 2003; Pirie 2005). The Asian Policy Forum, a regional network comprising of academics and institutions with expertise in financial regulation, largely endorsed the diagnosis and reform agenda pushed in Basle and Washington (Asian Policy Forum 2001; Shirai 2001a).[20] The "dual mismatches" that built up in a number of East Asian countries in the years before the crisis, involving foreign currency borrowing for domestic investment and borrowing short for long term projects, were seen as testimony to this regulatory failure. Poor disclosure standards, weak accounting rules, and poor corporate governance compounded the problem.

This dominant interpretation of the Asian crisis greatly strengthened the argument for international standard setting. International standards in financial regulation and supervision, corporate governance, accounting and auditing, insolvency regimes, and so on could assist domestic reform in Asia by providing best practice benchmarks. The G7 Finance Ministers, reporting to the heads of government meeting in Cologne in July 1999, argued that the promotion of global financial stability

> does not require new international organisations. It requires that all countries assume their responsibility for global stability by pursuing sound macroeconomic and sustainable exchange rate policies and establishing strong and resilient financial systems. It requires the adoption and implementation of internationally-agreed standards and rules in these and other areas. It requires the existing institutions to adapt their roles to meet the demands of today's global financial system: in particular to put in place effective mechanisms for devising standards, monitoring their implementation and making public the results; to have the right tools to help countries to manage crises; and to take steps to enhance their effectiveness, accountability and legitimacy. (G7 Finance Ministers 1999)

The argument for an international standards regime assumed that self-interest alone would not provide sufficient incentive for developing countries to improve regulatory governance. Furthermore, given the potential for contagion from developing country financial crises, the major countries evidently believed they had a right and an obligation to encourage detailed institutional reform in developing countries.[21] The G7 Finance Ministers' report of 1999 explicitly argued that "country adherence to standards should also be used in determining Fund conditionality," secure in the view that their own governments would never have to borrow from the IMF. Although these and other proposals to require the adoption of international standards were mostly dropped,[22] they encouraged opponents to portray the standards project as driven by narrowly Western and especially American corporate interests. To this was added the more direct evidence that over 60 percent of the loan conditionalities attached to the Indonesian, Thai, and Korean programs were related to financial sector reform (Goldstein 2001, 39), and the number of such "structural" conditionalities was unprecedentedly high (figure 1.1). The U.S. Treasury (2000, 1) subsequently boasted that many of these conditionalities were "supported by the vigorous use of the voice and vote of the USED [U.S. Executive Director] at the IMF."

The Rise of Regulatory Neoliberalism

The focus on domestic regulatory failures reflected more than a particular diagnosis of the crises that hit Asia in 1997. As Naim (1999) points out, the difficulties of the economic reform process in many developing countries had, by the mid-1990s, focused attention on the need to strengthen domestic institutions. A growing policy consensus about the basic principles of economic regulation in the major developed countries facilitated

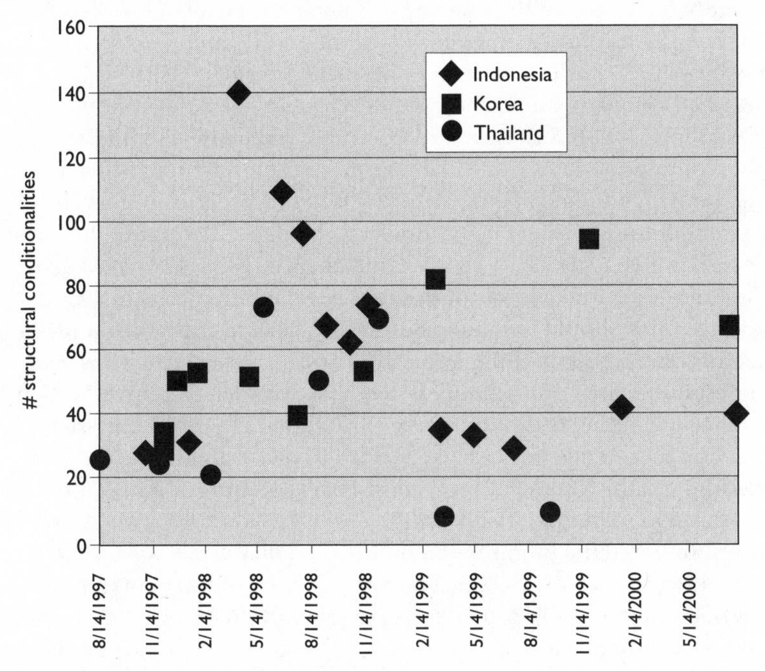

Figure 1.1. Structural conditionalities in IMF programs, Indonesia, Korea, and Thailand: 1997–2000

Sources: Goldstein (2001, table 7); IMF.

international regulatory agreements in the key international institutions that later were extended to the rest of the world. This new policy consensus derived in part from the "new institutional economics," which emphasized the importance of institutions in economic development (North 1990; Olson 2000). Successful economic reform and long term economic development was now said to require fundamental political and institutional reforms, including in East Asia, the supposed home of the hitherto successful "developmental state" model.

In the view of Chalmers Johnson (1982), the core characteristic of the developmental state was a strongly nationalistic focus on the goal of national economic development and catch-up with the West, combined with a relatively competent and autonomous bureaucracy that actively intervened in the market to promote long-run economic competitiveness.[23] After the crisis, the two countries most commonly associated with state developmentalism, Japan and Korea, were often portrayed by neoliberal critics as highly prone to problems of moral hazard and policy "capture."

The "embeddedness" of the state in business and societal networks (cf. Evans 1992) had, in the neoliberal view, undermined its ability to set policy objectives independently of particular business interests.[24] Although Johnson (1982) had clearly distinguished the developmental state from the "predatory" states of South East Asia and elsewhere in the developing world, the neoliberal critique in essence claimed that developmental states had a dynamic tendency to become predatory.[25] What was required, therefore, was a re-strengthening of state institutions via the depoliticization of economic policymaking (Chang 1999, 190; Jayasuriya 2000, 2005; Robison 2005).

One of the central aspects of this new regulatory consensus was that key policy agencies should be independent of political influence and staffed by technocrats implementing strict, transparent rules. This consensus was strongest in the area of monetary policy, with the idea of central bank independence becoming orthodox by the early 1990s. However, the principle of agency independence was easily extended to other areas of economic policymaking, notably financial regulation (Beck, Demirgüç-Kunt and Levine 2003; Das, Quintyn, and Taylor 2002). The argument for agency independence dominated the literature on monetary policy in the wake of an article by Kydland and Prescott (1977). Their argument was that many government policy decisions are subject to a "time consistency problem." Although commonly applied to tax and monetary policy, this theory had wide application, from nuclear deterrence to financial regulation. For example, there may be a conflict between ex ante and ex post optimal policy with respect to financial sector capital or solvency requirements. If it is socially optimal for the regulator to exercise forbearance (i.e., to waive temporarily the minimum requirements) in the event that one or more large financial institutions fall below the minimum, financial actors will realize this and may engage in excessively risky strategies. This produces a socially sub-optimal outcome. The regulator may try to deter this behavior by announcing ex ante that they will not (in the future) engage in regulatory forbearance, but financial actors will realize that they will have strong incentives to renege on this policy in the event of an actual financial crisis. In the absence of some kind of binding commitment mechanism, this policy will lack credibility, particularly given that politicians would also be likely to prefer a forbearance policy to avoid an economic downturn.

The standard solution in the area of monetary policy was to delegate the task of achieving a low rate of inflation to a conservative central banker with assured political independence (Rogoff 1985). Since the 1980s, many central bank reforms have aimed at both increasing the political independence of central bankers and requiring them to achieve specific, transparent targets (usually an inflation target). In many countries, central banks are also regulators, and so de facto this sometimes also extended the effects of agency independence to this policy area. The principle that independent regulators with transparent, statutory responsibilities could produce better financial regulation and supervision was also easily derived from the time inconsistency thesis (Beck, Demirgüç-Kunt, and Levine 2003; Majone 2005).

These arguments coalesced with more general arguments in favor of a neoliberal regulatory state that could enforce market-oriented rules and that would be immune from policy capture by industry and from political opportunism or predation by governments (Hay 2004). Well before the time inconsistency literature emerged, the German Ordoliberal tradition had emphasized the importance of politically independent state regulatory agencies able to enforce property rights, contracts, and to ensure the value of money (Sally 1998, 105–30). A similar emphasis subsequently reappeared in neoliberal theories of economic development that stressed the core state function as one of enforcing private property rights (e.g., North 1990, 35). When private disputes arise that require state intervention, regulation in this view should be predictable, fair, efficient, and depoliticized ("arms-length"). Operational independence both from government and from the regulated industry is emphasized, by way of the delegation of key responsibilities to technocratic agencies (Kahler 1990; Majone 2005; Thatcher and Stone Sweet 2002). Much of this literature drew upon an idealized understanding of the historical rise of a "minimalist" state in Britain and the United States.

The central principle of this emergent regulatory neoliberalism, then, was that economic regulation should be insulated from politics via agency independence.[26] Furthermore, such agencies should impartially enforce arms-length, transparent rules within a limited "zone of discretion."[27] Transparency of decision-making would deter capture by industry or political interests, and constraining agency discretion would limit the potential for the emergence of new time inconsistency and political legitimacy problems. By the late 1990s, this had approached the status of a "strong norm," witnessed in the trail of communication that it has generated (cf. Finnemore and Sikkink 1998, 891–92). This can be seen in the tendency of those countries that do not comply with the norm's formal requirements to argue that their central banks and/or financial regulators enjoy "practical independence."[28] It is difficult to find examples of governments who now openly defend the idea that financial regulators should be politically subordinated, or that prudential rules should allow for a high degree of flexibility in their implementation.

The practical model for this approach to financial regulation was the U.S. Federal Deposit Insurance Corporation (FDIC) Improvement Act of 1991. The savings and loan bailout of the late 1980s was widely blamed on forbearance by a regulator under substantial political pressure and which also wished to hide past regulatory mistakes (Jackson and Lodge 2000, 109).

The 1991 act sharply curtailed the scope for regulatory discretion in prescribing a system of "prompt corrective action" (PCA) for dealing with weakened financial institutions. The PCA rules were intended to trigger specific, mandatory regulatory actions by the FDIC when insured depository institutions fell below designated safety and performance thresholds, with the goal of reducing taxpayer losses.[29] This model has since been widely copied around the world, including by many Asian countries after 1997.

The BCP of 1997 are also consistent with the main principles of regulatory neoliberalism. The first principle, the "precondition" for effective supervision, advocates "operational independence...free from political pressure" for financial regulators, a clear set of responsibilities and objectives, limits on policy discretion, the power to enforce compliance, legal protection for supervisors, and sufficient financial resources (BCBS 1997, 13–14). As the BIS has stated, the BCP are intended to set the overall framework for strengthened market competition and private risk management.

> Only effective financial supervision can successfully counteract [unduly risky] behaviour by promoting adequate capital standards, effective risk management and transparency. This requires skilled supervisors, who can understand the risks in financial activities; identify the best ways to anticipate, manage and control these risks; and establish an adequate framework of prudential regulation. These strong leaders should have independent status and be backed up by institutional and legal support to help them enforce regulations and apply corrective measures.[30]

The BCBS and other international standard setters drew heavily upon institutional designs and practices in the major developed countries, especially those with the most sophisticated financial markets. The United States and the United Kingdom in particular provided the key regulatory benchmarks, with their relatively transparent fiscal and monetary policy frameworks, independent central banks and financial regulators, corporate governance codes and advanced accounting standards. This image of a new regulatory consensus was assisted by parallel (though not identical) regulatory innovation in this period by other Anglo-Saxon countries, including Australia, Canada, and New Zealand. After the Mexican and Asian crises of the 1990s, the United States and other governments advocated the extension of this approach to financial regulation to developing countries as well (e.g., U.S. Council of Economic Advisors 1999, 281). Argentina's currency board system, its independent bank regulatory agency (SEFyC), and its embrace of the Basle framework and IFRS, represented the culmination of this agenda in Latin America. Most of East Asia, by contrast, was left looking decidedly out of step on the eve of the crisis.

The ascendancy of regulatory neoliberalism was also reinforced by the seemingly spectacular resurgence of the U.S. economy in the 1990s. Robust

U.S. GDP and productivity growth, combined with flourishing financial markets,[31] seemed to confirm the superiority of the neoliberal model. Alan Greenspan among others argued that a permanent rise in productivity growth due to the information technology revolution had raised the sustainable level of economic growth in the United States and, perhaps, asset prices as well.[32] The German and Japanese challenges of the 1980s seemed a distant memory as the United States appeared poised to dominate the new technologies and entrench its preeminence across whole swathes of manufacturing and services. One indication of this perceived American dominance was the 2000 Financial Times-PricewaterhouseCoopers survey of chief executives, which ranked 15 American firms in the top 20 of the world's most respected companies and 8 in the top 10. Sony and Toyota, both Japanese, were the only non-American firms to make the top 10.[33] America's venture capital markets and associated innovation had become the envy of the world, reversing the view of a few years earlier that the U.S. financial system promoted "short-termism" (Porter 1992). The American model of corporate governance, with shareholder value as the primary corporate objective and boards of directors as the main monitor of management performance, was also triumphant.

Elsewhere, a similar narrative of success and failure was popular. "Neoliberal" Britain also seemed to be enjoying a comparative economic renaissance. Upon gaining office, Britain's New Labour government promptly made the Bank of England independent and created a new, integrated, independent financial supervisory agency. By contrast, in continental Europe, persistently high unemployment and other strains cast doubt on the long-term viability of the German and related economic models. However, it was undoubtedly Japan that suffered the most surprising reversal of fortunes, with growth barely positive by the mid-1990s, deeply troubled financial and corporate sectors, and some spectacular failures of financial regulation (Nakaso 2001). This weakened Japan's ability and willingness to resist U.S. and IMF attempts to impose regulatory neoliberalism upon the crisis-hit Asian countries in 1997–98 (Blustein 2001, 102). Since 1998, the Japanese government had itself decided to make the Bank of Japan independent, to establish a Financial Services Agency (FSA) modeled on British lines and an independent accounting standard setter, and to adopt Western-style corporate governance reforms.

The Politics of International Standard Setting

The association of the United States and the United Kingdom with the successful practice of regulatory neoliberalism helped to justify their traditionally dominant position within important international forums. New York's and London's status as the world's most important international financial centers gave American and British central bankers and regulators special expertise and authority within the key groups.[34] The UK Chancellor of the Exchequer since 1997, Gordon Brown, played an important role in promoting this agenda in the G7 Finance Ministers meetings in the wake of the emerging market financial crises of 1997–98. A key step was the commissioning of the Tietmeyer report on the international financial system in October 1998 by the G7 Finance Ministers and Central Bank Governors, which was presented to and endorsed by this body in February 1999. A former President of the German Bundesbank and a financial conservative, Tietmeyer saw financial instability as the product of poor domestic policy choices and weak regulation. Eisuke Sakakibara, then vice-minister at Japan's MOF and a participant in the G7 deliberations during the crisis period, said no one within the G7 objected to this basic analysis.[35]

The international reforms advocated in the Tietmeyer report were minimal, amounting mainly to increased coordination among the key international and national authorities involved in promoting financial sector stability. Although it advocated the involvement of major emerging market countries in this process, the main innovation was to establish the FSF, which would bring together the key Basle committees, IOSCO, the IFIs, OECD, IAIS, and mainly G7 national government representatives.[36] The core idea was to formulate and disseminate international best practice standards to promote domestic financial reform, particularly in emerging market countries. As Dobson and Hufbauer (2001, chap. 2) argue, the major countries implicitly assumed that their international financial firms and their own regulatory systems had been operating efficiently, despite the excessive international bank lending to Asia before mid-1997.

The major emerging market countries could not be excluded entirely from the reform discussions, but their involvement has been limited. After a pledge by President Clinton at the Vancouver APEC summit in November 1997 to promote a wide debate on the reform of the international financial architecture, the U.S. Treasury unilaterally convened the G22 grouping in April 1998, with strong representation of those developing countries Washington deemed systemically important, including the main Asian countries.[37] In Europe, particularly in France, this was interpreted as an effort to side-step the more Europe-heavy institutions such as the Interim Committee of the IMF (renamed the International Monetary and Financial Committee [IMFC] on September 30, 1999). The G22 established three working groups to discuss different aspects of international financial reform. Although domestic policy and regulatory reform were at the top of the agenda, the role of the IMF in crisis lending and the issue of ensuring private creditor "burden-sharing" were also seen as central.[38]

Among other things, the G22 reports (G22 1988a, 1988b, 1988c) recommended the establishment of a permanent "financial sector policy forum," an extension of IMF Article IV consultations to include observation of international standards, the automatic publication of a report on such observance, and the inclusion of financial sector soundness statistics in the SDDS. The reports offered little criticism of the IMF and were highly critical of financial regulation in the Asian countries in the run-up to the crisis.[39] That such criticisms were acceptable within a group with heavy East Asian representation reflected the substantial weakening of the East Asian model(s) in the collective imagination, including within East Asia itself. However, one report argued that "standards should be developed in a collaborative manner to ensure that both the developed and the emerging world have a voice in the standard-setting process" (G22 1998b, Executive Summary).

The G7 Finance Ministers created a broader forum to discuss international financial reform, the G33, in early 1999, but this group proved unwieldy.[40] In September, the G7 Finance Ministers agreed to establish the narrower G20 grouping, which included representatives from the major EU institutions and the IMF and World Bank (see table 1.3). For East Asia, the G20 grouping was less satisfactory than the G22, including only Japan, China, Korea, and Indonesia. However, the G20 subsequently played no role in standard setting, and its function seems primarily one of consultation and consensus building.

In practice, representation in the standard-setting process was determined by the G7 decision to delegate standard-setting authority to other institutions. Most of the standard-setting bodies have restricted memberships, but have drawn on other countries on an ad hoc basis. For example, the BCBS has 13 country members and is dominated numerically by European countries.[41] Nevertheless, the BCP drafting committee included representatives from Chile, China, Czech Republic, Hong Kong, Mexico, Russia, and Thailand.[42] The PCG drafting process included representatives from all OECD member states, which include some developing countries, and from various other international organizations with relevant expertise.[43] By contrast, the IASB, a private sector body, has always been predominantly Anglo-American in nature. As of mid-2002, the IASB consisted of three British members, including the chairman, four Americans, and one representative each for Australia, Canada, South Africa, France, Germany, and Japan. However, IASB also has working committees with developing country representation. One senior Japanese official argued that the IASB was actually more open to Asians and more willing to listen than was BCBS.[44]

Despite efforts to increase the legitimacy of the standard-setting process, many developing countries continue to see it as G7 dominated. One indication of this was the establishment in November 2000 of yet another forum, the Emerging Market Eminent Persons Group (EMEPG), consisting of former finance ministers and experts of 11 major emerging market

TABLE 1.3
Country membership of selected international organizations (2002)

	G7	BCBS	FSF	G22	G20	OECD
Argentina				X	X	
Australia			X	X	X	X
Belgium		X				X
Brazil				X	X	
Canada	X	X	X	X	X	X
China				X	X	
France	X	X	X	X	X	X
Germany	X	X	X	X	X	X
Hong Kong			X	X		
India				X	X	
Indonesia				X	X	
Italy	X	X	X	X	X	X
Japan	X	X	X	X	X	X
Luxembourg		X				X
Malaysia				X		
Mexico				X	X	X
Netherlands		X	X			X
Poland				X		X
Russia				X	X	
Saudi Arabia					X	
Singapore			X	X		
South Africa				X	X	
South Korea				X	X	X
Spain		X				X
Sweden		X				X
Switzerland		X				X
Thailand				X		
Turkey					X	X
United Kingdom	X	X	X	X	X	X
United States	X	X	X	X	X	X

Sources: BIS, G20, G22, OECD and IMF websites.

Notes: The membership of the G20 comprises the finance ministers and central bank governors of the G7, 12 other countries, the European Union Presidency (if not a G7 member), and the European Central Bank. The Managing Director of the IMF, the Chairman of the IMFC, the President of the World Bank, and the Chairman of the Development Committee of the IMF and World Bank also participate. Various committees of the BIS, and the heads of IOSCO, the IMF, the World Bank, OECD, and IAIS are also represented at the FSF.

countries. EMEPG's goal was explicitly to provide an alternative emerging market viewpoint to G7 on the international financial reform debate. In a report issued in October 2001, the group argued that "in most of the forums or agencies drawing up codes and standards, emerging market economies are not included or, at best, are underrepresented" (EMEPG 2001, 31). They also argued that international standards should be applied flexibly, that a one-size-fits-all approach should be avoided, and that their implementation should not be a prerequisite for access to official finance. Similar points were made by Asian representatives at the first Asia-Pacific meeting of the

FSF in October 2001.[45] Even so, it remains difficult for individual countries to reject international standards openly. As we shall see, most developing countries are visibly concerned to signal their willingness—and ability—to comply with such standards.

The Triumph of International Standards?

At the close of the 20th century, the G7 countries had established an international standards regime that aimed to promote best practice regulation globally, with best practice understood as principles consistent with regulatory neoliberalism. This model of regulation was an ideal type, though practice in the major Anglo-Saxon developed countries in the late 1990s was generally assumed to approximate it most closely. The Asian crisis was seen as verifying this model of economic regulation and thereby contributed to its ascendance. The various standard-setting processes associated with this model were sometimes, but not always, dominated by the United States and the United Kingdom.[46] American policy in particular in these years can be seen as an attempt to establish an idealized version of its own domestic regulatory framework as recognized international best practice. Despite this, the language employed by international bodies was designed to encourage widespread adoption: international standards were "generally accepted by the international community as being objective and relatively free of national biases" (FSF 2000a, 7 n. 3). Even though a number of developing country experts seemed inclined to accept this view, there were many dissenting voices who pointed out that they would bear the real burden of implementation (EMEPG 2001, 31–33).

In terms of the international standard-setting process, the U.S. attempt to dominate was not entirely successful. In both the OECD and IASB the Europeans and to a lesser extent the Japanese were able to resist U.S. attempts to dictate international standards. However, this resistance mattered less than it might appear because the growing intellectual dominance of regulatory neoliberalism enabled U.S. (and UK) regulatory agencies to offer their national practices as supplementary international standards in cases where international standards were ambiguous or too general. As we will see in later chapters, Asian developing countries have often looked to the major Anglo-Saxon countries for detailed regulatory benchmarks.

The ascendance of regulatory neoliberalism and its embodiment in the international standards project has caused some to argue that the major developing countries have little choice but to accept full convergence, despite its costs (Jayasuriya 2005; Pirie 2005; Soederberg 2003). However, the extent of convergence, particularly in the crisis-hit countries that were compelled to adopt international standards, largely remains undemonstrated. Before I investigate this empirical question, however, the next chapter will outline the main existing theories concerning compliance with international standards and will provide an alternative theory that is employed in the case study chapters.

2

A Theory of Compliance with International Standards

The previous chapter argued that the rise of regulatory neoliberalism and the associated international standards project raises important practical challenges for many countries, especially developing ones. This chapter has two primary objectives. First, it asks how we should understand compliance in the world economy and how this relates to the concept of convergence. Second, it outlines a theory of what determines compliance and noncompliance with international standards.

Existing theories of compliance, whether they emphasize ideational factors (Hall 2003) or international market or institutional forces (Jayasuriya 2005; Pirie 2005; Soederberg 2003), have often argued that states and private market actors will find it difficult to resist. Many such theories fail to address the possibility that compliance with international standards can be superficial rather than substantive. In contrast to these theories, I argue that there are good reasons to expect that mock compliance will often be widespread in developing countries, mainly for reasons of domestic politics.[1] Furthermore, under circumstances that I specify, such mock compliance is likely to be sustainable over long periods of time.

Compliance and Convergence in the World Economy

Before we discuss competing theories about the nature of and forces behind compliance with international standards, it is necessary to define our key concepts, compliance and convergence. Compliance with international rules and standards has been a focus of recent literature that developed out of the international regimes tradition in international relations (Krasner 1982; Keohane 1984). This literature is mainly concerned with how international law and regimes affect state behavior, though the behavior of nonstate actors can also be an important issue.[2]

Compliance signifies when the actual behavior of actors who are the targets of an international rule or standard conforms to the prescriptions of that rule or standard.[3] Most of us easily recognize when others act inconsistently with laws and social norms that prevail within countries or communities; most of the time, perhaps, most actors comply with most such laws and norms. International regimes generally aim at altering or constraining state behavior, including the behavior of actors within states. International standards related to financial regulation are voluntary, but are intended to provide principles that countries should adopt when revising national frameworks for both public and private sector behavior. Self-evidently, such standards are intended to have a constraining effect on national behavior and assume that many actors do not currently act in ways consistent with such standards.

If compliance occurs when actor behavior is consistent with accepted standards, *convergence* is the process by which previously different actors, groups, or organisms become more alike. As noted above, the main proponents of the international standards project have seen the promotion of compliance with such standards as a key means of fostering a general convergence toward regulatory neoliberalism. However, compliance with international standards and convergence upon regulatory neoliberalism need to be clearly distinguished for the following reasons.

First, although both compliance and convergence will always in practice be a matter of degree,[4] compliance is concerned with actor conformity to a specific rule or standard, whereas convergence relates to the overall nature of the system or organism. The core of regulatory neoliberalism is the transparent and neutral regulation of deregulated markets by independent supervisory agencies. This benchmark is an ideal type, which makes the assessment of convergence upon regulatory neoliberalism a different matter to the assessment of compliance, not least because there are many different ways in which actor behavior can fall short of this ideal type. Departures from this ideal type occur in those countries said to typify regulatory neoliberalism, such as the United States, though such departures may be less systematic than in other countries.

Second, even if all actors in a particular country were in full compliance with all existing international standards, this need not imply complete convergence upon regulatory neoliberalism. Even if, as argued in chapter 1, many international standards have been inspired by the ideals of regulatory neoliberalism, as products of often difficult international negotiation they are never likely to be full expressions of these ideals. As a result, different possible forms of compliant behavior are likely to exist, including some that depart from the ideal of regulatory neoliberalism.[5] This also implies that outright noncompliance with some international standards may be compatible with regulatory neoliberalism. In addition, as lawyers and economists have long recognized, even if rules appear to be consistent with particular objectives today, it is impossible to write "complete contracts" that encompass every possible future contingency.[6]

Some other distinctions are important. Generally, we can distinguish between rules that are legally binding ("laws") and those that are not ("standards" or "norms"). At the international level, many refer to such voluntary standards as "soft law" (Shelton 2003). International laws, by contrast, are agreed between states in the form of international legal treaties and often have some form of explicit compliance mechanism attached. International standards, voluntary even for states whose representatives were parties to their negotiation, may nevertheless be widely adopted (Jordan and Majnone 2002, 15). Once adopted, they may or may not be given legally binding status in domestic law.

We can also distinguish between technical and policy standards. Technical standards are intended to promote coordination and compatibility between international goods or services and/or the actors involved in related transactions.[7] Policy standards, with which this study is concerned, are minimum sets of best practice institutional designs and policy rules with which countries are encouraged to comply. According to the FSF, "standards set out what are widely accepted as good principles, practices, or guidelines in a given [policy] area."[8] Note too that international standards are not necessarily less stringent than international laws. As Raustiala and Victor (1998) argue, when compliance costs are uncertain and potentially high, states have incentives to choose soft rather than hard law so as to facilitate agreement on higher standards (i.e., legal binding might induce agreement on lower standards).

Most of the literature also distinguishes between implementation and compliance (e.g., Raustiala and Slaughter 2002, 539; Shelton 2003, 5). Implementation occurs when states adopt international standards in domestic legislation. However, such implementation may not prevent bureaucratic and private sector behavior that is inconsistent with these standards. This is illustrated in figure 2.1, which considers a sequential process from domestic adoption/implementation of international standards to bureaucratic and private sector compliance. Implementation is simply the first of these stages. This figure summarizes four different stages at which compliance may be blocked. I term these stages ratification failure, regulatory forbearance, administrative failure, and private compliance failure, respectively.

"Ratification failure" occurs when proposed reforms fail to be implemented, usually because they are not adopted by a legislature because of

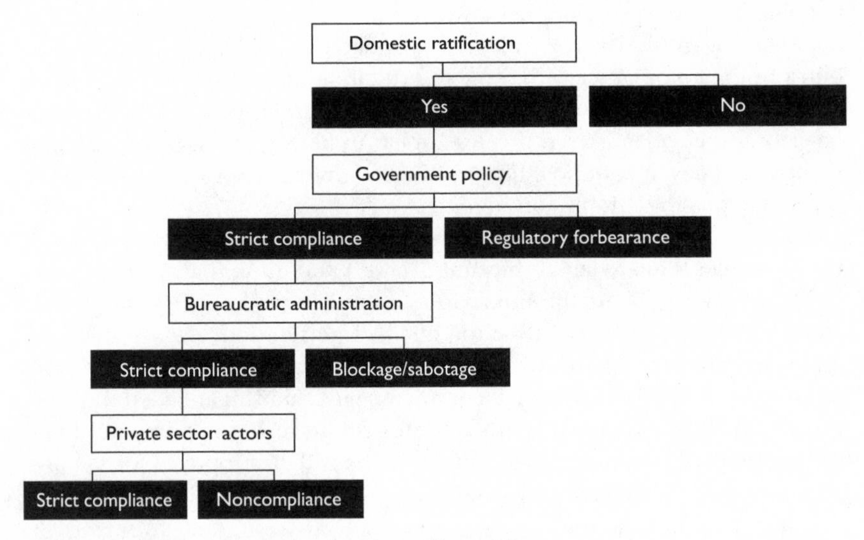

Figure 2.1. Four stages of compliance and compliance failure

organized political opposition to a given set of reforms. "Regulatory forbearance" occurs when the government itself intentionally refrains from strictly enforcing new standards, systematically or on an ad hoc basis (Hardy 2006, 4–5; Honohan and Klingebiel 2000, 7). "Administrative failure" occurs when implementing bureaucracies obstruct the government in its attempts to achieve full compliance, including via weak enforcement.[9] Finally, "private sector compliance failure" occurs when private sector actors who are the ultimate targets of regulatory action act in ways that undermine compliance.

Figure 2.1 suggests that we must distinguish between "formal," or merely superficial, compliance and "substantive" compliance. As should be clear, ratification may be insufficient to ensure that bureaucratic and private sector behavior is consistent with international standards. In examining compliance, we are interested not only in public policy content and policy instruments, but primarily in the extent to which these result in the convergence of behavioral outcomes (see Bennett 1991, 218–19). Government, bureaucratic and private sector actors may all have incentives visibly to signal compliance when in fact their underlying behavior is inconsistent with compliance. I call this "mock compliance."[10] I distinguish this from "substantive compliance," which occurs when underlying actor behavior is consistent with adopted standards. I call the gap between behavior consistent with substantive compliance and actual behavior the "real compliance gap." In a later section, I will explain why under specific circumstances mock compliance strategies are likely to be appealing to both public and private actors.

General Theories of Compliance

What determines compliance outcomes? There are two main approaches to explaining compliance with and defection from international agreements: rationalist and constructivist. The former emphasizes the material incentives for actors to behave in particular ways, while the latter emphasizes social learning and normative "logics of appropriateness" in explaining behavior. Although these approaches are commonly seen as opposed, recent work has argued for their potential compatibility (Checkel 2001; Finnemore and Sikkink 1998; Underdal 1998). After briefly reviewing both approaches, I give reasons why we should expect material incentives to dominate compliance outcomes by the major public and private actors in the short to medium term. I use this argument to develop my own theory of compliance with international standards, applied in the empirical chapters of this book.

Most rationalist approaches to compliance focus on cost/benefit calculations by actors motivated by given material interests.[11] In situations of uncertainty and potential multiple equilibria, international standards may act as "focal points" that facilitate coordination (Garrett and Weingast 1993).[12] Compliance costs include the "internal" costs of adapting past practices and systems to new standards or of recognizing losses that arise because new standards reduce the value of existing assets, or the "external" costs that may arise because markets or regulators sanction actors who must now reveal new and damaging information (Boughton and Mourmouras 2002; Ivanova et al. 2003; Mayer and Mourmouras 2002; Havrylyshyn and Odling-Smee 2001). The potential material benefits gained from compliance with international regulatory standards may include a mixture of market and regulatory benefits, such as higher levels and greater stability of inward capital flow, lower borrowing costs for governments and domestic firms, lower surveillance and listing costs for firms at home and abroad, and so on. Different actors are likely to have different expectations about the extent to which, for example, markets will sanction or reward their compliance with international standards.

Along these lines, Simmons (2001) argues that country compliance with international regulatory standards is determined by the market and political incentives for nonhegemonic countries to adopt them. Hegemonic countries are those with the market power to set regulatory standards unilaterally, though hegemons will have incentives to take into account the likely responses of other countries. For other countries, if the adoption of international standards raises (lowers) the profitability of their domestic firms, the incentives to emulate (diverge) will be strong. When adoption of particular standards is costly for some actors, rationalist approaches emphasize the importance of sanctions to deter noncompliance, either of the legal variety or of a decentralized form (e.g., Downs, Rocke, and Barsoom 1996; Oatley and Nabors 1998; Simmons 2000a).

Despite these insights, rationalist approaches to compliance have drawbacks. First, in emphasizing the material incentives for compliance that actors face, such accounts can underestimate the potential for deeper forms of social learning to promote compliance. Second, it can be difficult to make an accurate *ex ante* assessment of the costs and benefits of compliance and defection. Third, it is not always clear as to the appropriate level at which group interests should be aggregated, or which economic theory should be used to derive actor interests. Fourth, it is unclear how far-sighted actors are in calculating costs and benefits. Politicians, for example, may only be interested in short to medium term benefits, but this may be less true of firms and other actors.

Although in principle the rationality assumption can be separated from a materialist ontology, most rationalists in practice allow only a limited role for ideas in actor behavior. Constructivist approaches, by contrast, view shared norms and legitimacy as the primary driver of compliance with international agreements (Ruggie 1998; Risse, Ropp and Sikkink 1999). Behavioral norms may spread via technocratic, knowledge-based networks of authoritative experts ("epistemic communities") that transfer ideas and best practices across borders (Haas 1992, 1997; Ikenberry 1992; Slaughter 2004). International organizations may also play a socializing role, including via the professional training of individuals and groups with domestic policy influence (Finnemore and Sikkink 1998, 899). Cooperation within such international networks is said to be founded upon norms of reciprocity, common knowledge, and the desire of members to retain the respect of their peers (Aviram 2003). Simply put, national representatives can come to share values and to exhibit loyalty toward their network peers, and may be most likely to favor national compliance with the international standards they help to set.

What is much less clear is whether the norms shared by the technocratic experts that operate within these international networks will be shared by national political elites. Constructivists often argue that social activists, domestic and/or transnational, may also play a role in promoting government compliance with international norms, along with dominant states. Political elites can thus be pressured by transnational, international, and domestic social forces, as in the "boomerang model" advanced by Keck and Sikkink (1998). Unless elites "internalize" these norms, however, their expected behavioral response is compatible with and perhaps better modeled by rationalist accounts (Checkel 1999, 4). Over the longer term, if political elites internalize new norms via social learning, a much more significant role for norms in promoting cooperation and compliance would arise. Constructivists, like some rationalists, often allow a central role for crises in dislodging existing policy models and associated conceptions of self-interest in the minds of policymakers and other actors, facilitating the emergence of new ones (Blyth 2002; Hall 1989; Checkel 2001, 562).

If norms are internalized and change expectations about actor behavior, compliance with international standards may be de-politicized and become a technical, "managerial" problem (Chayes and Chayes 1993).[13] Noncompliance is seen mostly as a product of nondeliberate behavior by governments, the result of ambiguity in the nature of the rules, state capacity problems, and exogenous factors (Chayes and Chayes 1993; Weiss and Jacobson 1998). The presence or absence of external enforcement is therefore much less important than for rationalist theories.

Constructivist approaches face the major problem that social norms and processes of social learning are difficult to observe and measure (Checkel 2001, 553–56). In the early stages of norm establishment, we should expect to see signs of argumentative persuasion by "norm entrepreneurs," who seek to convince other social groups of a new message or policy model (Blyth 2002). In later stages, when norms are internalized, we should expect to see "communication trails" whereby actors seek to explain their behavior in normative terms. Checkel (2001) and Underdal (1999) also attempt to specify "scope conditions" for social learning: such learning is more likely in novel circumstances or crisis, when the group or society has few prior beliefs inconsistent with the new message; when the persuader and the new policy model have authority and legitimacy; when policy groups share common professional backgrounds; when there is a high density of interaction amongst participants; when reasoned argument rather than coercion is employed; and where the process of argumentation occurs in a relatively de-politicized setting.

These conditions are more likely to be met in the international standard-setting process than in the domestic compliance process. International standard-setting bodies may be composed of relatively like-minded experts who meet frequently over long periods of time, engage in persuasive argumentation and information sharing, and acquire loyalties to the network. By contrast, the compliance process in developing countries, on which this study focuses, tends to involve a much wider set of actors and is often very politicized. Crises may de-legitimize existing regulatory approaches and make the formal adoption of international standards more likely. However, this does not mean that substituting international regulatory standards will be uncontroversial and that substantive compliance will be forthcoming. As we have seen, politicians, bureaucrats, and corporate actors, who may not have internalized the new norms, often control the domestic compliance process.

In fact, most constructivists accept that widespread internalization tends to happen only (if at all) in the latter stages of a norm's life cycle (Finnemore and Sikkink 1998, 895–98; Risse 2000, 28–29).[14] When norms first emerge, they typically compete with existing norms. Within regulatory agencies, bringing in top personnel who share the new norms may be insufficient if resistance is strong further down the hierarchy. Resistance from other ministries and politically powerful interest groups who lose from the adoption of new standards can be strong and may derail compliance. International standards are usually very susceptible to the charge by such opponents that international standard-setting processes are illegitimate and reflect hegemonic interests. Under such conditions, as Underdal (1998, 22–24) argues, compliance outcomes are usually better modeled by rationalist approaches.

A Theory of Compliance with International Financial Standards

Constructivist approaches can help to explain why international standards are set and adopted, particularly in the wake of crises. However, as regards the process of compliance after formal adoption, for the reasons outlined above, I focus here on the distributional aspects of compliance in the short to medium term, when social learning is unlikely to be deep and compliance costly and controversial. Below, I outline a theory focusing on the circumstances under which mock compliance with international regulatory standards is likely to emerge. The main argument is that domestic political factors largely drive compliance outcomes because external pressures for substantive (as opposed to formal) compliance are often weaker than many suppose. Although there are likely to be domestic political forces that support international pressure for compliance, well organized interests upon whom most of the costs of compliance fall are often in a position to block substantive compliance. Mock compliance strategies specifically are more appealing and more viable under the following three conditions: (1) private sector compliance costs are relatively high; (2) the costs of outright noncompliance are perceived to be high; and (3) third party compliance monitoring costs are relatively high. Below, I consider each of these in turn.

International Financial Regulatory Standards: Compliance Costs and Benefits

The net costs or benefits of compliance with international standards (the difference between gross compliance costs and gross compliance benefits) in the short to medium term will depend upon the stringency of international standards compared to existing domestic standards. For "hegemonic" countries that succeed in having their own domestic standards adopted as international standards (or for countries in the happy position of having existing standards similar to the hegemon), compliance costs will approach zero. For these "producers" of standards, there may also be substantial economic benefits to be gained from compliance with international standards by other countries.[15]

For countries that are "consumers" of standards, compliance will generally be comparatively costly, especially for developing countries whose existing domestic standards are likely to be less stringent. However, proponents of international standards such as the major IFIs often argue that the gross benefits of compliance will be highest for developing countries, including lower borrowing costs for the government and the private sector, higher levels of financial market development and investment, and greater financial stability. One difficulty with this argument is that some proportion of the benefits of developing country compliance might accrue to international investors from developed countries. Furthermore, these purported benefits are uncertain and are unlikely to be large in the short to medium term. Even in the longer term, such benefits may depend upon complementary institutions that may be weak or absent in many developing countries, from functioning legal systems to various social institutions (Bebchuk and Roe 1999; Hall and Soskice 2001; Pistor 2000a, 2000b; Rajan and Zingales 1998; Williamson 1999). Moreover, even if we assume that the gross compliance benefits for developing countries are large, such benefits tend to be widely distributed and often take the form of collective goods. In contrast, compliance costs are likely to fall heavily upon particular private sector groups or individuals and must often be incurred in the short run. Under these conditions, collective action theory suggests that, like free trade, compliance will often be difficult and may depend on enforcement mechanisms that impose substantial costs for noncompliance.[16]

This implies that compliance outcomes are likely to differ across international standards. When compliance costs fall largely on the public sector rather than the private sector, the quality of compliance is likely to be higher. By contrast, when compliance costs fall largely upon particular private sector groups, the quality of compliance is likely to be relatively poor. In the case of SDDS, for example, compliance costs are borne by the public sector; compliance may even produce net benefits for the private sector if it reduces sovereign borrowing costs, as some studies have claimed (Cady 2005; Christofides, Mulder, and Tiffin 2003; Glennerster and Shin 2003; IIF 2002).[17] By contrast, for international standards in the areas of banking supervision, corporate governance, accounting, and auditing, substantial compliance costs are likely to be borne by particular groups in the private sector, making high quality compliance less likely.

The size of the private sector costs of compliance with these kinds of international standards is also likely to vary inversely with the economic cycle, falling during upturns and rising during downturns. In downturns, more firms will be threatened with bankruptcy or the need to reduce costs, making substantive compliance with more stringent regulatory standards more difficult. In full-blown economic crises of the kind that hit some East Asian countries in 1997–98, the rapid increase in the level of economic distress in the private sector is likely to make the absorption of compliance costs associated with more stringent international standards impossible for many firms.[18] This should raise the incidence of compliance-avoidance strategies by distressed firms. For example, firms on the edge of bankruptcy may oppose the introduction of new financial disclosure or new banking standards, since these might force banks to crystallize new nonperforming loans (NPLs). For this reason, crises are also likely to increase the likelihood of collusion between debtors and creditors (e.g., agreement to roll over distressed loans). Deep crises can also weaken administrative capacity and raise both the supply of and the demand for bribes.

Some groups in crisis-hit countries may favor substantive compliance. Taxpayers might prefer higher quality compliance if they blame the crisis on poor past regulation, but perhaps not if this would necessitate additional public bailouts of failed banks or firms. Depositors concerned about the safety of their savings may also favor stricter compliance, though they are arguably more likely to prefer blanket government deposit guarantees than regulatory policies that produce bank closures. Such broad interests might be supported by nongovernmental organizations (NGOs) such as activist consumer groups, anticorruption campaigners, and institutional investors, as well as by public sector actors such as technocratic reformers and those bureaucrats that stand to gain influence. Relatively strong firms within regulated sectors may also favor substantive compliance. For example, well-capitalized and managed banks, in contrast to weak banks, might prefer the real compliance gap to be relatively small so as to put pressure on weaker competitors. However, strong banks or firms might be able to achieve the same results through different means, such as a higher credit rating, an international equity listing or new investments.[19]

Hence, even some important pro-compliance groups are likely to have mixed or weak incentives to lobby the government to promote substantive compliance. Furthermore, such pro-compliance interests may be less well organized and politically influential compared to the concentrated private sector interests that oppose it, except perhaps during elections. Weak banks and nonfinancial firms threatened with their very survival have greater incentives to lobby against substantive compliance than strong ones have to lobby for it. After elections, NGOs, voters, and depositors will be hard-pressed to ensure substantive compliance, while governments will likely face strong anticompliance pressure from the private sector and hence will have an incentive to renege on electoral promises. Below, I give reasons why pro-compliance institutional investors and technocrats will also tend to have limited influence.

Beyond business cycle and organizational factors, there are a range of characteristics common to many developing countries, including many in East Asia, which are likely to increase the level of private sector resistance to substantive compliance even after economic recovery occurs. First, in the bank-based rather than capital markets-based financial systems that predominate in most developing countries, financial and nonfinancial sector preferences on compliance are more likely to be aligned and thus politically influential (Demirgüç-Kunt and Levine 1999; Henning 1994, 20–31). Second, compliance failures are more likely in countries with lower institutional capacity, a lack of complementary institutions and higher levels of corruption. Third, the dominant form of corporate ownership in most developing countries—indeed in most countries other than the United States and the United Kingdom—is family-owned firms. Related to this, banks and nonfinancial firms often form part of the same larger family-controlled groups.[20] As corporate ownership becomes more concentrated, the interest of controlling shareholders in exploiting "outside" or "minority" shareholders by taking large perquisites, asset stripping, cross-subsidization, etc, tends to increase. Insiders often resist any transparency that might expose such exploitation (Bebchuk and Roe 1999, 13–18).[21] They often prefer debt to equity finance, even at the expense of a higher average cost of capital, since issuing more equity can dilute control and increase transparency.

The Costs of Outright Noncompliance: Market and Official Pressure

What if external forces, such as international investors and the IFIs act to raise the costs of noncompliance such that these exceed the net costs of compliance for affected actors? This could considerably increase the political leverage of those domestic actors pushing for compliance. Various scholars have argued that either or both of these forces will often be capable of enforcing compliance with dominant international norms and standards (Gill 1995; Hansmann and Kraakman 2000; Simmons 2001; Soederberg 2003).

Market compliance pressure might work through various mechanisms. First, governments and firms that depend heavily upon international capital markets may come under pressure to comply with international standards if creditors deem this to be an important indicator of creditworthiness. Second, over time, equity and direct investors might migrate toward more efficient and less risky jurisdictions, placing pressure on other jurisdictions to improve their regulatory environments. Third, domestic banks and firms with international operations may favor national compliance if they are compelled to comply with international standards in foreign jurisdictions.[22]

Lastly, inward foreign direct investment (FDI) from countries in which compliance is relatively strong might introduce new compliance incentives for domestic firms.

It is difficult to judge a priori how powerful each of these sources of market pressure is likely to be. There are indications that the first is weak in practice because international lenders and investors generally do not see compliance with international standards as an important indicator of creditworthiness.[23] On the second, there is conflicting evidence. Some developing country governments have been concerned that outright noncompliance might raise the cost of foreign borrowing or deter inward investment.[24] However, there is also evidence that too-big-to-fail considerations and perceived political connections may also play a role in encouraging foreign equity investment in large firms in emerging market countries, regardless of the quality of their compliance (FSF 2000b, 23–24). In any case, these "pull" factors tend to be swamped by "push" factors like the level of liquidity in developed country financial markets, which is the primary determinant of the level of equity flows into emerging market countries (IMF 2001a, 40–41; Maxfield 1998).

As for the importance of compliance pressure on internationalized firms operating in foreign jurisdictions, this is likely to vary by standard. International equity listings can trigger requirements for such firms to comply with local corporate governance and financial reporting requirements.[25] However, this does not always produce greater compliance pressure in home countries.[26] One reason why this is so is because host country regulators tend only to be concerned with firm-level rather than home-country compliance with domestic standards, and they do not always require listed foreign-owned companies to adopt local standards.[27] The same applies to the treatment of international banks in major centers like New York and London, where host regulators have not required the branches of international banks operating in their jurisdictions to adhere in important respects to local standards.[28] In practice, host regulators apply a mixture of both local rules and considerable reliance upon regulation in the foreign bank's home country (i.e., the principle of "national treatment").[29]

Finally, inward FDI might well improve the average level of firm-level compliance in particular areas, if it is significant relative to the size of the relevant sector and if such FDI comes from high compliance jurisdictions. Foreign-owned firms may introduce better risk-management techniques and may also support more stringent supervision generally if they are compelled to comply with stringent standards on a global basis. Much will depend upon the sectoral importance of such FDI: if it is significant, it might increase pressure on domestic competitors to improve average compliance. However, this mechanism might only operate if better compliance has positive effects on efficiency and profitability, which is not obviously true.

If there are good reasons why market pressures for compliance will often be weak, what about compliance pressure from the IFIs? As noted in chapter 1, the IFIs have put considerable pressure upon developing countries to adopt international standards ever since the Asian financial crisis. This has been especially true for countries that have borrowed from the IMF since this time, including Indonesia, Korea, and Thailand. However, the IFIs do not possess the legal instruments to enforce substantive compliance. Most importantly, as noted earlier, IFI lending to member states has not taken into account the quality of compliance with international standards. The IFIs are therefore in a position to exhort countries to comply, but they do not have the ability to shift the balance of domestic political forces affecting compliance. This is unsurprising, given the low levels of legitimacy enjoyed by the IMF in many developing countries, including in pro-compliance NGO circles. Finally, given the weaknesses of the FSAP/ ROSC assessments of compliance noted in chapter 1, it is doubtful that the IFIs are able substantially to reinforce the pressure that markets can place on countries that exhibit poor quality compliance.

To summarize, market and official pressures are likely to raise the cost of outright noncompliance with international standards for many developing countries and thereby support the efforts of domestic pro-compliance groups. Particularly after crises, governments may find it difficult to avoid commitments to the adoption of international standards should they borrow from the IFIs, should they depend upon the resumption of private capital flows, and should other peer countries also visibly adopt international standards (Simmons and Elkins 2004). In addition, as emphasized by constructivists, deep crises can have the effect of de-legitimizing existing policies and practices. In such circumstances, ideas and external interests can push in the same direction. As argued in chapter 1, regulatory neoliberalism was pushed by the IFIs and major Western countries as a solution to the root causes of the crisis, and international standards were offered as the only viable blueprint for reform. When a new policy discourse becomes entrenched, this may also raise the costs of outright noncompliance with international standards.

However, although such external forces increase the likelihood of formal compliance, it is doubtful whether they have much affect upon the likelihood of *substantive* compliance with international standards. Those groups who are persuaded on ideational grounds of the need for compliance may lack the ability to convince others to comply. Governments and private sector actors in developing countries may judge that they can avoid both the costs of outright noncompliance and of substantive compliance by adopting mock compliance strategies. If, under such circumstances, mock compliance strategies are attractive, the central question becomes: When will mock compliance strategies be sustainable?

Third Party Monitoring: The Implications of Asymmetric Information

Mock compliance strategies will only be viable if insiders in the regulatory process (both the regulators and the regulated) believe it will be difficult or costly for outsiders (other private market actors, domestic voters, NGOs, neoliberal reformers, taxpayers, depositors, foreign governments, and the IFIs) to monitor the real quality of compliance and to use this information to punish poor quality compliance. Much, therefore, depends upon the transparency of compliance outcomes (Mitchell 1998). If this transparency is low, mock compliance strategies will be both more attractive and sustainable.

The degree of transparency of actor behavior and hence the likelihood of mock compliance outcomes is likely to vary by international standard. In the case of technical product standards, for example, firm-level compliance is relatively easy to verify and there are often powerful legal or market incentives for firms to reveal information about such compliance. In the case of the main macroeconomic data transparency standard, SDDS, the quality of compliance is fairly visible compared to most other policy standards. This is mainly for the simple reason that it is the one international standard on which the IMF provides an explicit, public yes/no compliance judgment.[30] By comparison, monitoring the quality of compliance with the BCP, PCG or IFRS can be difficult or even impossible for outside parties (Hegarty, Gielen, and Hirata Barros 2004, 9). This reinforces our expectation, deriving from the preceding consideration of the distribution of compliance costs, that mock compliance outcomes are more likely in these areas than for SDDS.

Some might argue that the IFIs possess inside information on the quality of compliance and are therefore able to encourage compliance across all international policy standards. However, it can be difficult for the IFIs to monitor regulatory forbearance and administrative failure when governments and regulators collude to hide it. Even when IFI monitoring is possible, the IFIs have historically had weak incentives to report and to sanction noncompliance. Their desire to promote member country "buy-in" of international standards, to avoid provoking capital flight, and the tendency of executive board creditor countries to favor the continuation of financial assistance for political reasons mean that sanctions and forthright criticism is rare. It should be kept in mind that the IMF has often failed in the past to sanction noncompliance even with the core macroeconomic policy conditions applied to borrowing countries, which has led to calls for greater domestic "ownership" of conditionality.[31]

If the quality of compliance with some international standards is difficult for outsiders to monitor, this might undermine the credibility of compliance commitments by all actors and so reduce the benefits of compliance for all (cf. Rodrik 1989, 757). Could this erode the incentives for any form of compliance with these international standards? This is unlikely for a range of reasons. First, formal compliance decisions are usually undertaken by political executives, senior officials and private sector managers, who may hope to use new policy standards to bring pressure to bear on others to modify their behavior. Second, actors with strong compliance intentions and capabilities may find ways of signaling these intentions to outsiders (e.g., by visibly costly over-compliance).[32] Third, even actors with weak compliance intentions may calculate that they have little to lose from formal compliance and the potential to achieve some gains, such as the avoidance of regulatory sanctions for firms or, for governments, cooperation with the IMF and major developed countries.

Thus, mock compliance is a likely outcome when private sector compliance costs are high, when the costs of outright noncompliance are high, and when outsiders find it difficult to monitor the true quality of compliance with international standards. This conclusion is reinforced by consideration of the compliance preferences of major government agencies. Financial regulatory agencies may support compliance with international standards, should this empower them relative to other agencies or should it increase the potential supply of bribes. However, they are also prone to regulatory capture when there is a dominant banking sector preference (Hardy 2006). The ministry of finance (MOF) might favor compliance were this to reliably reduce the government's cost of borrowing, but might oppose it if it believed it would crystallize large private sector losses, which the public sector would then be forced to absorb (Honohan and Klingebiel 2000). If third party monitoring costs are high, both government agencies may favor mock compliance in an attempt to achieve conflicting objectives.

Figure 2.2 summarizes the prediction that mock compliance strategies are likely as the severity of crises increases, given high outsider monitoring costs. The real compliance gap, relative to international standards, is AC.[33] This may be divided into "overt" (AB) and "hidden" (BC) compliance gaps, keeping in mind that the transparency of compliance will really be a matter of degree. Overt compliance consists mainly of formal adherence to international standards, including ratification. The hidden compliance gap, which measures the extent of mock compliance and increases with crisis severity,[34] reflects an undisclosed policy choice by government (regulatory forbearance), or its inability to ensure administrative and/or private sector compliance with the adopted standards. The rationale for the inverted U-shape of the substantive compliance curve is that at moderate levels of economic distress the external pressure for compliance will be strong, but the costs of substantive compliance will be relatively easily absorbed. At very high levels of distress, substantive compliance becomes nearly impossible for large parts of the private sector.

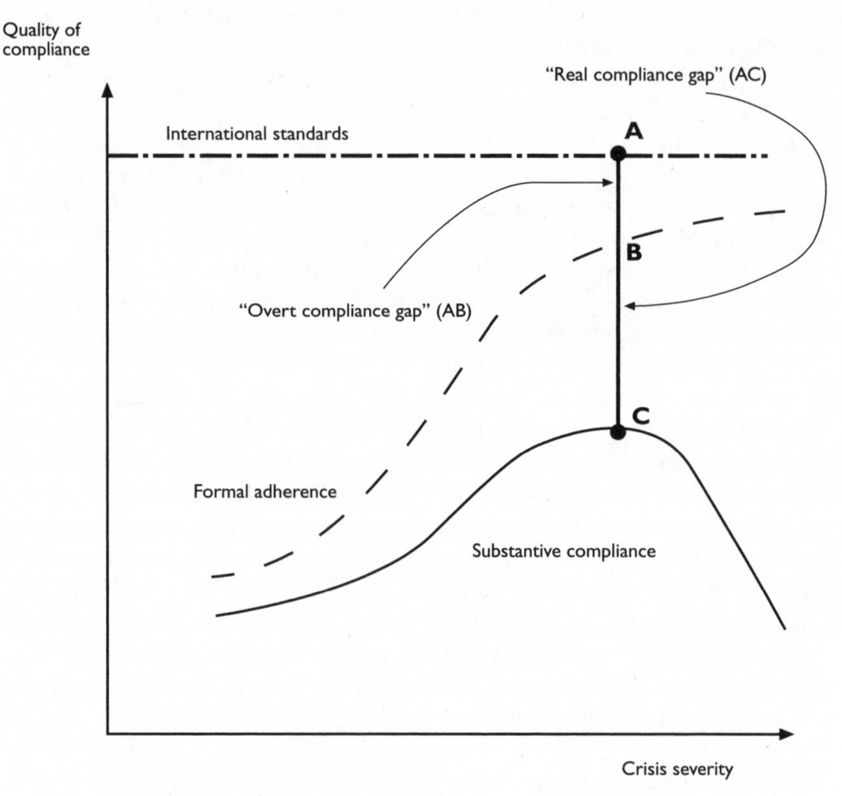

Figure 2.2. Effects of crises on compliance (international standards with high monitoring and private sector compliance costs)

Measuring Compliance and Its Sources

The empirical analysis in the following chapters depends on our ability to detect and to measure different compliance outcomes. Measuring formal compliance with international standards is relatively straightforward; this is largely a matter of assessing the extent to which domestic law and formal regulatory policy is consistent with established international standards.[35] However, measuring the real quality of compliance is far from easy, given that often insiders in the compliance process will have strong incentives to conceal it. For example, data are available on whether individual countries require, allow, or disallow listed companies to use IFRS for financial reporting purposes.[36] However, this data only measures formal compliance by country with IFRS; measuring substantive compliance requires a detailed investigation of the actual conformity of corporate financial reporting with specific IFRS. In this case, the ability of firms to engage in mock compliance with international or domestic standards depends upon the quality and independence of internal and external auditors, and on the strength of enforcement agencies. Measuring these country and firm-level attributes is also difficult, and the available data are generally poor. Similar considerations apply to the measurement of compliance with financial supervision and corporate governance standards.[37]

Unfortunately, this also means that finding direct evidence of sources of mock compliance outcomes is also likely to be difficult. This is because mock compliance can involve illegal or potentially politically damaging collusion by public authorities with individual private sector actors who stand to lose from the strict enforcement of rules. If this were simply a study of formal compliance outcomes, we could focus among other things on the ratification process in the legislature and observable political lobbying by organized interest groups. However, since we are primarily interested in investigating whether actual regulatory behavior is consistent with formally implemented rules, such relatively observable phenomena are less useful. Relatively rarely in recent years have supervisory agencies explicitly justified regulatory forbearance on public interest grounds. At the other extreme, where private sector actors bribe regulators to forbear the application of particular rules, there is no incentive for either party to reveal it to others.

Nevertheless, telltale signs of mock compliance and its sources do emerge, albeit often only after the event. Apparently solvent firms or financial institutions can unexpectedly collapse. Audits of bankrupt firms or banks may reveal misclassified loans, hidden debts, and outright fraud, as well as supervisory negligence and collusion. Sometimes "whistle-blowers" with inside knowledge make this knowledge public. Private sector analysts with detailed local knowledge can also have strong incentives to identify mock compliance should this affect investment performance. It is also possible to compare, for example, the detail of sample outcomes in financial disclosure and corporate governance across firms and countries. Although this kind of evidence is imperfect and often difficult to quantify, it can provide useful qualitative data on mock compliance and its sources. In the empirical chapters that follow, such qualitative forms of evidence are used to supplement more widely available evidence relating to formal compliance.

With respect to measuring compliance outcomes, the ambiguity or complexity of international standards adds to the problem of measurement because of the difficulty of specifying a clear compliance benchmark. As Shelton (2003, 16) points out, it is more difficult to measure compliance with the norm of free speech than with a detailed rule concerning limits on the discharge of toxic waste into water.[38] Many international financial standards are similar to the first example, with the possible exception of

IFRS.[39] To take one relatively well known case, the sixth BCP declares that regulators should set minimum capital adequacy standards requirements for all banks consistent with the (amended) 1988 capital adequacy accord, which set a minimum capital benchmark of eight percent of risk-weighted assets (BCBS 1988, 1997, 5). However, the 1988 accord allowed much flexibility for countries and banks as to how they would meet this rule, with the inevitable result that it has often been easy for many banks and their regulators to satisfy the letter of the standard while circumventing its intent (to promote "prudent" capitalization).

At the same time, particular national standards often emerge to fill the gaps or to clarify ambiguities in international standards, and these national standards come to constitute recognized international best practice. Typically, both regulators and market actors look to detailed regulatory practices in the major developed countries, particularly the United States and the United Kingdom, for such best practices. There are two related reasons for this. First, the American and British approaches to core financial regulation are often relatively stringent and conservative, though they are not always the most stringent.[40] Second, London's and Wall Street's position as the world's dominant financial centers confers a preeminent status upon British and American regulatory agencies, which are also very influential in international standard-setting bodies. As the chairman of the BCBS Accounting Task Force recently noted, "the unavoidable conclusion is that banks need to address... compliance challenges in their risk management programs on a global basis, and that the most stringent requirement quickly becomes the [global] benchmark."[41] Of course, sometimes rules in the two dominant centers diverge, as is currently the case with equity listing standards in the United States and the United Kingdom, and hence a process of regulatory competition can ensue. Nevertheless, the global importance of U.S. and British standards and their tendency to become focal points for convergence makes it convenient to use them in most cases as supplements to official international standards in cases where the latter provide ambiguous benchmarks. As we will see, this eases somewhat the task of measuring the quality of compliance with a range of international standards.

Summary of Predictions

To conclude this theoretical discussion, it will be helpful to clarify how my theory of compliance differs from others and what precisely it predicts. First, other theories of compliance do not always specify how compliance can be largely superficial, or of the mock compliance variety. Second, in contrast to many other theories, I argue that domestic pro-compliance lobbies,

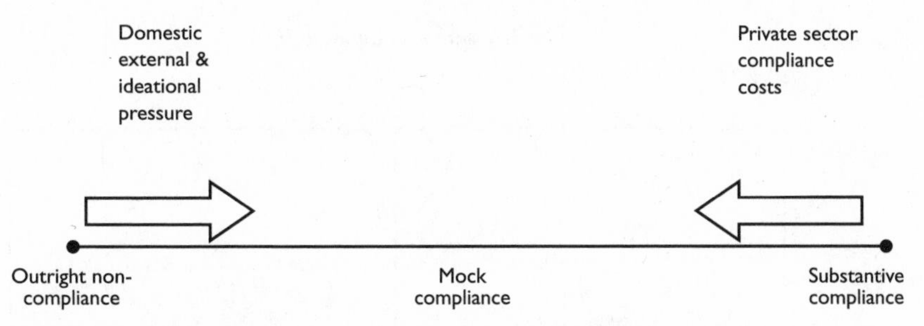

Figure 2.3. Pro-compliance pressure and domestic compliance costs favor mock compliance outcomes

Note: For international standards with high private sector compliance costs and high third party monitoring costs.

international market forces, IFI conditionality, and ideational convergence all tend to promote formal compliance, though they will often be insufficient to promote substantive compliance with international standards. This prediction is summarized in figure 2.3. Third, my theory also abstracts from other factors, such as institutional capacity, except insofar as such capacity is endogenously determined by the domestic political factors upon which I focus. In doing so, I do not wish to deny the importance of "exogenously determined" institutional capacity[42] for compliance outcomes, especially for the least developed countries. However, since the focus of this book is upon some of the most successful middle-income developing countries,[43] the research design is simply intended to focus on compliance outcomes in countries in which exogenous institutional capacity constraints are less severe.

What does my theory predict in terms of compliance outcomes across different standards? The average quality of compliance should be relatively high for SDDS: where compliance costs are mostly socialized, private benefits may be positive, and transparency of compliance makes market sanctioning more effective. By contrast, compliance quality should be much lower for those international standards which entail higher private sector compliance costs and greater monitoring difficulties for outsiders. This prediction is summarized in figure 2.4, where the quality of compliance is expected to be significantly better in quadrant 1 than in quadrant 4. As noted in the introduction, compliance with SDDS is judged by the IMF to be complete in all four of our countries, so in the empirical chapters to follow, I focus only upon on the first three areas identified in quadrant 4.[44]

As for compliance across countries, for those areas in which mock compliance does occur, the real compliance gap should be greatest in those

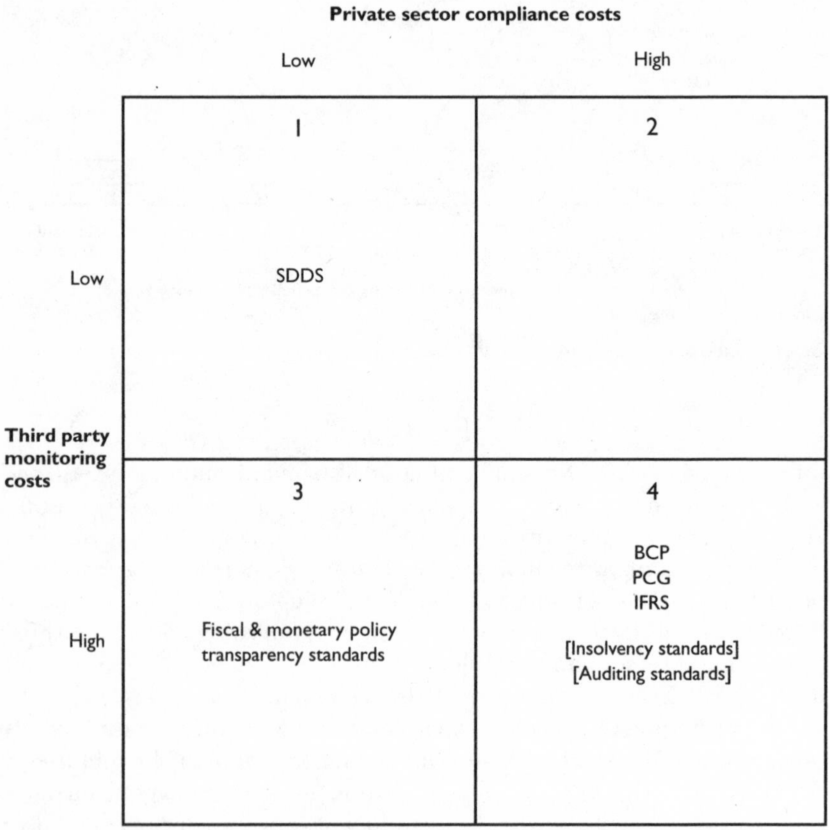

		Private sector compliance costs	
		Low	High
Third party monitoring costs	Low	1 SDDS	2
	High	3 Fiscal & monetary policy transparency standards	4 BCP PCG IFRS [Insolvency standards] [Auditing standards]

Figure 2.4. Private sector compliance costs and third party monitoring costs by standard

countries most deeply affected by the crisis, Indonesia and Thailand. This also implies that over time the quality of compliance should improve most for those countries in which economic recovery was more vigorous (Malaysia and Korea). However, we should once again distinguish between outcomes for different international standards. Economic recovery reduces the level of financial distress in the economy and thereby increases the ability of banks and firms to absorb the costs of compliance with new banking regulation and (to some extent) financial reporting standards. However, noncyclical factors such as the predominance of family and state ownership in Asian countries will likely remain important limitations on the quality of compliance with corporate governance standards (and to some extent financial reporting transparency as well). Hence, we would expect more improvement over time in the quality of compliance with banking regulation and supervision standards compared with accounting standards and especially corporate governance standards.

In the empirical chapters that follow, I assess this theory against the alternative theories that emphasize the role of international market forces, international institutions, and ideational convergence in fostering compliance.

3

Banking Supervision in Indonesia

After a deep economic and political crisis over 1997–98, the Government of Indonesia (GOI) portrayed the goal of compliance with international banking supervision standards as a core plank of its reform strategy for the banking sector and the financial regulatory framework. More broadly, given Indonesia's still bank-dominated financial system, banking supervision has been a key plank of the neoliberal reform project in Indonesia (Hadiz and Robison 2005). Fundamental failures in banking regulation and supervision were generally recognized to have been an important factor in the depth of the crisis. Furthermore, given the extensive nationalization of the banking sector that resulted from the crisis and the strong support given by the IFIs to the bank regulatory agency, the Bank of Indonesia (BI), the prospects for financial regulatory reform were arguably promising. BI was tasked with upgrading the regulatory framework and conducting bank supervision in ways consistent with international standards.

Consistent with the theory of compliance outlined in chapter 2, the GOI ultimately found it impossible to avoid committing itself to the adoption of international standards favored by a coalition of external forces and a group of domestic neoliberal reformers. In some cases, formal compliance itself failed. Even more often, mock compliance resulted as a large gap remained between new formal rules adopted in the post-crisis period and the actual practice of banking supervision and bank management. In the past, chronic regulatory failures were closely associated with the predatory political structure of the New Order state, which President Suharto had dominated (MacIntyre 1993, 151–53; Robison and Hadiz 2004, 80–96). After Suharto's political demise, the process of democratization produced a series of weak governments that remained highly susceptible to the strong anticompliance preferences of important parts of the private and public banking sectors, nonfinancial industry, and the bureaucracy. This susceptibility was partly due to the very depth of the crisis and the anemic economic recovery that followed it, but also because anticompliance forces were able to forge extensive links with new political actors. Consistent with our theory, the extent of mock compliance has diminished as economic recovery has accelerated in recent years, but substantive compliance remains elusive.

Formal Commitment to the Basle Core Principles

Financial sector problems emerged early on in the crisis as the continuing depreciation of the rupiah undermined the mostly unhedged balance sheets of major Indonesian firms, who had borrowed heavily offshore in hard currencies. With many firms unable or unwilling to service their international or domestic debt, the great majority of domestic bank loans became nonperforming. The IMF's and the government's inexperience with banking sector problems led to a series of disastrous mistakes that compounded financial and corporate sector collapse, though weaknesses in supervision also contributed to this result (IEO 2003, 11–15).

There is no doubt that the broad impact of the crisis and of associated IMF conditionality was to substantially increase the level of formal commitment to international standards in Indonesia. However, even this formal commitment proved highly volatile over the first six months of the crisis.[1] In the first Letter of Intent (LOI) outlining the GOI's reform commitments to the IMF, there was an explicit commitment to raise Indonesian banking regulation and supervision standards to international levels:

> Prudential regulations and enforcement procedures will be strengthened in line with the Basle Committee's Core Principles of banking supervision.... The instruction issued by the central bank to raise capital adequacy to 9 percent by end-1997, and 12 percent by end-2001, will be strictly enforced. The Bank Supervision Department of Bank Indonesia will be strengthened to effectively implement risk-based oversight of the banking system, with due regard for the need to strengthen the banks' capacity to provide credit only to solvent borrowers.[2]

In addition to increasing the leverage of the IFIs in Indonesia, the crisis also considerably improved the position of the government's team of economic technocrats, who also favored the adoption of international standards, especially relating to banking regulation and supervision.[3] As a subsequent review by the IMF's own Independent Evaluation Office suggested, "[i]nternal [IMF] documents show that both [IMF] staff and management perceived the crisis as an opportunity to assist the reformist economic team in carrying out financial sector reform and deregulation, both areas that were earlier emphasized in IMF surveillance" (IEO 2003, 29). Above all, the reformers wanted to restore the operational independence of the key policymaking ministries and the central bank by eliminating the chronic political interference and corruption of the Suharto regime.[4]

However, the limits of the influence of this reform coalition of external and domestic actors were soon made clear, repeating a pattern established in the past (MacIntyre 1993, 155). Key political actors in the Suharto regime, not least the President himself, were closely associated with major businesses that stood to suffer directly from the implementation of the IMF's structural conditionalities. Hence, on numerous occasions from November 1997 through May 1998, the President backtracked on several of the commitments made to the IMF and, implicitly, to domestic reformers (Blustein 2001, 101–2). This prompted a series of tense renegotiations with the IMF followed by more backtracking.[5] Even when commitments to the IMF were finally adopted, such as with the introduction of full tax deductibility of banks' loan loss provisions in April 1998, the IMF and its Indonesian allies remained in a weak position to enforce general commitments like that to "strengthen BI's bank supervision department and strengthen enforcement" (see table 3.1).

In addition to many of the governance reforms contained in the LOIs being very general in nature, they often consisted of "targets" or "benchmarks" rather than "performance criteria" that would trigger the cessation of disbursements in the event of nonimplementation (table 3.1).[6] Jack Boorman, then Director of the IMF's Policy Development and Review Department and one of the senior Fund officials intimately involved in the Indonesian program, subsequently defended the first LOI from the criticism that it was overly intrusive:

> Contrary to popular perception, almost all structural measures included in the first LOI were general in nature and were meant to be implemented over the course of the program, thus giving the government the necessary leverage to pursue the reforms, but the discretion to advance them at a pace deemed most appropriate. (Boorman and Richter Hume 2003, 9)

As it turned out, such flexibility simply allowed the Suharto regime to engage in virtually outright noncompliance with international standards. In this regard, things changed considerably after Suharto's resignation on 21 May 1998. The new government, led by former Vice-President B. J. Habibie, recognized that it had little choice but to implement the major reforms

TABLE 3.1
Banking regulation-related conditionalities in Indonesia's IMF programs

Prior actions	Performance criteria	Benchmarks	Targets	Other conditions for completing next review
		November 1997 LOI		
	By end-December 1997, establishment of quantitative performance targets for state-owned banks together with monitoring mechanisms	Audits of state-owned banks by international accounting firms by end-March 1998 * Introduction of full tax deductibility of loan loss provisions by end-March 1998		
		January 1998 MEFP		
			Revision of central bank and banking laws by end-1998 Require banks immediately to publish audited annual reports Submission of draft law on the elimination of foreign ownership restrictions on listed banks by June 1998	
		April 1998 Supplementary MEFP		
Introduction of full tax deductibility of loan loss provisions by end-March 1998		Audits of state-owned banks by international accounting firms by end-June 1998 *	Upgrade reporting and monitoring procedures for banks' foreign exchange by end-June 1998	Restore IBRA banks to 8% CAR by end-1998

TABLE 3.1—cont.

Prior actions	Performance criteria	Benchmarks	Targets	Other conditions for completing next review
Announce minimum capital requirements			Strengthen BI's bank supervision department and strengthen enforcement	
			Submit to Parliament a draft law to institutionalize Bank Indonesia's autonomy by end-1998	
		July 1998 MEFP and LOI		
	Submit to Parliament a draft law to institutionalize BI autonomy by end-Sept 1998			
		October 1998 LOI		
			Issue new regulations on loan classification and loan loss provisions by 15 November 1998	
			Issue new regulations on connected lending, liquidity management, and foreign currency exposure by end-November 1998	

November 1998 LOI			
		Issue three new prudential regulations on connected lending, the capital adequacy ratio, and the semi-annual publication of financial statements by 15 December 1998	
March 1999 MEFP and LOI**			
		Pass amended Banking Law by end-March 1999 Finalize assessment of further amendments to regulatory framework by end-June 1999	

Sources: IEO (2003, Appendix A1-1), and IMF website.

Note: Prior actions are required before the IMF Executive Board can consider a program; Performance criteria are required for disbursements to continue; Benchmarks and Targets do not govern disbursement but may be subject to discussion at review.

* = not implemented

** A number of subsequent LOIs and MEFPs (Memoranda on Financial and Economic Policies) were issued, the last being in June 2003, but there were no further commitments made with respect to banking sector regulation.

agreed with the IMF and to agree a series of new reforms that would restore confidence in the shattered financial system. Toward the end of 1998, the GOI also made commitments to upgrading various key regulatory standards in the areas of capital adequacy, loan loss accounting and provisions, and connected lending. In the LOI of May 1999, the GOI noted that Parliament had approved the new Central Bank Act (no. 23/1999) on 17 May, which gave BI considerable legal independence and which required it to improve its supervisory and examination activities by the end of June, including its on- and off-site supervision.[7] The BI Master Plan, mentioned in the January 2000 LOI, envisaged conformity with most of the BCP by the end of 2001. However, there was no specific performance requirement in the IMF program for such compliance, and the date for its achievement was later extended to end-2002.[8]

Nevertheless, despite these public commitments to compliance after May 1998, the GOI chose to limit external scrutiny of its performance in this area. Notably, as of late 2006 it has so far refused either to participate in the FSAP process or to publish a number of relevant reports prepared by IMF staff (Boorman and Richter Hume 2003, 14).[9] Although this makes the assessment of the quality of Indonesia's compliance with the BCP more difficult, I argue below that what evidence there is suggests that this was often poor in the early post-crisis years.

Compliance with the Basle Core Principles

In 2000, an IMF technical assistance team began an assessment (unpublished) of Indonesia's degree of compliance with the BCP; it was completed in September 2002. According to the IMF, the results were "fairly bad."[10] The general conclusion was that BI's understanding of the intent of the rules was in many cases poor. The GOI chose not to publish this report, but BI provided a summary assessment in its 2002 annual report (Bank Indonesia 2002, 153–54). Although this reported some progress over 2000–2002, full compliance had been achieved for only 2 of the 25 BCPs. Indonesia was judged materially noncompliant or wholly noncompliant for 13 others (see table 3.2). BI adopted a plan to rectify these deficiencies, including adopting new regulations and considerable staff training. In early 2004, a new self-assessment by BI judged Indonesia as fully compliant with 16 of the 25 BCPs (IMF 2004b, 22).

I argue below that there was more behind compliance failures in Indonesia than "poor understanding" by BI staff of new rules and other kinds of institutional capacity problems. The assessment that follows is based upon a variety of publicly available material as well as interviews with Indonesian officials and independent experts. Rather than go through all 25 BCP

TABLE 3.2
IMF assessment of Indonesia's BCP compliance, September 2002

Level of compliance	September 2000	September 2002	September 2002: Core principles (number)
Fully compliant	2	2	1, 2
Largely compliant	5	10	3, 5, 6, 14, 15, 18, 21, 22, 24, 25
Materially noncompliant	16	12	4, 7, 8, 9, 10, 12, 13, 16, 17, 19, 20, 23
Noncompliant	2	1	11

Source: Bank Indonesia (2002, 154) (based upon an IMF technical mission assessment).

identified above, I focus only on some of the most important: regulatory independence; rules on capital adequacy, loan classification and provisions; legal lending limits; and disclosure requirements.[11]

Independence of Regulators

The principle of regulator independence was seen as pivotal by the IFIs and domestic reformers and is embodied in the first BCP. The BCBS holds that compliance with this principle requires that "there is, in practice, no significant evidence of government or industry interference in the operational independence of each agency, and in each agency's ability to obtain and deploy the resources needed to carry out its mandate" (BCBS 1999, 12). The IMF assessment team in 2002 judged Indonesia to be fully compliant with this principle, presumably because the new Central Bank Act of May 1999 granted substantial legal independence to BI (see also Quintyn, Ramirez, and Taylor 2007).

Certainly, before this point, BI was both legally and in practice subordinate to the MOF and the GOI in regard to banking supervision. The BI Governor was a Cabinet member, and the finance minister chaired BI's Monetary Committee; but it was Suharto who effectively controlled all the major levers of financial policy. Regulatory limits on bank credits to single or group borrowers were routinely flouted because of the political connections of large borrowers. Inevitably, politically directed lending resulted in serious insolvency problems in both banks and borrowers. The IFIs had been aware of these supervisory failures, but institutional and high politics prevented them from being aired.[12] Attempts by BI to enforce prudential rules against connected borrowers resulted in Suharto's removal of the BI Governor in 1992 and the Minister of Finance in 1996 (Cole and Slade 1998, 65). State banks, in particular, had long been used to direct credit toward strategic sectors for broad developmental purposes, but politically connected businessmen received the bulk of large public sector contracts and state bank loans from the 1980s (Enoch, Frécaut, and Kovanen 2003; Pangestu and Habir 2002, 32; Robison and Hadiz 2004, 80–83). Even if BI had been consistently willing to enforce regulations against state banks and politically connected private banks, which is doubtful, it lacked the autonomy to do so.[13]

In any case, before May 1999 BI possessed few real enforcement powers, since many rules were indicative rather than mandatory. Banks that exceeded regulatory limits simply got lower scores on their overall CAMELS ratings, with no automatic punishment for nonobservance of specific regulatory standards.[14] The exception was for minimum capital adequacy ratios (CARs), provisioning requirements, and legal lending limits (LLLs), which in theory could lead to administrative sanctions or cease and desist orders in the event of noncompliance (Binhadi 1995, 220, 229).[15] However, since compliance with these "mandatory" rules was also extraordinarily low, it demonstrated that the problem was not with the rules as such but with the political system in which BI was deeply embedded.

BI's political subordination continued well after the crisis began, even though a stricter "exit" policy for bad banks was announced at the beginning of the IMF program. The government, with IMF support, had tentatively begun to manage the banking crisis by announcing the closure of 16 relatively insignificant, insolvent banks on 1 November 1997, three of which were connected to members of the Suharto family (Blustein 2001, 110; Boorman and Richter Hume 2003, 8; IEO 2003, 126). Although these bank closures signaled a shift to a stricter exit policy, especially because only small depositors were to be compensated, the strategy had the disastrous effect of precipitating a series of runs on large connected private banks such as BCA, as depositors placed their money in the "safer" state-owned and foreign banks.[16] This undermined the credibility of the new exit policy, since BI was compelled to provide emergency liquidity to other banks to keep them afloat (IEO 2003, 29). Termed "BLBI," this ongoing liquidity support to the banking sector led to a massive expansion of the monetary base and dramatic currency depreciation.[17] Many of the largest bank recipients of these funds were in violation of various key regulatory limits, and most of the funds were used for purposes other than recapitalization, including repayment of creditors, intra-group investments, and capital flight (Robison and Hadiz 2004, 193). In effect, state funds were lent to banks that were in turn raided by their owners to avoid the collapse of their corporate empires.[18]

Corruption, which remained extensive after Suharto's demise, undermined compliance with international standards in other ways. The Bank Bali scandal, which broke in August 1999, proved only the first of many, but it prompted the IMF, World Bank, and ADB to suspend cooperation temporarily with the GOI in September 1999. Bank Bali, controlled by the government's Indonesian Bank Restructuring Agency (IBRA), had channeled illegal funds to Golkar, President Habibie's political party. This implied either incompetence or collusion by IBRA and BI officials. The BI Governor was sentenced to three year's jail in connection with the scandal, though he refused to resign from his position.[19] Low civil service pay is often said to contribute to corruption, though it is also widespread in the better-paid private financial sector.[20] Furthermore, although post-Suharto governments have been unable to prosecute successfully the most flagrant cases of corruption from the Suharto era, many public officials fear that the corruption of the judicial process might render them liable to future prosecution.[21] The prosecution of current and former senior BI staff, including the two previous governors, has underlined the risks involved.

From May 1999, the level of formal compliance with international standards in this area improved markedly. The new Central Bank Act explicitly ruled out BI being used as a source of subsidized finance for favored borrowers, and the rules for the provision of emergency liquidity support to banks were also tightened.[22] The act provided for a fixed five-year term for its governor, who would no longer sit in Cabinet. Importantly, it also described BI's responsibility for banking regulation and supervision as one of the three key pillars of its monetary policy independence. In principle, the new regulatory regime also gives BI considerable new powers in the area of banking supervision.[23] If banks should violate regulations, BI could now apply administrative sanctions. BI officials were also granted legal protection in the conduct of supervisory functions, including off-site supervision and on-site examination, though as noted above there are limits to this protection. In cases where specific regulations are enforceable through criminal sanctions, such as in the case of the LLL regulation, BI should report the finding to the police and/or the attorney general. A Special Unit for Banking Investigation was established to deal with these more serious violations. A stricter interpretation of BI's fit and proper test for senior management threatened the traditional system of political patronage in the financial sector. Finally, a new exit policy was specified in which failed banks would either be closed, or, in the case of banks deemed too big to fail, recapitalized and transferred to IBRA.[24]

Under the new rules there are three increasingly intensive forms of bank supervision: "normal," applied to banks with CARs above 8 percent, "intensive," applied to banks with CARs between 6–8 percent, and "special," applied to banks with CARs between 4–6 percent (banks with CARs persistently below 4 percent were supposed to be closed or transferred). Normal supervision focuses on risk-management, an enhancement to the old CAMELS approach. Undercapitalized banks would be required to submit recapitalization plans within six months. After this time (with a three-month grace period), if the bank was still under-capitalized, it could be transferred to IBRA if the various problems were deemed rectifiable (e.g., if CARs could be raised to the 8 percent minimum within a year). Banks would be placed under intensified surveillance if their NPLs were above 5 percent and would be required to take actions to reduce them below this level (BI 2005, 23). Unsurprisingly, BI insists that this new policy has been strictly applied since May 1999.

The extent of executive branch intervention in banking supervision does appear to have decreased dramatically since May 1999. Under the presidency of the freely elected Abdurrahman Wahid,[25] BI's deteriorating relations with the government were one indication of this independence.[26] However, although BI is more independent of the executive branch today than before 1999, it is less independent of Parliament. Senior managers and the Board of Governors of BI have in practice been elected by Parliament's Commission IX for financial affairs. Some claim money politics dominated this appointment process, so that corruption continues to intrude into BI's governance at the highest levels.[27] As Robison and Hadiz (2004, 205) noted, the danger of insulating BI supervision from the political process was that it might allow predators within BI more freedom to exploit corrupt linkages with private sector interests outside of the Bank.

In any case, the extensive nationalization of the banking sector due to the crisis meant that IBRA, rather than BI, became the focus of political intervention in financial regulation. It was here that the key battle was played out between the GOI (or rather, those in the government with real reformist intentions) and the major debtors and former owners of banks who had suffered major losses but who were fighting to preserve the remains of their business empires. Given the high stakes and the ability of these powerful private sector actors to influence both IBRA and the courts, it was a battle the reformers could not win. By mid-1998, all of Indonesia's largest private banks were back in state hands (along with many other assets of sometimes dubious value). IBRA also had supervisory responsibilities for banks under its control (Hadiz and Robison 2005, 226–29; Pangestu and Habir 2002, 20). By mid-2002, ten banks still remained on IBRA's books, constituting about 70 percent of the banking sector's total assets. When IBRA was closed in April 2004, the total proceeds from asset sales and debt recovery delivered to government since 1998 had been Rp 168 trillion, giving a recovery rate on IBRA assets of only 28 percent.[28]

This represented a massive transfer of wealth from taxpayers to depositors and to some powerful private sector players who will never have to repay the bulk of their debts to the government. Bank nationalization, as Hamilton-Hart (2000, 115) notes, often had the effect simply of relieving bank owners of their liabilities to depositors and other creditors, even while the government tried, mostly unsuccessfully, to recover banks' loans to these same owners. Many concerns were also raised over the fact that the government's desperate need to raise cash meant that banks could in some cases be sold back to their original owners at a substantial discount.[29] Various IBRA oversight mechanisms existed, including an Ombudsman, Audit Committee, and Oversight Committee, but their criticisms of IBRA-led restructurings and sales rarely changed the outcome (IMF 2002, 36).

In the case of "joint recap" banks, in which both the government and private owners had injected capital, the latter were often able to retain control and in some cases continued to evade prudential oversight. A notorious example is BII, formerly majority-owned by the Widjaja family associated with the Sinar Mas group. IBRA took a 57 percent stake in BII in 1999 with a Rp 6.6 trillion injection of recapitalization bonds; it also assumed BII's Rp 12 trillion exposure to the Sinar Mas group.[30] Surprisingly, an additional Rp 15 trillion worth of additional capital was subsequently injected into BII, even though this did not provide the government with additional equity or control. With disastrous consequences, IBRA allowed family members to retain management control until May 2002.[31] The management team was replaced only after it was disclosed that BII's CAR had deteriorated to minus 47 percent at the end of 2001 due to previously undisclosed NPLs. It is unclear if this treatment stemmed from too-big-to-fail considerations or from collusion between former BII managers and IBRA officials.[32]

Another sign of IBRA's politicization can be found in the high turnover of its chief executives (in dramatic contrast to BI). Over 1998–2004, IBRA had seven directors: more than one resigned in frustration, and the government replaced others. IBRA reported to the Financial Sector Policy Committee, a cabinet-level body headed by the coordinating minister for the economy. The committee was initially under the MOF, but was moved to the Ministry of State-Owned Enterprises (MSE) when Megawati Sukarnoputri took over the Presidency after Wahid's ejection from office in July 2001. Bank recapitalizations then had to be approved by the MSE, the MOF, and Parliament, increasing the points at which political influence could be exerted.

To summarize, although BI's independence from government increased substantially from May 1999, politics, especially within the legislative branch, has continued to intrude into the regulatory process. BI itself has not been able to escape allegations of political corruption and negligence, though the major problems appear to have been in IBRA, where there were more opportunities and even greater reason for powerful private interests to subvert the supervisory process.

Rules on Capital Adequacy, Loan Classification, and Provisioning

Capital adequacy requirements had been phased in from the early 1990s, with a minimum required CAR of 7 percent by March 1993 and 8 percent by end December 1994, consistent with the Basle minimum (Binhadi 1995, 204–5). However, the underlying definitions showed considerable laxity compared to Basle norms. Tier 1 capital included, in addition to the usual core equity, 50 percent of the current year's profit after tax (increased to 100 percent in 1993). As for risk weightings, domestic interbank claims were weighted at only 20 percent, the same as claims upon prime international banks; claims on state-owned banks were weighted at 0 percent; and claims on SOEs were reduced from 100 percent to 50 percent in 1993 (Binhadi 1995, 91, 207–8). For these reasons, Indonesian bank CARs were considerably overstated compared to most developed countries before the crisis.

Indonesia's loan classification system dates to 1971, but was also updated in 1991 and 1993. There were four categories: current, substandard, doubtful, and loss, on which provisioning requirements were 0.5 percent, 3 percent, 50 percent, and 100 percent respectively. The definitions were very lax by U.S. and UK standards.[33] Loans could be defined as "current" even if they were substantially in arrears (by up to 6 months on principal for credits with installment periods of 4 months or more—compared to 3 months in the United States and the United Kingdom). Substandard loans were defined as those in interest arrears of up to six months (Binhadi 1995, 225–28). Most importantly, given the standard practice of lending against collateral, banks were permitted to deduct collateral values from the outstanding nominal loan amount of noncurrent loans in order to calculate the provisioning requirement (up to 100 percent for cash or near-cash equivalents or 75 percent of the value of less liquid collateral). However, there were few stipulations regarding appropriate methods of collateral valuation and little regulation of appraisal companies. Hence, the pre-crisis rules allowed Indonesian banks to overstate capital and to understate NPLs compared to banks in major developed countries.

After the crisis, the government's economic team and the IMF aimed to raise the amount of real capital in the banking system. As noted above, the first LOI was very optimistic, aiming to raise required capital well above the 8 percent Basle minimum, on the reasonable grounds that this was necessitated by the extensive connected lending in the Indonesian system.[34] However, it soon became clear that even the 8 percent minimum was unattainable after the crisis, let alone 12 percent. In early 1998, when average CARs hit *minus* 13 percent, BI quietly dropped the 12 percent target, stating that Indonesia would reach the standard Basle 8 percent minimum by end-2001, with an interim 4 percent minimum.

At the same time, capital definitions were gradually tightened, though they were not made completely consistent with Basle standards. From November 1998, only general provisions on current loans could be counted toward Tier 2 capital (rather than, as before, all provisions). From June 2000, specific loan-loss provisions had to be deducted from the total value

TABLE 3.3
Classifications of Indonesian bank inspections, 1998–99

Type of bank	Category A (CARs >4%)	Category B (–25% <CARs <4%)	Category C (CARs <–25%)	Total
State banks	–	–	7	7
Private national banks	32	62	34	128
Banks taken over	–	–	4	4
Regional development banks	12	10	5	27
Joint venture banks	12	16	4	32
Foreign banks	10	–	–	10
Total	66	88	54	208

Source: Bank Indonesia.

of earning assets for CAR calculations.[35] BI regulation No. 3/21/PBI/2001 of 13 December 2001 also excluded investments in subsidiaries from capital, which significantly reduced reported CARs for some banks. However, loans to SOEs remained risk-weighted at only 50 percent, in contrast with the Basle standard of 100 percent (IMF 2004b, 20).

From March 1998, foreign specialists were brought in to help BI to assess bank capitalization (Enoch, Frécaut and Kovanen 2003, 80). Based on inspection reports, banks were divided into A, B, and C categories. Category A banks were those with CARs of at least 4 percent, category B those with CARs between –25 percent and +4 percent, and category C those banks with CARs less than –25 percent. Category C banks were, in principle, automatically to be deemed nonviable and closed. That most banks fell into category B indicates both the severity of the Indonesian crisis and the laxity of precrisis supervision. All state banks were placed in category C and all foreign banks were in category A (table 3.3). However, no state banks were actually closed: four were merged to form Bank Mandiri, while others (BNI, BTN, and BRI) were restructured and recapitalized. Thus, again, considerable discretion was allowed in the application of the closure rules, with too-big-to-fail and political considerations playing a role.

BI also promulgated new loan classification and provisioning standards on 27 February 1998. A "special mention" category was added to the existing loan classification system, consistent with international best practice (table 3.4). BI allowed banks to upgrade NPLs to substandard after three repayments were made (i.e., often within three months) and to current or special mention after a further three months. This was consistent with standard practice in the major Western developed countries in the early 1990s, but international best practice had since moved on to the use of "forward-looking criteria" (FLC) in loan classification.[36] BI argues that its system is now semi-forward looking, in that new regulations require banks

TABLE 3.4
Indonesian asset classification and provisioning standards, post-crisis

Provisioning category	Asset classification	Provisioning requirement as percentage of asset face value
General provision	Current	1%*
Specific provision	Special mention	5%
	Substandard	15% (after deducting collateral value)
	Doubtful	50% (after deducting collateral value)
	Loss	100% (after deducting collateral value)

Source: Directorate of Banking Research and Regulation, Bank Indonesia.
* Excepting government bonds and Bank Indonesia Certificates of Indebtedness (SBIs) from 12 November 1998.

to consider, in addition to any payment delinquency, both the future prospects of each debtor and its industry. However, the adoption of a true FLC system of loan classification is dependent upon a substantial increase in risk management capacity in the banking sector and in BI itself.

The increases in provisioning requirement compared to the pre-crisis regime relate to the current, special mention, and substandard categories and meet international standards. These increases were phased in from 31 December 1998 to 30 June 2001, by which time banks were required to meet them in full. However, banks are still able to deduct up to 70 percent of the value of collateral attached to loans classified as substandard and below (up to 50 percent for securities). Assets backed by cash collateral are classified as current and require no general provision; nor do holdings of government-backed debt.[37] BI issued new rules relating to collateral valuation in November 1998 that required banks to take into account the difficulties in gaining possession of the collateral through the foreclosure process (Song 2002, 18). Banks must obtain a recent valuation (within the previous six months), issued by a MOF-approved valuer. If no market price is available, banks must use the tax accounting price, which should be the most conservative available.[38] Bankers complain that these rules are very conservative, forcing them to value collateral on a fire-sale basis.[39] Even if this is true, the Indonesian provisioning regime remains a much less conservative system than in the United States and in Korea, where collateral cannot be used to offset provisions.

The published figures on bank CARs suggest great improvement from the depths of 1998 to early 2002 (figure 3.1), though there was substantial variation across different major banks (table 3.5). By the end of 2000, the average commercial bank CAR in Indonesia was over 20 percent, well above the minimum requirement, and has remained high ever since. However, there are reasons to think Indonesian banks are considerably less well capitalized than official figures suggest. In the absence of a functioning

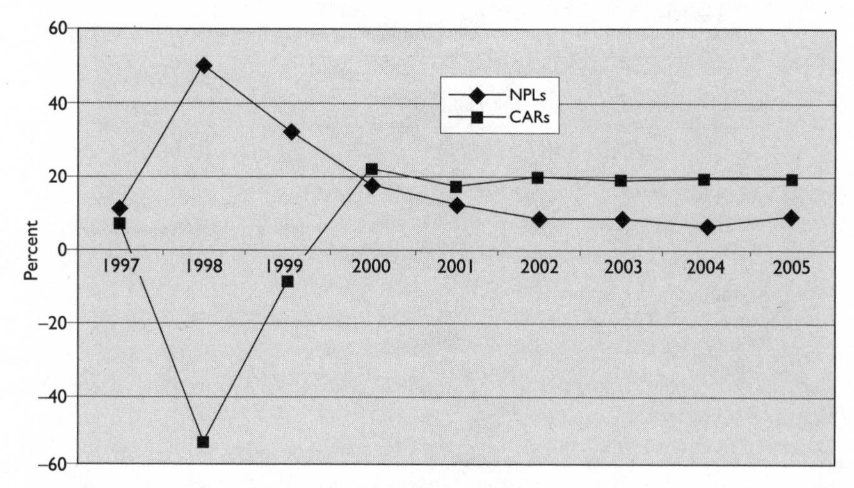

Figure 3.1. Indonesian banks: CARs and NPLs, 1997–2005

Sources: IMF, Bank Indonesia.
Note: CARs are calculated as total Basle capital as a percentage of risk-weighted assets for the banking sector. NPLs are nonperforming loans as a percentage of total banking sector loans. Figures are end-of-period averages, so do not show the peaks, troughs, or within-period variations.

system of financial intermediation, income from government bonds became the major source of bank income.[40] Many banks still hold large amounts of government recapitalization bonds on their balance sheet, which is not surprising given that these bonds are weighted at 0 percent for capital calculation purposes. Also, government bonds held for "investment purposes" (which made up the bulk of such holdings) were valued at 100 percent of face value, even though they traded on secondary markets at a discount. The 50 percent risk-weight for SOE loans also continues to flatter official CARs.

The most important question, however, is whether Indonesia's new loan classification and provisioning standards were strictly enforced. Unfortunately, published data (on the BI website) does not include information on the value of collateral attached to loans, so we must take BI's and the banks' word that collateral valuation is now consistently conservative. Even if this were true, however, the difficulties of foreclosing on collateral in Indonesia's dysfunctional legal system must imply consistent under-provisioning. As for loan classification, private analysts commonly claimed in the years after the crisis that superficial restructuring of loans remained standard practice in Indonesia and that BI persistently turned a blind eye to this (IMF 2002, 59, 2004c, 21). Certainly, many Indonesian corporations remained effectively bankrupt over 2001–2, and often it was in the interest of both bank and

TABLE 3.5
Official capital and NPL ratios, major Indonesian banks, first quarter 2002

Bank	Official CARs (%)	Official NPLs (% of total loans)
BCA	40.1	11.3
BII	-14.6	20.2
BNI*	15.6	28.7
BRI*	13.7	13.7
BTN*	13.8	12.4
Buana Indonesia	23.2	1.3
Danamon	38.8	3.8
Lippo	25.4	8.6
Mandiri*	26.4	15.4
Mega	11.4	0.3
Niaga	17.5	15.1
Pan Indonesia	36.9	10.6
Universal	2.2	11.9

Sources: Bank Indonesia and individual bank websites.
Note: CARs are calculated as total Basle capital as a percentage of risk-weighted assets. NPLs are non-performing loans as a percentage of total bank loans.
* State-owned banks (as distinct from those banks owned by IBRA).

debtor to restructure loans so as to treat them as performing. State banks remain especially weak, since they continue to be the main port of call for politically connected but problematic borrowers.

The BI website now provides much more data on NPLs than before 1998. For example, it provides monthly data on restructured loans that have been reclassified as performing (i.e., from lower categories to current or special mention). In late 2001 to early 2002, each month the major Indonesian banks were reclassifying as performing past NPLs worth on average about 3 percent of their total loan book (with wide variation across banks). Some of these included unrestructured NPLs repurchased from IBRA, and BI regulations allowed forbearance in classifying these loans for one year (World Bank 2004a, 24). Moreover, BI itself admitted that bank inspections have shown that Indonesian banks continued to underestimate the level of NPLs well after 1998 (BI 2004, 26). Estimating the "true" level of NPLs remains difficult, despite the increased availability of some data. By the end of 2002, official bank NPLs had fallen to 8 percent of total loans, but total NPLs including those held by IBRA were still 45 percent of total loans outstanding. If restructured loans were added back to official NPLs, as some analysts suggest is necessary, this put total NPLs at about double the official rate, and considerably higher for state banks. Compared to other countries, provisioning levels also looked quite low: loan-loss provisions covered only 37 percent of these re-estimated NPLs in May 2002, compared to well over 100 percent in Korea and Malaysia.[41]

More recently, additional doubt was cast on the veracity of reported NPLs. In May 2005, Bank Mandiri, Indonesia's largest and still majority state-owned bank, announced that as a result of new, tighter BI loan classification regulations, its reported NPLs would rise. As it turned out, these increased from 7 percent of Mandiri's total loans at the end of 2004 to 25 percent by September 2005. Over 40 percent of its corporate loan book was still classified as nonperforming. This revelation occurred at a time when Mandiri's senior management was under investigation for making illegal loans.[42] NPLs at state-owned banks generally increased three-fold over 2005, 70 percent of which was due to tightening of loan classification rules (IMF 2006, 11; Fitch Ratings 2005). However, it was unclear why this regulatory tightening should only have produced substantially higher NPLs for Mandiri and BNI, the two largest Indonesian banks, rather than across the board. This provides further evidence of past forbearance and/or bank-level compliance failures, suggesting that borrowers could have been borrowing from one bank to repay NPLs to another (Ernst & Young 2006, 25). However, it also shows that BI continued to tighten regulation as economic recovery took hold.

Legal Lending Limits

Continuing compliance weaknesses can also be found in other prudential rules, notably LLLs. Legal limits on lending to unconnected and connected single and group borrowers had already been introduced in 1988 (Binhadi 1995, 69–73, 220–23).[43] Initially, the LLL for unconnected debtors was 20 percent of bank capital for single debtors and 50 percent for a group of debtors (reduced to 20 percent in 1993).[44] There was no limitation placed on loans to management or staff other than that repayment ability should be assessed with respect to their bank salary. LLLs for bank commissioners were limited to 5 percent of bank capital for individual commissioners and their companies and 15 percent for a commissioner and his group of companies. Banks could also lend to shareholders with 10 percent or more of a bank's shares up to 10 percent of bank capital for single borrowers and 25 percent for group borrowers (reduced to 10 percent by 1997). LLLs were inapplicable for government-guaranteed credits. Although these rules were very lax by international standards, the more fundamental problem was that even these limits were persistently ignored in the pre-crisis and the BLBI period as owners used banks as sources of finance for family businesses (Rosser 2002, 51–84).[45]

Unsurprisingly, the October and November 1998 LOIs set the prompt revision of LLLs as key targets. On 31 December 1998, LLL provisions were updated, but the main objective was to bring banks into conformity with the existing rules. Again, however, what was desirable from the perspective of regulatory neoliberalism and what was politically possible were very different things. Requiring banks to come rapidly into conformity with the LLL provisions would have had a severe contractionary effect on bank lending and the economy generally. Inevitably, the GOI decided that the newly enforced rules would be phased in gradually over the following four years. For unconnected borrowers (single and group), LLLs were set at 30 percent of bank capital until the end of 2001, 25 percent throughout 2002, and 20 percent from 1 January 2003. By the beginning of 2002, then, Indonesia aimed to be in compliance with the Basle-recommended limit of 25 percent. For connected parties, however, a Basle-consistent LLL of 10 percent of bank capital was to be implemented immediately in 1999.

Indonesia was still judged to be materially noncompliant or noncompliant in the relevant BCPs (numbers 9 and 10) in this area by the IMF assessment team in September 2002. This judgment was replicated in 2004 (IMF 2004b, 24). In the absence of the unpublished reports, the reasons for these judgments are unclear. Certainly, the apparent intention to enforce the new LLLs has been onerous for banks and some borrowers; BI argued that even phased enforcement contributed to the collapse of bank lending after 1997 (BI 2000, 23). There is also some evidence of regulatory forbearance in this area, as the deadline for bringing LLLs into conformity with the revised regulations was extended in June 2000 for debtors involved in debt restructuring under an official agency (BI 2000, 100).

However, despite this slippage, there seems to have been a dramatic improvement in this area since 1997. Banks must now report their single and group lender exposures to BI on a monthly basis and must disclose in their public financial reports whether they breach the maximum specified levels. Violations are also published on the BI website. When violations of these limits are judged to be intentional, BI can press criminal charges. Assuming the data itself is accurate, from 1998 to early 2002, only "unintentional" violations occurred (such as those due to unexpected foreign exchange movements), in which case banks are given nine months to reduce the exposure to acceptable levels.[46] Reported related party loans for the major private banks have also been reduced to well within the maximum allowable amount. Without inside knowledge about the accuracy of financial reporting, however, it is impossible to reach a definitive judgment on compliance in these areas.

Disclosure Requirements

Bank financial disclosure requirements have been improved considerably since the crisis. This might promote "market regulation" even in the presence of regulatory agency failures (Barth, Caprio, and Levine 2006). In the January 1998 LOI, a target requiring banks to publish audited annual financial statements was included (it may have surprised many to learn that this was not already the case!). The November 1998 LOI also required banks to publish semi-annual reports. In late 2000, BI required banks, private companies, and individuals to provide data to BI on all foreign borrowings and monthly reports on foreign exchange positions (BI Regulation No. 2/22/PBI/2000 and Circular Letter No. 2/28/DSM). Later, in March 2001, BI required Indonesian banks to publish detailed financial reports monthly and quarterly. Much of this data is now published at the insistence of the IMF on the BI website. In addition, BI issued revised Indonesian Banking Accounting Guidelines (PAPI) in 2000, effective from 13 December 2001. These included the principle of consolidated reporting for subsidiaries in which a bank has a majority interest. However, penalties for nonobservance were surprisingly small, being limited to less than US$10,000; the public naming of nonobservant banks may be a greater sanction.[47]

The main accounting standard-setting body was KSAK, the Committee on Financial Accounting Standards of the Indonesian Institute of Accountants (IIA). This was renamed DSAK, the Financial Accounting Standards Board, in 2001. Since 1994, KSAK's strategy was to use IAS/IFRS as the basis for setting Indonesian Financial Accounting Standards ("PSAK"), though in some cases U.S. GAAP is used.[48] A taskforce was established in 1999 to recommend improvements for bank accounting in Indonesia. The committee, led by IIA, also had representation from BI, the Indonesian Bank Association, practitioners and academics. It reported in March 2000, and the new standards on "Accounting for Banking" (PSAK 31) were effective for reporting for 2001. These are largely based upon IFRS, with new standards in areas shown to be important by the crisis.

In September 2002, the IMF judged BI to be "largely compliant" with the accounting and disclosure provisions of BCP 21. Local IMF staff thought the degree of transparency of financial sector information in Indonesia as good as the G7 average.[49] Nevertheless, some divergences with relevant IFRS remain. Indonesia's definition of related party transactions (PSAK 7) is comparable to that in IFRS and U.S. GAAP. However, there is no requirement (unlike under IFRS and U.S. GAAP) to disclose related but "uncontrolled" parties if there have been no transactions with them (PricewaterhouseCoopers 2001, 54). Also, in contrast to IFRS, there are no rules relating to de-recognition of financial assets (IFRS 39.35), or requiring disclosure of fair values of financial assets and liabilities (IFRS 32.77).

Internal enforcement within banks is the task of the compliance director and the audit committee. In theory, the Board of Commissioners is responsible for ensuring that the independence of the internal audit unit from management is guaranteed. In 1999, BI also issued new requirements concerning standards for internal audits.[50] External auditors have also been required, since 2001, to notify BI within seven days if they discover any undisclosed and materially important problems in banks' accounts. If auditors fail to do so, either through incompetence or collusion, BI can bar them from auditing banks, and can require the audited bank to re-publish financial statements. It can also ask BAPEPAM, the securities regulator, to remove individual auditors from the list of approved auditors of all public companies. Regulators argue that the banning of some auditors has generally induced conservative behavior by external auditors.[51] Some argue evidence of this can be seen from the differences in loan classifications reported by banks in their March and April monthly reports.[52]

However, despite these undoubted improvements in bank financial disclosure, there have been a number of serious accounting and criminal frauds at a number of the major Indonesian banks since 1998, including at BII, BNI, BRI, Asiatic Bank, Bank Global International, Bank Mandiri, and Bank Bali. In most cases these banks were under the control and supposedly close supervision of government agencies. Not only does this suggest weaknesses in the supervisory framework, it also reveals crucial ongoing weaknesses in the internal and external auditing of banks (and companies in general) in Indonesia. Furthermore, such accounting frauds cast doubt on compliance claims in other areas (e.g., the general observance of LLLs noted above). Hence, although greater financial transparency might partly compensate for weaknesses in regulatory agency supervision, the effectiveness of market monitoring is likely to depend considerably on the quality of the auditing process. In Indonesia, this still seems to be a key source of weakness.

Explaining Compliance Outcomes

As we have seen, since the crisis, Indonesia has made major changes to its formal framework of banking regulation and supervision, but a considerable real compliance gap persists in a range of areas. Only a few years after the crisis, Hamilton-Hart's (2000, 109) judgment was harsh: "The reform process has done virtually nothing to improve financial governance even though the reforms have brought changes to the law and upgraded the technical qualifications of those administering it." This assessment is broadly consistent with our own argument about the size of the real compliance gap in Indonesia, though from the perspective of 2007, it would be wrong to deny that there has been improvement in the quality of compliance with international banking supervision standards since 1997. Nevertheless, some important compliance gaps persist even in terms of the formal rules in place in Indonesia and, most significantly, in the actual behavioral practice of regulators and banks.

Is this compliance pattern consistent with our own theory? On balance, the answer is yes. As noted earlier, Indonesia was declared by the IMF to be in full compliance with the SDDS macroeconomic data transparency standard in June 2000. In contrast, the IMF has not been able to date to convince the GOI to undertake a public assessment of its compliance with banking supervision standards, though unpublished assessments suggest that the quality of Indonesia's compliance in this area has been quite poor, even if improving. The same appears to be true in some other areas in which private sector compliance costs are relatively high and the transparency of compliance outcomes low.[53]

The depth of the crisis in Indonesia meant that the real compliance gap in banking supervision was large in the first four to five years after 1997. Notably, the GOI (and the IMF) had no choice but to renege on early commitments to bring Indonesia's regulatory standards rapidly up to (and in some cases beyond) international levels. In key areas such as capitalization standards, provisioning standards, and the enforcement of LLLs, banks were given up to four years (from late 1998) to bring themselves into line with minimum international standards. The reason is obvious: given the catastrophic collapse of the system of financial intermediation and widespread economic distress, neither the New Order regime nor the weak democracy that followed it could have borne the political costs of rapid substantive compliance.

The political limits on compliance went beyond these cyclical factors and were considerably more pernicious than mere electoral pressure. President Wahid was elected in 1999 by the county's highest representative body without the personal baggage of corruption and business linkages that tainted the Suharto and Habibie governments. However, he proved unable to push reform in the face of powerful organized interests in the business sector that had deep links with the bureaucracy and Parliament (Robison, Rodan, and Hewison 2002; Robison and Hadiz 2004, 216). Wahid's cabinet included some moderate reformers in key positions, including Laksamana Sukardi, Kwik Kian Gie, and (later) Rizal Ramli, but various other important cabinet posts were also given to the military and to other political parties, including Golkar, with whose support Wahid had been elected. Meanwhile, predatory interests reconfigured around a much weakened but still unreformed state apparatus and found new sources of patronage in Parliament. Wahid's own presidency collapsed after only 13 months, plagued by its own dabbling in money politics and associated corruption scandals.

Like Wahid, his successor, former Vice-President Megawati Sukarnoputri, was associated with the domestic reform movement and appointed prominent reformers to key economic posts, including Boediono, Dorojatun Kuncoro-Jakti, and Laksamana. However, her party's indiscipline and corruption and its weak position in Parliament led to a series of compromises with other parties, the military and business interests. This severely weakened the influence of pro-compliance domestic reform lobbies, which included parts of an often highly critical press, academia, and neoliberal technocrats.[54] In spite of the massive transfer of distressed assets to the public sector and other forms of bailout of banks and firms, not all of the concentrated private sector compliance costs could be socialized by the government (not least, the public debt looked potentially unsustainable by 2001–2). The Megawati administration proposed substantially easing repayment terms for the major individual state debtors. Some of these debtors had developed relationships with Megawati's husband, the ambitious politician-businessman Taufik Kiemas, who assiduously cultivated relationships with major businessmen and New Order era political figures.[55] The public backlash against these proposed deals forced a government retraction, but subsequent prosecutions were ineffectual, with key debtors slipping out of the country before verdicts were handed down and in some cases living openly in Singapore.[56]

Of course, those aspects of (temporary) formal noncompliance were visible to third parties, but the GOI and IMF hoped that by signaling an intention to adopt international standards, Indonesia would not be punished by markets. The assessment of whether this judgment was correct is beyond the scope of this chapter, but the low level of capital inflows into Indonesia during these years suggests it may not have been. The perceived need to converge only gradually upon key international standards also implied an intention on the part of the authorities to enforce the rules on the books, in contrast to the past.

However, there is still much evidence of even more hidden forms of regulatory forbearance and compliance failures behind the scenes. Regulators consistently found banks to be underestimating NPLs. Best practice methods of NPL estimation were not generally introduced, and the IMF had strong doubts about the reliability of financial reporting. Collateral, much of which would not have been easily collectable in reality, also assisted banks in limiting required provisions. This, as well as lax definitions of some of the risk weightings of some asset categories, allowed banks to report inflated CARs. BI may have been more independent of government after May 1999, but the politically subordinate IBRA was responsible for supervision of the many banks under its control and clear failures of oversight occurred, as demonstrated by the large incidence of fraud and other scandals at IBRA-controlled banks. Formal financial reporting rules were upgraded, but auditors, perhaps even more than elsewhere, often failed to detect serious fraud until it was too late. Finally, it is difficult to find a major institution in Indonesia that is not tainted by allegations of corruption and incompetence.

Also consistent with our theory, economic recovery eventually produced improved compliance, both formal and substantive. New LLLs were apparently enforced by 2002–3, and loan classification rules were tightened further in 2005, forcing the two largest banks to report dramatically increased NPLs at a time when the economy had much improved. However, compliance continues to be retarded by more deep-seated political factors that are unlikely to disappear. The political pressures on the government to improve economic prospects in the poorest parts of this diverse country have increased after democratization. In 2005, in addition to the tightening of loan classification rules, two new BI regulations relaxed lending rules in the poorest regions.[57] Corruption also remains a powerful constraint on substantive compliance at all levels. The state-owned banks continue to be especially prone to this. In April 2005, senior executives of Mandiri were investigated for allegedly extending loans to some technically insolvent debtors in return for bribes.[58] The chief executive was subsequently removed and arrested, amid allegations of illegal loans to, among others, a major Suharto-family linked pulp and paper company. In July 2005, the former chief executive and two former directors of the country's second-largest state bank, BNI, were also arrested in a corruption investigation dating back to 2003.[59] Earlier scandals in other state-controlled banks show these are not isolated events.

How does this explanation of banking compliance outcomes compare with others? Hamilton-Hart's (2000) main explanation for failure of reform was that Indonesia chronically lacked the necessary "administrative capacity."[60] There is little doubt that of the four countries examined in this book, Indonesia's lower level of economic development and limited supply of appropriate skilled human resources has significantly constrained the quality of compliance with international standards. However, others disagree with this assessment (Pangestu and Habir 2002, 28).[61] BI has taken on more staff, including foreign experts, improved in-house training, and the number of supervised banks has fallen considerably. The organization of regulation has also been improved. Two directorates were made responsible for off-site supervision of banks and two directorates for on-site examination. At the prompting of the IMF, on-site examiners were given a permanent position within the compliance and audit sections of the most systemically important banks to monitor risk management practices. These examiners are present in addition to the internal compliance director within banks. Nevertheless, it would be wrong to deny the importance of capacity problems, partly because bringing in foreign experts and new supervisory staff to fill human resource gaps in the regulatory agencies is different from building real centers of administrative expertise (Hamilton-Hart 2000, 120–27). Similarly, continuing capacity problems in banks' internal management and compliance functions can be an obstacle to substantive compliance (BI 2005, 25–26).

However, this capacity argument is less at odds with my own than might at first appear, because some of the important constraints on institutional capacity it identifies have political origins. Although it is difficult to make a sharp distinction between politically exogenous and endogenous capacity constraints, it is reasonable to include political interventions in the regulatory process and political corruption in the latter category, as well as (to some extent) political decisions about staff levels and salaries in supervisory agencies.[62] Political interventions and corruption were both relatively centralized in the Suharto era, but the recent process of Indonesian democratization has eradicated neither. Powerful private and public sector interests, for whom substantive compliance and effective regulation would be very costly, have been able to subvert and distort the process of financial supervision, as well as the whole process of financial restructuring since 1997. The level of outright fraud and clear failures of regulation, not least in banks that have been majority-owned and under the watch of BI and IBRA, has been extraordinary even by the standards of the other main crisis-hit countries.

As for the compliance effects of external forces, it is clear that the IFIs played an important role in encouraging the GOI to adopt international standards, particularly in the final year of the New Order regime.[63] The IMF program, which expired at the end of 2003, notably provided support to the beleaguered Indonesian economic technocrats who largely shared its agenda. However, as we have seen, although IFI pressure pushed the GOI in the direction of formal compliance, it was incapable of doing much more, let alone of producing substantive compliance. As the IMF's own independent assessment (IEO 2003, 142) concluded, "[the IMF] placed too much faith in the ability of [Indonesian] reformists to deliver policies, and failed to explicitly consider the various political constraints on policy making." It is possible that IMF conditionality actually increased the initial size of the real compliance gap, by promoting more rapid formal compliance than would otherwise have occurred, and by worsening the severity of Indonesia's economic crisis. Neoliberal ideas have had even less effect on compliance outcomes. Neoliberal technocrats have had fluctuating but generally weak levels of political support. Their closest allies have arguably been the IFIs, and like them Indonesian neoliberals have never enjoyed much influence over the actual practice of supervision and enforcement. Nor did many of the pro-compliance NGO critics wish to be seen to be siding with Washington-style neoliberalism.

Finally, as for market forces, these were unable significantly to affect the quality of compliance in the main supervisory agencies. The trauma suffered by the country's major banks and firms after 1997 meant that foreign equity listings and hence foreign regulator pressure was a negligible factor. Certainly, however, it was true that international creditors and investors largely shunned Indonesia until 2004–5 when growth recovered, and this increased the pressure for compliance. Some international institutional investors like CalPERS publicly shunned Indonesia for its poor regulatory and political framework. The government's desperate need to revive growth so as to ameliorate some of Indonesia's deep internal problems was undoubtedly significant in its continuous public commitment to compliance with international standards. Even so, such pressure was insufficient to promote substantive compliance in many areas, since the country's political leaders could not follow through on these commitments.

However, in one area market pressure has arguably been important. Inward foreign direct investment (FDI) in the Indonesian banking sector has been an exception to the general flight of FDI from Indonesia since 1997. Foreign strategic investors have purchased controlling stakes in various banks: BCA, Bank Danamon, Bank Niaga, BII, Bank NISP, Bank Buana, Bank Lippo, and Bank Permata. Moreover, this trend accelerated from 2004. In some of the more recent cases, family owners may have sold out to foreign banks because of doubts about their ability to compete in this more internationalized banking environment (Fitch Ratings 2005, 1). By mid-2005, 8 of the top 12 Indonesian banks were controlled by foreign banks or investor consortia, 3 by the state (Mandiri, BNI and BRI) and only 1 by a family (Pan Indonesian). Even in the latter case, a foreign strategic investor (ANZ bank) has a 29 percent stake.

For foreign banks, compliance costs are relatively low, because in most cases parent banks must meet international standards abroad. Their ability to introduce better risk management techniques is in many cases superior to domestic banks. In Indonesia, they have focused on expanding lending to the SME and retail sector rather than on relationship lending to large firms. Furthermore, they arguably have a strong interest in more stringent supervision of their domestically owned Indonesian competitors. This foreign competition raises the stakes considerably for poorly managed domestic banks and has undoubtedly increased the average quality of compliance in the sector since 2003–4. The problem is now concentrated in the remaining state-owned banks, which remain important, and the many smaller indigenous banks. However, the increasingly important role of foreign banks may ultimately prove to be the most powerful factor promoting compliance in Indonesia's banking sector, since foreign control has the distinct advantage of largely bypassing the endemic problems of official regulation and supervision in this country.

Crisis, Collusion, and Mock Compliance

When financial crisis hit Indonesia in late 1997, the Suharto government resisted giving a clear commitment to comply with a range of international regulatory standards. Although the international forces pushing for compliance, including the IFIs, foreign governments, and international investors significantly raised the costs of outright noncompliance for the government, it saw the domestic costs of compliance as too high. These compliance costs were especially high for business interests in and close to the ruling family itself.

However, this situation was unsustainable because it deepened the levels of uncertainty and associated capital flight. The attempt to resist foreign compliance pressure in the name of Indonesian nationalism also rang increasingly hollow as it became clear that the regime was largely protecting its own. Domestic reformers, emboldened by pressure from the IFIs, foreign governments, and the deteriorating economy, demanded greater regulatory effectiveness, transparency, and especially the elimination of collusion between the government and the private sector. With the eventual collapse of the Suharto regime, the commitment of the GOI to new elections meant that a public commitment to compliance with international standards could no longer be avoided. Hence, a combination of pro-compliance domestic and external forces promoted a considerable degree of formal compliance with international banking supervision standards. What is most striking, however, is how far the actual behavior of public and private sector actors in Indonesia subsequently diverged from this formal commitment.

It is clear that ratification failure has not been the main obstacle to substantive compliance in Indonesia. Although there were delays in legislation and implementation after Suharto's departure, most of the formal regulatory framework was in place by the end of 1999. Given this, private sector opposition to compliance shifted to less visible forms. It is difficult to judge the relative importance of regulatory forbearance, administrative failure, and private sector compliance avoidance in substantive compliance failures, because all three are often interrelated in the Indonesian case. Official forbearance occurred, for example, in the form of delays to implementing stricter LLLs and official CARs in response to powerful banking and corporate sector opposition. Despite this considerable official relief granted to the private sector, serious noncompliance persisted, most notably perhaps in the chronic underreporting of NPLs at state-controlled banks and collusion between banks and large borrowers. That these banks remained highly prone to fraud and corruption since the crisis suggests that the root cause of substantive compliance failure has been a set of deeply ingrained collusive relationships between government, bureaucracy, and the private sector. Given this situation, it is unsurprising that the GOI has so far remained unwilling to submit its regulatory practices to external assessment in the form of a public FSAP.

Thus, high and concentrated private sector compliance costs and continuing obstacles to third party monitoring of compliance, combined with a government apparatus in which private sector influence remained embedded, produced deep compliance failures. This frustrated the efforts of domestic pro-compliance lobbies, which mainly consisted of neoliberal technocrats and intellectuals, though these groups had never enjoyed decisive influence in Indonesian policy. Such lobbies lost most of their influence when it came to regulatory agency and private sector behavior. More strikingly, given the claims of much recent literature about the power of external forces to promote policy convergence, domestic politics trumped compliance pressure from the IFIs, bilateral creditor governments, and private creditors. The exception to this generalization is the way in which increased foreign control of the domestic banking sector has improved compliance at the level of individual banks. Over time, if this further erodes the importance of relationship lending and political intervention in domestic finance, it may prove to be the most important legacy of the crisis.

4

Corporate Governance in Thailand

This chapter evaluates Thailand's compliance with international corporate governance standards since 1997. At the outset of the crisis, there was no single set of recognized international standards in corporate governance. The G7-designated standard setter in this area, the OECD, set up a task force only in April 1998 and issued the Principles of Corporate Governance (PCG) in May 1999. Various other bodies in the meantime were competing to fill this vacuum, including the International Corporate Governance Association (ICGN), the Commonwealth Association, the (U.S.) Business Roundtable, as well as various national stock exchanges (notably those in the United States and the United Kingdom), regulatory bodies and ad hoc commissions. When the PCG were finally promulgated, their general nature and their attempted melding of different traditions of corporate governance made them difficult to use for reform purposes.[1] In this somewhat confusing situation, Asian governments looked to Western models of corporate governance to provide more detailed benchmarks for post-crisis reform, particularly those in the United States and the United Kingdom.[2]

The difficulties of finding an appropriate reform benchmark did not deter the IMF or the new Thai government from committing Thailand to adopting international corporate governance standards (in addition to most other international standards). Chuan Leekpai, the Democratic Party politician who became prime minister in a coalition government at the end of 1997, was publicly committed to this solution. His government embraced the IMF program and emphasized the need to restore the confidence of international investors in the Thai economy and Thailand's regulatory framework (Hewison 2000, 206).

However, the fragmented coalition and party system made it difficult for the Chuan government to gain autonomy from opponents of reform and compliance, who were not in short supply (Haggard 2000, 92–100). As we will see, this often meant that even in terms of formal compliance, outcomes diverged considerably from the government's initial hopes. Opposition to the government's program soon emerged from various quarters of society, including from powerful Thai business families whose industrial and banking empires had been built during the previous decades of rapid growth. After the elections of 2001, won by the party of Thailand's most prominent businessman, Thaksin Shinawatra, political power was re-centralized and the government's commitment to compliance with international standards significantly declined. However, under both governments the average quality of compliance with international corporate governance standards has been poor.

Corporate Governance before the Crisis

Corporate governance was little known or understood in Thailand before the crisis. The Securities and Exchange Commission (SEC) Act of 1992 and the Guidelines on Disclosure of Information of Listed Companies (May 1993) required companies to "disclose information necessary for decision making to the general public ... [that is] correct, sufficient and timely," and to "give investors in the Exchange equal access to the information." Such information included major dealings with employees, customers and suppliers, and "significant" changes in shareholdings of insiders or controlling persons. However, Thai accounting standards lagged IAS considerably in key areas, and auditing practices were often inadequate. Corporate disclosure was typically very poor and enforcement very patchy. Insider trading was prohibited but was rarely reported or investigated; fines were rare and usually derisory (Nikomborirak 2000, 29).

More significantly, a Stock Exchange of Thailand (SET) requirement of 1993 specified that independent directors of listed firms should be truly independent of the company and related companies, should own less than 0.5 percent of the company's stock, and required them "to take care of the interest of all shareholders equally."[3] However, this provision had little impact on listed companies, which, like most Thai firms, were family-owned and controlled.[4] Although pyramid structures and cross-shareholdings are less important in Thailand than in other East Asian countries, informal alliances between families produced similar outcomes (DFAT 2002, vol. 2, 110). Given that nominee shareholding accounts are ubiquitous in Thailand, it was often impossible to discern precisely who owned what, therefore making it easy to disguise insider trading (Nikomborirak 2000, 8). Sometimes family-controlled holding companies would remain unlisted, while particular companies within a group would be listed for tax purposes, increasing the opacity of corporate governance. Such holding companies were not required to disclose related party transactions or to have them approved by shareholders. Indeed, related party transactions were completely normal in the Thai business community before the crisis, and few company managers or directors thought to question them.[5] The inevitable result, given high levels of ownership concentration, was that outside (or "minority") shareholders[6] were systematically disadvantaged.

Even what minimal legal requirements were in place were poorly observed and enforced (Nikomborirak 2000). The legal enforcement of outside shareholder rights against company managers and insiders was extremely weak. Although banks, given their dominant position in corporate financing in Thailand, were potentially in a position to exercise influence over the managements of their clients, typically they failed to do so. Relationship lending, poor corporate governance, and poor risk management practices predominated in Thailand's banking sector, as in many other Asian countries. In short, Thailand's corporate governance culture before the crisis was in most important respects wholly at odds with a Western ideal-type model in which outside shareholder rights were prioritized, though self-evidently this had not prevented sustained high growth until 1996.

Compliance with International Corporate Governance Standards

As noted earlier, the Chuan government, between 1997–2001, appeared to be strongly committed to bringing about convergence upon Western standards of corporate governance, supporting the IMF's own agenda in this area.[7] However, the new government was unable to ensure that key legislation was passed into law, reflecting considerable domestic opposition to this reform agenda. As a result of this legislative impasse, most of the new initiatives in corporate governance came from the SET, which has been able to set new rules for listed companies without relying upon new parliamentary legislation. However, SET rules for listed companies generally take the form of recommendations rather than requirements; therefore, this approach did not fully compensate for the legislative blockage.

In January 1998, the SET released a "Code of Best Practices for Directors of Listed Companies." These recommendations encouraged companies to undertake various reforms, such as to establish audit, nominations, and remuneration committees at the board level, and to ensure outside director independence (SET 1998).[8] In June 1999, the SET also issued the more substantial Best Practice Guidelines for Audit Committees (SET 1999). An SET Committee on Corporate Governance released new voluntary guidelines in 2000, which have since been revised several times. From financial year (FY) 2002, the SET has required listed companies to report on their observance of the SET's 15 principles of good corporate governance and to justify any departures from them in their annual reports.

Despite these initiatives, the general perception of outsiders has been that Thailand lagged regional leaders, such as Singapore and Malaysia, on corporate governance reform. Moreover, there is a widespread perception of a persistent large gap between the new standards and actual company behavior (CLSA Emerging Markets 2003, 16). In what follows, I assess the quality of compliance with international corporate governance standards in Thailand in the following four key areas: the independence of boards of directors, audit and other board committees, minority shareholder rights, and corporate governance in the financial sector. Although this does not cover all aspects of corporate governance reform, these are the main areas upon which attention was focused during and after the crisis.

Given that what constitutes best practice in corporate governance is often open to debate, in table 4.1. I compare the new corporate governance rules in Thailand as of 2003–4 with best practice (read: the most stringent rule) in Asia. Many of the best-practice rules in the final column of table 4.1 emulate corporate governance standards in the United States and the United Kingdom, though in some areas Asian standards are more stringent, including shareholder approval of related party transactions and shareholder voting rights generally, board legal responsibility, and separation of chairman and CEO roles.[9] As a cursory glance of this table reveals, a number of Thailand's formal standards of corporate governance often now approach or meet best regional practice. However, as we will see, relatively stringent formal rules do not translate into high quality compliance.

Board Independence

The SET Code of Best Practice for Directors of Listed Companies of 1998 drew upon similar codes in the major Western countries and explicitly sought to increase the independence of corporate boards as a counterweight against controlling owner-managers. The 1998 code simply recommended that boards include at least two independent directors. In 2002, in its fifteen principles of good corporate governance for listed companies, the SET increased the minimum number of recommended independent directors to one-third of the board total, with three as the minimum.[10] Although this represents a move toward international best practice, it lags more stringent

TABLE 4.1
Selected corporate governance rules, Thailand, and Asian best practice, 2003–4

	Thailand	Asian best practice
Boards		
Cumulative voting for board members permitted?	Yes (default; but most companies choose to opt out)	Pakistan (mandatory)
Limit on how many company boards an individual may serve?	No, except for bank directors (5)	Korea (2 for non-executives)
Minimum number of board meetings per year	4	Thailand
Fit and proper test for directors?	Yes	Yes
Legal responsibility of board for financial statements	Liable if statement is made knowingly	Hong Kong (fully liable)
Company prohibited from indemnifying directors?	No	Malaysia
Continuing training required for directors?	No	Malaysia
Legally required separation of chairman and CEO?	No	Malaysia
Independent directors required?	Yes (at least 3)	Korea (majority for banks and large companies)
Audit committees required?	Yes	Yes
Audit committees: minimum number of independent directors required	All, incl. one with expertise	Thailand
Remuneration and nomination committees required?	No, but recommended	Philippines (Yes)
Disclosure		
Quarterly and annual reporting	Yes	Yes
Consolidated financial reporting?	Yes	Yes
Annual reports provide information and any divergence from CG codes	Yes	Yes
Shareholder participation		
Can shareholders vote to remove directors?	Yes, special resolution (>75% of votes)	Malaysia
Do shareholders vote on issuing capital?	Yes (>75% of votes)	Thailand
Do shareholders vote on board remuneration?	Yes (>50% of votes)	Thailand

TABLE 4.1—cont.

	Thailand	Asian best practice
Do shareholders vote on major corporate transactions (acquisitions, disposals, etc)?	Yes (75% of votes), if transaction >50% of NTA	Malaysia
Minimum % shareholder votes required to call an extraordinary shareholder meeting	20% (or 25 shareholders with 10%)	Korea (3%)
Minimum % shareholder votes required to place issue on shareholder meeting agenda	33.30%	Korea (1%)
Corporate control		
Notification threshold in event of substantial acquisition of shares	5%	5%
Threshold for mandatory offer for all shares	25%, 50%, 75%	Taiwan (20%)
Related party transactions		
Disclosure of related party transactions	Yes	Yes
Shareholder approval of related party transactions?	Yes (>75% of votes), if >10m baht or >3% of NTA; interested party must abstain	Thailand
Shareholder redress		
Derivative action	Yes (minimum 5 shareholders or 20% of shares)	Yes (Hong Kong, India, Korea, Singapore, etc)
Class action	Draft bill proposed	Yes (Hong Kong, India, Singapore, etc)

Sources: OECD (2003, Appendix A); Nam and Nam (2004, table 1).
Note: NTA = net tangible assets.

regional and international standards requiring a majority of independent directors on boards. For example, the NYSE requires independent directors to be in a majority on corporate boards, as does the Korea Stock Exchange (KSE) for banks and large listed companies.[11]

The Thai code is also less stringent than some in that it is open on the question of whether the CEO and board chairman roles should be separate. Traditionally, these roles were often merged (as continues to be the case in the United States, though much less so in the United Kingdom). An early 2002 survey by the Thai Institute of Directors (IOD) showed that of the top 100 Thai listed companies, only 27 percent had separated the positions of CEO and Chairman.[12] However, this practice is becoming less common in the very largest Thai companies. For the top 50 Thai listed companies in 2002, in only 12 percent of cases were these two roles held by the same individual, though these companies did not usually disclose whether CEOs and Chairmen had family ties, as is common in Thailand (Standard & Poor's 2004a, 5; Nam and Nam 2004, 71). In this area, major listed Thai firms appear to be gravitating toward the global standard rather than the Thai domestic standard, suggesting that investor pressure is playing a role in promoting formal compliance here.

However, it is doubtful whether these rules to enhance the monitoring role of the board make much practical difference in the Thai context. In the country's most prominent corporation, Shin Corp, owned until January 2006 by the prime minister's family, CEO and Board Chairman positions were separated, but the Chairman, Bhanapot Damapong (the prime minister's brother-in-law and business partner), was a major shareholder, holding over 13 percent of the shares of the company. Generally, it remains common in Thailand for controlling shareholders to dominate both boards and senior management, whatever the formal arrangements. As of 2002, even formally independent directors accounted for one-third or less of the board for the majority of the top 50 Thai listed companies. A more recent survey found that independent directors were in a majority on the boards of only 12 percent of major companies in Thailand, and for 37 percent of companies surveyed independent directors accounted for less than 25 percent of board membership (Nam and Nam 2004, 71). Another study found that half of the top 100 Thai listed companies had only two independent directors on the board, whereas the average board size was over 12 (Nikomborirak 2004, 226). Thus, many listed companies do not meet even the relatively lax Thai domestic standard.

Furthermore, surveys of directors on company boards often revealed considerable ignorance concerning their roles and responsibilities, despite much publicity on the corporate governance reforms.[13] A shortage of qualified directors was a major problem, though the IOD and SET both now provide training. Boards meet reasonably frequently in Thailand, but most companies do not report individual directors' attendance—nor are they required to do so (Standard & Poor's 2004a, 4). There is no maximum number of boards on which individual directors may sit (though the maximum is five for banks), raising doubts about their ability to be effective. Although the SET code requires that independent directors must satisfy the general criteria of independence from management and major shareholders (SET 1998, 2.2.1), this is of course not true for non-independent directors. Nor can it guarantee that directors act independently, though this is true in any country.

Unsurprisingly, various surveys show that Thai company boards rarely constrain managers and controlling owners, a conclusion also reached by the World Bank's ROSC assessment team in 2004–5 (World Bank 2005b, ii). Family shareholders tend to control boards and dominate senior management, who in turn propose "independent" and non-independent directors to boards. In 2004, the CEO of over a third of major listed companies was from the founding family (Nam and Nam 2004, 51). The same survey found that 51 percent of directors believed it to be "unthinkable" that director candidates proposed by management could be rejected by shareholders; the rest thought it could happen only rarely (Nam and Nam 2004, 67). Hence, although in recent years the boards of Thai listed companies have appeared to be moving toward the ideal Anglo-Saxon type of independent boards, on average relatively little has changed in behavioral terms.

Audit and Other Board Committees

Audit committees have been required of all Thai listed companies since 2000 and best-practice guidelines for directors and audit committees have been issued by the SET (1999), largely following the U.S. Blue Ribbon Committee (1999). The standard for audit committee independence is higher than for company boards and is close to the U.S. standard. Audit committees must meet quarterly and must have at least three members, all of whom must be independent of management, and at least one must have relevant expertise (SEC Thailand 2002, 2). Audit committees and company boards must also scrutinize and approve all material related party transactions.[14]

In practice, however, a few years after its propagation, many listed companies had not complied with this domestic standard. In 2002, of the top 50 listed companies, 10 did not have a fully independent audit committee and 7 did not even have a majority of independent directors (Standard & Poor's 2004a, 9–10). A 2003 survey found that 35 percent of major Thai firms' audit committees actually had a minority of independent directors (Nam and Nam 2004, 76). Again, the shortage of qualified directors in Thailand seems to be a major constraint.

In practice, as in many other countries, Thai audit committees with some exceptions have often not lived up to their responsibilities to scrutinize company accounts, transactions, and strategies in the interest of all shareholders. Directors often have limited understanding of the concepts of fiduciary duty, duty of care, and duty of loyalty embodied in the law (World Bank 2005b, iii). Even when they do, a majority vote at an annual general meeting can pardon directors for violating fiduciary responsibilities (DFAT 2002, 2:126). Audit committee members are legally liable for the decisions they take and potentially subject to derivative suits (see below), but none have been prosecuted.

Thai listed companies are also encouraged, but not required, to establish remuneration and nomination committees to promote greater control over executive pay and over the nomination of company directors.[15] This lags more stringent requirements elsewhere. In practice, however, very few companies have remuneration and nomination committees. Again, this is not true of the largest companies, which do often have both, but independent directors are usually in the minority on these committees and do not seriously constrain controlling shareholders and managers (Standard & Poor's 2004a, 7–8; Nam and Nam 2004, 76). In the case of nomination committees, this has meant that friends and family of large shareholders have commonly been reappointed as directors and managers with little scrutiny (Nikomborirak 2004, 228).

Shareholder Rights and Financial Disclosure

Formal shareholder rights and financial disclosure have improved considerably in Thailand since the crisis and appears on paper to be an area of relative strength (table 4.1). The SEC proposed in 2003 to require disclosure of beneficiaries of nominee shareholding accounts, albeit phased in over 2003–8.[16] Listed companies are now required to disclose their top ten shareholders, including the ultimate beneficiaries of such shareholdings. They are also required to provide audited quarterly financial reports, as in the major developed countries and now in much of Asia. As in the United States, CEOs and chief financial officers (CFOs) of listed companies are now required to certify financial statements.

Since 1997, there has also been an effort to bring Thai accounting standards into conformity with IFRS and/or U.S. GAAP. The SEC also issues accounting disclosure regulations for listed firms and for public bond offerings that in some cases go beyond approved Thai accounting standards; it also inspects financial statements of listed firms, although it depends heavily upon auditors in ensuring that companies comply with its requirements.[17] From FY2006, auditors for listed companies must be rotated every five years and non-audit fees paid to auditors must be disclosed, mirroring the 2002 Sarbanes-Oxley legislation in the United States.

Since these tightened disclosure requirements have been put in place, a number of Thai companies have voluntarily de-listed from the Stock Exchange, claiming that the new requirements force them to release sensitive information for little benefit. Although this does not mean that compliance with new financial disclosure rules for listed companies is low (on the contrary), it does reflect the perception that the costs of compliance for listed companies are considerable and may be best avoided altogether. For the relatively few Thai companies that are listed, formal convergence with IFRS does seem to be occurring. Thailand announced in 2005 that it intended to adopt IFRS fully by 2006 (World Bank 2005b, i). Despite the issuance of new draft accounting standards that aim to bring about such conformity, this had not been achieved by mid-2007.

The gap between formal standards and behavioral practice in these areas is also large. For example, the voluntary SET code stipulates that a minimum of 10 percent of votes and 25 shareholders is required to call an extraordinary shareholders' meeting. However, the chairman of the board may simply fail to respond and pay only a small fine. There are various loopholes by which controlling shareholders can ensure that key decisions are approved without putting them to a general shareholder vote (Nikomborirak 2004, 223).

Related party transactions have been a particular focus of concern, as these have often been linked with the most egregious forms of outside shareholder exploitation. From 1993, a majority of shareholders needed to confirm related party transactions and the issuance of stock warrants to majority shareholders, but this requirement simply left the door open for the abuse of minority shareholder rights.[18] In May 2001, the SET merely confirmed the 1993 rules, but it revised them in November 2003. These revised rules considerably strengthened the disclosure and voting rules on related party transactions, requiring their disclosure and approval by at least 75 percent of shareholders.[19] However, the unrevised Public Company Act of 1992 remains considerably less stringent in this regard and it is unclear if noncompliance with the SET rules constitutes a violation of the law (Nikomborirak 2004, 222). This substantially limits the SEC's enforcement capacity in this crucial area.

The Thai rule on disclosure in this area simply requires firms and auditors to report additional detail for "non-normal business transactions." However, auditors in practice tend to report simply that the price of transfers between related parties is "agreed" and may not investigate them closely. A further problem is that consolidated accounting between parents and subsidiaries is only required for majority-owned subsidiaries. This relatively lax rule means that transfers of funds between parents and directly and indirectly controlled subsidiaries remains relatively easy (Nikomborirak 2004, 224; SEC interviews, March 2002).

Voting mechanisms also remain unconducive to the exercise of minority shareholder rights. As in Indonesia and Korea, Thailand introduced cumulative shareholder voting for directors after the crisis as the default rule for listed companies.[20] In practice, however, cumulative voting remains very rare because most companies simply opt out, presumably because it threatens the control of block shareholders (World Bank 2005b, ii). Also, a relatively high threshold of 75 percent of shareholders who hold 50 percent of the votes is required to remove directors, making such removal difficult in practice (World Bank 2005b, 5). Thus, shareholder meetings are often perfunctory affairs.

Possibilities for shareholders to seek legal redress also remain limited. Class action suits as a mechanism for enhancing minority shareholder rights have been proposed but have faced powerful domestic opposition that has blocked their adoption in Parliament.[21] Even if they are introduced in the future, shareholders may not be able to obtain sufficient information from companies to utilize such powers effectively. Derivative lawsuits are allowed but rarely initiated, perhaps because the Public Company Act is unclear about who would bear the expenses in such cases (World Bank 2005b, 10).[22] Thailand, like many Asian countries, has no tradition of litigation of these kinds.

As a result, most of the burden of legal enforcement of shareholder rights has fallen upon the SEC. The SEC has imposed more fines for breaches of securities law and blacklisted some auditors and individuals (for management or directorship positions) in recent years. A major difficulty is that although company directors are criminally liable for failing to perform their duties under the 1992 Public Companies Act, the standard of proof is very high. The SEC is unable to settle with directors for breaches of the Act and to impose fines, as in other countries in the region and elsewhere. Despite the large number of corporate scandals in Thailand since the crisis, few directors have been indicted and prosecuted (Barton, Coombes, and Wong 2004; Nikomborirak 2000, 12). The SEC has pushed for such powers, but the SEC Act (1992) remains unrevised despite much drafting (World Bank 2005b, i). Furthermore, as discussed below, the SEC remains subordinate to government and hence subject to considerable political constraints on its enforcement capacity.

Corporate Governance in the Banking Sector

In many countries, financial regulators, central banks, and finance ministries specify separate corporate governance requirements for banks and other financial firms that can go beyond normal requirements for listed companies. This was seen as especially important in Asia after the crisis because of the dominance of banks in the region's financial systems. Not only was better corporate governance within banks important in itself, but it might enhance the role of banks as monitors of borrowing firms (as they had often failed to do before the crisis).

From September 1999, the Bank of Thailand (BOT) issued a set of corporate governance requirements for banks that go beyond SET rules. Since this date, independent directors of Thai banks are not permitted to own more than 0.5 percent of the bank's outstanding shares; they may only have a maximum of three directorships, and they may not borrow from the bank. The appointment of bank directors is now also subject to BOT approval. Since 2002, commercial banks were required to establish risk, remuneration, nomination, and audit committees, the latter of which must consist of three members, two of which must be independent.[23] In early 2002, the BOT also produced a set of guidelines on corporate governance intended to inform bank directors of their responsibilities (BOT 2002).

Compliance with these rules seems good compared to that of nonfinancial listed companies with standard SET rules. The average number of independent directors on Thai banks was 3.9 out of 12 board members in total, slightly less than one third, meeting the minimum SET standard (Polsiri and Wiwattanakantang 2004b, 28). Nevertheless, as for all companies, the quality of bank directors sometimes remains poor. It has been difficult for banks to recruit new outside directors, partly because of the small pool of experienced candidates and partly because potential directors have been concerned about the limited compensation and large potential personal liabilities they may incur.

After the crisis, the BOT also required disclosure of related-party lending and imposed limits on such lending of 50 percent of a related company's equity, 25 percent of its total liabilities or 5 percent of the bank's own tier-I capital, whichever is the lower (BOT 2000, 28). Commercial banks may own no more than 10 percent of the stock of a listed company. These rules are mainly consistent with BCP 10, except in that this standard suggests regulators deduct any lending to related parties from capital when calculating CARs (BCBS 1999d, 25–26). Although it is doubtful that there are open breaches of these regulations, the limits are wide and related party lending remains substantial for some banks.

There is so far little sign that Thai banks have played an active role in raising standards of corporate governance in the corporate sector generally, perhaps because the slow recovery of lending to the corporate sector meant that banks' leverage over their corporate clients was limited. The Thai government's emphasis upon bank lending to the small and medium enterprise (SME) sector, which has notoriously poor corporate governance standards and upon whom there is least pressure for change, is another obstacle. For example, the state-owned Krung Thai bank was encouraged by the government to lend aggressively to the SME sector over 2002–3, resulting in a further buildup of NPLs. This conflicted with the BOT's attempts to restore its own battered regulatory credibility, leading to an open clash with the government. Eventually, the BOT Governor, Pridiyathorn Devakula, forced the resignation of the government-promoted Krung Thai president and asked the police to file criminal charges against nine officers for reckless lending.[24]

Rather than new formal standards, the main impact of the crisis on corporate governance in banking, as in Indonesia, has occurred through the impact of financial restructuring on bank ownership. Before the crisis, politicians and bureaucrats commonly sat on bank boards, reflecting the close relationship between business and politics in Thailand, along with founding family members and (often) senior management (Polsiri and Wiwattanakantang 2004b, 2). Family control of banks was widespread.[25] In government-intervened banks after 1997, the equity of existing shareholders was written down close to zero, and new boards were created on which BOT nominees sat. Crucially, at IMF urging, existing restrictions on foreign ownership of Thai banks (to 25 percent of total shares) were also completely lifted for ten years in July 1997 in order to encourage foreign investment in the sector.

As in Indonesia, the results of bank restructuring on ownership have been considerable. In 1996, families were the largest shareholders in 12 of 15 Thai banks; by 2003, this was true for only one of 13 banks. The number of banks for which foreign investors were the dominant shareholders rose from none in 1996 to seven of 13 in 2003. Banks in which the state was the dominant shareholder doubled from two to four over this period. Nevertheless, as of 2003, families still retained important stakes in three banks, with both directors on the board and a family member in the Chairman or CEO position (Polsiri and Wiwattanakantang 2004b, 24–28). Foreign controlled banks even more than others have focused on retail rather than corporate lending, limiting their impact on corporate governance in the nonfinancial sector, where families still dominate. Even so, there is little doubt that this has improved the average level of corporate governance in the banking sector itself, which is significantly better than in the nonfinancial sector (CLSA Emerging Markets 2005, 84–85; Standard & Poor's 2004a).

To summarize the overall situation on compliance with corporate governance standards since 1997, there has been improvement in the formal rules. Formal shareholder rights are now much more extensive than before 1997, notably including the approval of related party transactions. However, even the formal Thai standards relating to board independence and board committees generally lag those in Korea, the Philippines, and the United States, with the exception of Thailand's standard on audit committee independence. Despite these areas of formal noncompliance, the main weaknesses are to be found in the area of enforcement and the quality of compliance by companies.

This conclusion is supported by comparative surveys and contrasts markedly with Thailand's full compliance with SDDS from May 2000. A 2002 survey of corporate governance in Asia argued that many of the changes introduced in recent years were merely cosmetic and that poor compliance was widespread, including in Thailand (CLSA Emerging Markets 2003). This study is probably the most authoritative comparative empirical assessment that exists for the Asian region, though it should be interpreted with caution (table 4.2).[26] This survey noted the large perceived gap between the formal

TABLE 4.2
CLSA summary corporate governance scores, Asia 2002

	Rules and regulations	Enforcement	Political/ regulatory environment	Adoption of IFRS/ US GAAP	Institutional mechanisms and CG culture	Overall country score
China	5	4	5	5	3	4.3
Hong Kong	8	6.5	6.5	9	7	7.3
India	8	6	6	7.5	6.5	6.6
Indonesia	4.5	1.5	4	5	2.5	3.2
Korea	7	3.5	5	7	6.5	5.5
Malaysia	9	3.5	4	7	6.5	5.5
Philippines	6.5	2	2	6	4	3.7
Singapore	8.5	7.5	6	9	8	7.7
Taiwan	7	5	5	7	6	5.8
Thailand	7.5	3	4	6	4.5	4.6

Source: CLSA Emerging Markets 2003, 16.

rules and the quality of their enforcement in Thailand, comparable to that in Indonesia, Malaysia, Korea, and the Philippines but larger than in Singapore, Hong Kong, and India. The 2005 CLSA survey (CLSA Emerging Markets 2005, 84–85) suggested that little had changed since 2003 in terms of enforcement, though the SET had taken some new headline initiatives to raise awareness of corporate governance issues.

In another survey that used a scorecard for corporate governance disclosure, researchers from Standard and Poor's and the National University of Singapore gave a mean score of only 38 for the top 50 listed Thai companies in 2002–3, 140 being the maximum score. This compared with an average score of 81 for Singapore companies.[27] Given that Thailand's largest listed companies are almost certainly those with the best quality of disclosure, this survey underscores the general reluctance of Thai firms to disclose information about their corporate governance practices (see also Nam and Nam 2004, 97–101). By contrast, although the World Bank (2005b) ROSC assessment also makes some guarded criticisms of the state of corporate governance in Thailand, the generally uncritical tone of the report shows the extent to which the IFIs are politically constrained in their assessments of compliance. Unsurprisingly, the Thai government used this one relatively positive assessment to claim that all is well in corporate governance in Thailand.[28]

Explaining Compliance Outcomes

This overall outcome is broadly consistent with our theory of compliance. The obvious direct losers from the adoption of a new set of corporate governance rules that aimed at shifting the balance of power in firm governance from insiders to outside shareholders have been the major Thai corporate families. Resistance to the practical consequences of the new rules has been concentrated in the nonfinancial sector, where family ownership remains dominant. In 2004, 26 families controlled 66 percent of the SET's market capitalization, compared to 75 percent in 2001 (Polsiri and Wiwattanakantang 2004a, 26; World Bank 2005b, 1). The compliance costs for Thai family firms of Western corporate governance standards are high and, as a result, the average quality of their compliance with the new domestic standards introduced since the crisis is low.[29] As noted above, in the banking sector, where family control is markedly lower than average, the improvements have been greater.

Corporate families have not only resisted substantive compliance with these new rules within their firms, but they have also actively used the political system to block key pieces of legislation that might make such resistance more difficult. Important parliamentary bills that have remained in draft or debate stage for years after the crisis include the Bank of Thailand Act (1942), the Currency Act (1958), the Commercial Banking Act (1962), the Public Limited Companies Act (1992), the Civil and Commercial Code (1992), the Securities and Exchange Act (1992), and the Finance, Securities and Credit Fonciers Act (1979). Although there has been much talk since 1997 of revisions to these laws, none had been revised as of late 2006. Despite the ability of the SET and SEC to take some initiatives in this area under existing law, the large gap between the new voluntary code for listed companies and existing legislation creates real obstacles to enforcement.

One reason given for the legislative blockage is that the decentralization of political power in Thailand has increased the number of veto points in the system (Haggard 2000, 92–100). In cases where legislation has been passed (e.g., the Bankruptcy Act, revised in 1998, 1999, and 2004), it was often watered down, because particular interests had to be assuaged, including debtor interests that were directly represented in the Senate.[30] However, since 2001, the legislative impasse continued under a much more centralized political system in which Prime Minister Thaksin Shinawatra's Thai Rak Thai (TRT) party enjoyed a large parliamentary majority.[31] This continuity of outcomes under different political circumstances suggests a deeper explanation: what remained before and after 2001 was the embeddedness of major corporate families in the political process.

Indeed, Thaksin's electoral victory in 2001 embodied the reaction of the domestic business elite to the neoliberal reform agenda of the Chuan government and its support for a more pro-domestic business agenda.[32] In the electoral campaign, Thaksin successfully painted the Chuan government as pro-foreign rather than pro-Thai. In office, the TRT government, in which a number of business families besides Thaksin's were represented at the Cabinet level, reversed attempts to promote independent agencies, openly attacking the new agencies created in the 1997 constitution and attempting to silence or isolate other sources of dissent. The TRT government also imposed extensive political control over the bureaucracy, appointing associates and businessmen to key bureaucratic and SOE jobs on the grounds that the public sector needed more "managerial" experience. Thaksin openly admired the more authoritarian Malaysian and Singaporean governments and disparaged the independent media, academics, and other critical voices (Pasuk and Baker 2003). From the perspective of the domestic business elite, the acceptance of Western-style corporate governance standards was a distraction or worse, more in the interests of Western investors than of Thai business. Hence, although the Thaksin government made some gestures concerning the need to improve corporate governance in Thailand, the actual legislative results were extraordinarily low despite its large parliamentary majority.[33]

In the absence of changes to corporate and related law, the SET and SEC have had limited legal powers and even less political autonomy to enforce the standards that have been adopted. This has been especially clear in the case of the former prime minister's own business interests. The scandal of early 2006 over the Shinawatra family's use of offshore nominee companies to hide some of its shares and to avoid taxes on the sale of its holdings of Shin Corp was only the last in a long series of scandals. The purchaser, Temasek (the Singapore government's holding company), also managed to obtain SEC waivers on its obligation to make mandatory tender offers on two Shin Corp subsidiaries, to the detriment of minority shareholder interests.[34] In 2001, in the wake of TRT's first election victory, the independent National Counter Corruption Commission had found that Thaksin breached electoral laws on the disclosure of assets. Controversially, the SEC subsequently ruled in favor of Thaksin after the Constitutional Court's own narrow vote to acquit him.[35] In 2005, the SET conspicuously failed to investigate the causes of a sharp rise in the share price of a Shin Corp subsidiary, iTV, the day before better than expected results were released (CLSA Emerging Markets 2005, 84). Shin Corp itself has exhibited what might be described as a relaxed attitude to corporate governance. A leading survey of corporate governance in the Asian region consistently rated the quality of Shin Corp's corporate governance in the bottom quartile of Thai firms, themselves ranked very poorly on average (CLSA Emerging Markets 2005, 85). Nevertheless, as Thaksin's critics often pointed out, during his time in office, Shin Corp's share value rose four-fold on the back of several favorable government decisions to the benefit of his family.[36]

The World Bank assessment of Thailand's corporate governance record was much less critical. Although it noted that the SEC is insufficiently independent of the executive branch in terms of enforcement, it claimed that

SEC enforcement in cases of fraud had improved over time (World Bank 2005b, iii, vii). One possible sign of this occurred in March 2006, when the SEC fined Panthongtae Shinawatra, the prime minister's son and one of Thailand's richest men, for several violations of the SEC Act.[37] However, the modest fine of about $150,000 appears to have resulted from the intense political pressure on the SEC to act in the wake of the sale of Shin Corp to Temasek. Moreover, although strengthening the SEC's independence from government has been proposed in a draft revised SEC Act, this has never been passed.[38]

Thus, pro-compliance domestic lobbies have never been strong enough to promote corporate governance in Thailand in more than a tentative way. Groups such as the Thai Investors Association have promoted the cause of investor rights, but the absence of large private institutional investors in Thailand has weakened the pro-compliance coalition (DFAT 2002, 2: 118; World Bank 2005b, 1). NGO groups focused more on the shortcomings of the Thai political process than on the details of corporate governance. Although the relatively independent media actively investigated the relationship between these two facets of Thai society, the Thaksin government harassed journalists and academic critics systematically, employing populist rhetoric to cast doubt upon their patriotism and their sympathy for rural voters. Foreign institutional investors are more active, but this activism is confined only to the largest listed firms (World Bank 2005b, 1). Moreover, many appear to have been keener to invest in stocks with good growth prospects (including Shin Corp) rather than those exhibiting good corporate governance. Finally, during the Thaksin era, foreign investors suffered considerably reduced political influence.

To summarize, the poor quality of compliance with even domestic corporate governance standards in Thailand is primarily the result of the domestic business community's opposition to a real enhancement of outside shareholder rights. Until 2001, this business opposition used the fragmented political system to block the Chuan government's attempts to introduce legislation that threatened to introduce enforceable, Western-style investor rights. After Thaksin's election in 2001, the need to employ such tactics was much reduced because the government itself put the interests of the Thai business elite above all else.

Consistent with this explanation, the quality of compliance did not generally improve as economic recovery from the crisis proceeded. As the economy has recovered along with the profitability of their companies, this has not increased the incentive for family owners to devolve greater control over the corporate cash flow to outside shareholders. Thus, in contrast to compliance with banking supervision standards, there appears to be no strong effect of economic recovery on compliance in this area. Indeed, one could argue that economic recovery has actually reduced incentives for high quality compliance with corporate governance standards by reviving the economic prospects of listed companies with relatively poor corporate governance (CLSA Emerging Markets 2005, 86).

How far do alternative explanations get us in understanding the Thai pattern of compliance in this area? As in Indonesia, capacity constraints do appear to be important in some areas of compliance, notably the shortage of qualified independent directors for company boards. To the extent that capacity problems arise in the SEC's enforcement section, however, this is arguably politically endogenous. In fact, the main problem has not been with enforcement capacity but with the SEC's political subordination to government.

As for the role of external forces, the IFIs were arguably even less able than in Indonesia to shift the domestic balance of political power in favor of pro-compliance reformers. In its various LOIs to the IMF, the Thai government consistently committed itself to compliance with a range of international standards. However, even the Chuan government, dominated by a rhetorically pro-reform Democratic Party, was unable to push significant legislation through Parliament. After the election of the Thaksin government in 2001, with its anti-IMF and pro-business stance, the political leverage of the IFIs in Thailand diminished further still—well ahead of July 2003 when the government repaid its outstanding IMF borrowings. This low degree of external institutional leverage is underlined by the tentative World Bank ROSC assessment of Thailand's corporate governance framework in 2005. This report, which was used as evidence in support of Thailand's claims of progress in this area, was at odds with most independent assessments and demonstrates the political difficulty encountered by the IFIs in assessing compliance in important emerging market countries.

As for neoliberal ideas, these too have had little effect upon the quality of compliance outcomes in this area. Certainly, the Chuan government seemed openly accepting of the neoliberal critique of Thai capitalism offered by the IMF, foreign governments, and international investors (Hewison 2005, 317). However, the appeal of neoliberal ideas proved very limited, especially in domestic business circles. The neoliberal critique was easily portrayed by various groups opposing the reforms as pro-foreign and anti-Thai and it was swept aside in the 2001 elections.

As for market forces, these have been surprisingly weak in terms of their effect on average levels of compliance in the corporate sector.[39] One possible reason is that concentrated ownership and low stock market liquidity limits the impact of market pressure on listed companies to improve corporate governance. Since few Thai corporations are listed abroad, the influence of foreign regulators is negligible. Also, as noted earlier, there are no large private Thai institutional investors, since this sector is dominated by government-owned and controlled pension funds.

What, however, of pressure from the much larger foreign institutional investors? CalPERS, one major U.S. institutional investor, indicated in 1998 that it would withdraw investments from Thailand, along with China, Indonesia, Malaysia, and the Philippines, citing governance failures at the corporate and broader political level.[40] However, CalPERS appears to have been the exception among foreign institutional investors. On the face of it, most major Thai listed companies have dramatically improved their corporate governance since 1997, with independent directors now sitting on boards and lengthy corporate governance statements to be found in most annual reports. But it remains very difficult for outsiders to know how deep such changes go. Given this, institutional investors have generally focused on profitability and shareholder returns rather than assessing governance. The results have been plain: on average, domestic and foreign investors alike appear to have in recent years favored Thai stocks with relatively *poor* corporate governance, including, for example, Shin Corp (CLSA Emerging Markets 2005, 86). In such circumstances, it is not surprising that controlling block shareholders in many large listed Thai firms have perceived little to gain and much to lose from paying more than lip service to corporate governance standards.

Again, a partial exception to this generalization must be made for the banking sector. This is not because investors and other creditors have necessarily preferred banks with relatively higher quality corporate governance. As noted above, this "capital cost" effect seems very weak and may even work in the opposite direction. Rather, it has been because the restructuring of the Thai banking sector after the crisis had the effect of supplanting family owners with state and foreign owners. Today, foreign investors control about a third of major Thai banks, a dramatic transformation given the formal limits on foreign entry into this sector (temporarily waived for 10 years in 1997). Although the state-owned banks have not necessarily exhibited good quality corporate governance (e.g., Krung Thai), foreign-owned banks have found it both easier and more attractive to meet Thailand's minimum corporate governance standards—and often to exceed them. Hence, as in Indonesia, inward FDI flows have had some effects in the banking sector, though it should be noted that nationalist sentiment against foreign control of major Thai corporations has increased in recent years.[41]

Finally, part of the blame for poor compliance outcomes lies with the international standards themselves in this area. As noted above, these have been vague and arguably contradictory, particularly in the case of the PCG. When the Thai authorities looked elsewhere for more detailed rules, such as U.S. rules relating to board independence, these were rules that had often conspicuously failed even to achieve their stated objectives at home. This made it very unrealistic for the IFIs to expect that the governance of

Thai firms would be transformed through the importation of rules whose effectiveness had always largely depended upon voluntary compliance by the interested parties. In Thailand, as in much of the rest of Asia, a low average level of corporate sector interest in such voluntary compliance has been the determining factor.

Ratification Failure and Mock Compliance

The Thai case clearly demonstrates that the costs of both compliance and noncompliance can be very concentrated and asymmetrically distributed. This has meant that domestic politics has been much more important than external pressure for compliance outcomes. For the Chuan government, facing a collapse of investor confidence in the Thai economy and pressure from the IFIs, the costs of outright noncompliance were seen to be very high. In pledging Thailand's willingness to adopt international standards, the government responded both to this external pressure and to its desire to resolve deep domestic economic and political problems. However, the Thai corporate sector saw this strategy as shifting unacceptably large costs onto private business owners and opposed compliance from the outset. High levels of family ownership have been at the core of corporate resistance to substantive compliance in this area. Granting more rights to outside shareholders has been perceived by controlling shareholders as a direct threat to their interests.

As in the Indonesian case, the various sources of compliance failure are interrelated. More than in any other country examined here, the level of formal compliance with international standards has been lower than expected. In spite of the Chuan government's public goal of compliance with all the main international regulatory standards, it found it impossible to push key pieces of legislation through Parliament. The SET and SEC upgraded the corporate governance framework for listed companies, but legislative blockage has meant that legal enforcement of this new framework has been difficult. Ratification failure thus weakened the ability of the bureaucracy to enforce compliance with the new corporate governance framework and emboldened the corporate sector to engage in mock compliance strategies. The evident desire of the corporate opponents of compliance to block key legislative reforms suggests that they have been concerned that in the event of successful legislation, levels of enforcement might rise considerably, imposing substantial costs on controlling shareholders.

The key reason for ratification failure and low levels of bureaucratic enforcement has been the embeddedness of the Thai business elite in the political process. Over 1997–2001, this left the Chuan government and the pro-compliance lobby generally hostage to the many points of potential blockage in Parliament. After the election of the TRT government in 2001, the new government's large parliamentary majority had little positive effect, because the business elite now effectively controlled the political agenda, symbolized by Thaksin's own prime ministership. From this entrenched position, Thai business families were easily able to resist further pressure from the IFIs and domestic and international investors for improved corporate governance. This reduced the need for regulatory forbearance, compared to other countries. However, sometimes political pressure from the government on key enforcement agencies deterred the latter from using their already limited powers against key figures in the Thai corporate and political elite.

Nor did market forces work systematically to discourage mock compliance, since firms could engage in mock compliant behavior without serious negative consequences. Investors found it very difficult to detect the difference between compliant and mock compliant behavior by individual firms, and concentrated on investing in firms with profitable businesses. Perversely, as the economy recovered from the crisis, market forces generally favored rather than punished firms with poor corporate governance. The partial exception to this generalization has been in the banking sector, where increased foreign investor control has allowed more improvement in corporate governance outcomes. Generally, however, the long-term effect of the crisis on the quality of Thai compliance with international corporate governance standards has been remarkably limited.

5

Banking Supervision and Corporate Governance in Malaysia

Malaysia is a rather different case to Indonesia and Thailand. Of the four countries most affected by the crisis, only Malaysia managed to avoid IMF intervention and conditionality. Even so, Malaysia's government joined its neighbors in committing itself to convergence upon international best-practice standards in spite of its reputation for macroeconomic unorthodoxy. In this chapter, I assess Malaysian compliance outcomes in the two areas covered in the previous two chapters, banking regulation and corporate governance.

There are other respects in which Malaysia differs from Indonesia and Thailand. First, Malaysia's British colonial legacy and common law legal tradition would lead some to expect considerably better compliance outcomes compared to Thailand and Indonesia (La Porta, Lopez-de-Silanes, and Shleifer 1998b; Shleifer and Wolfenson 2000). Second, Malaysia is financially more developed than Indonesia and Thailand, which should also favor compliance. Indeed, by some measures, Malaysia has one of the most capital markets–based financial systems in the world, comparable to those of Singapore and Hong Kong in the Asian region (Beck, Demirgüç-Kunt, and Levine 1999). A third difference has more ambiguous implications for compliance: political power in Malaysia has been consistently more centralized than in both Indonesia and Thailand. The enhancement of executive power and the subordination of the judiciary was a marked characteristic of the Mahathir era, which lasted from 1981 to 2003 (Gomez and Jomo 1999, 183; MacIntyre 2003, 45–48; Woo-Cumings 2003, 216).[1] The attitude of the executive branch of government toward compliance with international standards has therefore been crucial, but this has varied considerably over time.

As in Indonesia and Thailand, mock compliance outcomes in banking supervision and corporate governance were clearly in evidence in the years after the 1997–98 crisis. The quality of Malaysia's compliance with international standards in both areas has been better than that in Indonesia and Thailand, but it has still lagged that in the best performing countries in the region. In banking supervision, the quality of compliance improved considerably along with economic recovery. Interestingly, this also seems to have occurred in the area of corporate governance, in contrast to the Thai experience. I argue that this has largely been due to a more positive attitude toward compliance by the Malaysian political leadership since 2001.

Compliance with International Standards of Banking Supervision

The Malaysian government's response to the Asian crisis has often been said to have been unorthodox and at odds with those elsewhere in the region, particularly in the three countries in which the IMF intervened (Indonesia, Korea, and Thailand). However, the initial policy response, led by Finance Minister Anwar Ibrahim in November 1997, was wholly orthodox in its macroeconomic aspects, "an IMF program without the IMF." Only after Anwar's ousting in September 1998 did the Malaysian government adopt capital controls and a reflationary macroeconomic policy. A month later, Prime Minister Mahathir remarked that "Bank Negara [the central bank and regulator] and those responsible for supervising the economy [i.e., Anwar]...were completely taken in by the IMF, which was perceived to be the authority in economic policy."[2]

Nevertheless, in the area of financial restructuring and regulation, Malaysia's response remained fairly orthodox even after Anwar's ouster, with some exceptions and with some explicit forbearance.[3] As in the other crisis-hit countries, early in the crisis the government provided emergency liquidity to banks and a blanket guarantee of bank deposits; established state agencies to purchase NPLs from the banking sector and to recapitalize banks (Danaharta and Danamodal respectively); and another agency to restructure corporate sector debt (the Corporate Debt Restructuring Committee, or CDRC). Unlike the other three countries, Malaysia did not promote foreign takeovers of domestic banks, focusing instead on a strategy of indigenous financial sector consolidation centered around a prescriptive "master plan" (IMF 1999b; Meesook et al. 2001). With this exception, the Malaysian government's response in the area of financial reform, both before and after Anwar's demise, was broadly similar to that in the IMF countries. In March 1988, the government committed itself to bringing prudential regulation and supervision up to international best-practice levels.

In international and regional forums, the attitudes of Malaysian representatives to the promotion of international standards were very supportive.[4] In the judgment of an IMF report,

> The [Malaysian] authorities...pursued fundamental reforms in the financial and corporate sectors, including a bank consolidation program and an upgrading of prudential regulation and supervision in line with international best practice. (Meesook et al. 2001, 2)

The March 1998 package included measures to strengthen the regulatory framework, disclosure standards, and risk management practices. A further package in April 1999 tightened the regulatory framework and this included disallowing bank lending to controlling shareholders, given that connected lending had been rife before the crisis. In November 1999, a framework of risk-based supervision and risk management for banks was adopted (Meesook et al. 2001, 14). Before assessing the results of this formal commitment to compliance with international banking supervision standards, we must briefly review banking supervision in Malaysia before the crisis.

Banking Supervision before the Crisis

The Malaysian government had adopted financial reform measures well before the 1990s crisis. After the failure of several financial institutions in 1986, the central bank, Bank Negara Malaysia (BNM), was granted wide powers to license and to regulate all financial institutions. The revised Banking and Financial Institutions Act (1989) formalized and strengthened the prudential framework. Compared to the other three main crisis-hit countries, this regulatory framework was comparatively robust and BNM enjoyed a long-standing reputation for administrative competence (DFAT 1999, 7; Jomo and Hamilton-Hart 2001, 74–79). BNM enforced a provision that prohibited banks from owning more than 10 percent of the stock of nonbank companies and from sitting on company boards (DFAT 2002, 2:135). In addition, regulatory limits on foreign borrowing by banks were largely enforced, in marked contrast to Korea and Thailand, so that most of the large foreign capital inflows in the 1990s came in the form of equity investment and FDI. Due to its relatively developed capital markets, Malaysia's financial system was also less bank-dominated than elsewhere in Asia and its average levels of corporate leverage significantly lower (Meesook et al. 2001, 4–5).[5]

Malaysia's comparatively good prudential reputation is somewhat surprising given that the Mahathir government had subordinated prudential considerations to its explicit policy of promoting "bumiputera" (indigenous Malay) business interests. This priority was set in the ruling coalition's New

Economic Policy (NEP), adopted in 1970 to promote greater social harmony between the country's ethnic groups. A key goal of NEP was to create an indigenous Malay business community to counter-balance traditional Chinese business dominance and reduce inequalities of wealth across ethnic groups. Over time, this policy actively fostered close linkages between bumiputera business interests and the ruling Barisan Nasional coalition, especially the dominant party within the coalition, UMNO (Gomez and Jomo 1999).[6]

A few key banking groups were particularly close to the ruling party, and in these cases it was more difficult for BNM to regulate effectively (Gomez and Jomo 1999, 60–66). One was Bank Bumiputera Malaysia, established by the government in 1966 and used to provide loans to well-placed bumiputera entrepreneurs. Bank Bumiputera's deep involvement in the financing of Malay business effectively allowed it to ignore existing prudential rules. In 1985 and again in 1989, the government was forced to rescue the bank as NPLs accumulated.[7] At the time, Daim Zainuddin, a key promoter and beneficiary of the NEP and one of the country's wealthiest bumiputera entrepreneurs, was also Finance Minister and UMNO Treasurer. Daim was also owner of another bank, UMBC, later sold to the partly government-owned Sime Darby Group. BNM also failed to enforce systematically the rule that single shareholders should control no more than 20 percent of a commercial bank, a rule intended to limit connected lending. Bank mergers or takeovers in the 1990s that breached this limit and were not disallowed by BNM all involved close associates of leading members of UMNO. As political interventions increasingly eroded BNM's supervisory mandate, its good reputation was somewhat tarnished in the years before the crisis (Hamilton-Hart 2002, 123–25; Jomo and Hamilton-Hart 2001, 87–88).

Banking Supervision after the Crisis

Like Indonesia and Thailand, Malaysia has not so far agreed to undertake a FSSA or ROSC assessment of banking supervisory practices, though it was urged to do so by some IMF executive directors in its late 2002 Article IV consultation.[8] The government conducted an early self-assessment that reached very optimistic conclusions. BNM claimed that by mid-2000, it was in compliance with 23 of 25 Basle Core Principles and would be in full compliance with all by the end of 2000, once market risk was included in its capital adequacy framework.[9] However, as we will see, this assessment is problematic in various ways. Below, I assess the quality of Malaysian compliance with international banking standards in three key areas: independence of regulators; rules on capital adequacy, loan accounting, and provisioning; and other prudential rules.[10]

Independence of Regulators

Under the 1989 Banking and Financial Institutions Act (BAFIA, section 126), BNM and the Minister of Finance both have the power to recommend the regulatory guidelines they deem necessary. However, BNM's legal independence from the government is low, representing a major departure from a key norm of regulatory neoliberalism. Interestingly, unlike in Singapore, where a similar system prevails, there is little attempt by the government to argue that BNM is operationally independent in practice, even though there is a reasonable case to be made in the area of monetary policy.[11] The governor and deputy governor positions are explicitly political appointments; since 1985 these have tended to come from outside BNM (Hamilton-Hart 2002, chap. 5). The MOF Secretary-General is an ex-officio member of BNM's board, while the BNM governor has been involved in other institutions central to the government's economic policies. On a few occasions BNM governors and other senior officials have been forced to resign, notably Ahmad Don, in August 1998, who was associated with Anwar. Referring to this event, Mahathir explicitly criticized BNM for ignoring the recommendations of the National Economic Action Council (NEAC), which was created by Mahathir in January 1998 to consolidate his control over economic policy (and later headed by Daim).[12]

BNM responded to the crisis by increasing the number of bank examiners and the frequency of bank examinations (IMF 1999b, 56, 69). As the recession intensified in Malaysia over 1998, NPLs grew rapidly and banks stopped lending, in part due to the enhanced prudential standards adopted months earlier by the Anwar team (see below). Macroeconomic austerity and bank and corporate restructuring directly threatened a number of the bumiputera business interests that had benefited from the government's policy; a number of bumiputera loans were among the worst performing in the financial system (Khoo 2001). Mahathir came to see the threat to the NEP posed by these policies as part of a general attempt by the IMF and associated domestic forces to impose neoliberalism on Malaysia and thereby to undermine its social and political stability. Anwar's economic policy dominance and his campaign against cronyism and nepotism also threatened Mahathir's own personal position, as well as that of his economic advisor, Daim, and their political and business allies.[13] In September 1998, Anwar was sacked (and jailed) and replaced by Daim. As I show below, BNM exercised forbearance on loan classification and provisioning standards in the face of pressure from the prime minister's office.

The concentration of problems created by the government's favoritism toward bumiputera business interests was reflected by the fact that in 1999, Bank Bumiputera Group and Sime Bank Group dominated the NPLs in Danaharta's portfolio at 29.3 percent and 33.2 percent, respectively, of the total.[14] This highly concentrated NPL problem in turn pointed to powerful connected debtors such as the Renong group, a company originally established by Daim as the finance arm of UMNO itself. In 1998, the government recapitalized Bank Bumiputera in return for selling some of its NPLs to Danaharta, before it in turn was sold to the Bank of Commerce. Sime Bank was merged with RHB Bank, also subsequently recapitalized by Danamodal. In addition, 30 percent of RHB's shares were purchased by Khazanah Nasional Berhad, the government-owned investment corporation. Those NPLs purchased by Danaharta from Bank Bumiputera were at an 85 percent discount, the highest of any bank (Danaharta 2003, Appendix 2).

Hence, although the process of recapitalization and merger of banks was relatively transparent and efficient in Malaysia,[15] the bailout of various companies connected to the UMNO elite was not (Haggard 2000, 166–71). These bailouts made clear the government's desire to socialize the business risks incurred in the name of the NEP. This policy attracted growing criticism within the grassroots of UMNO itself and added to the Muslim voices who felt that Anwar had been poorly treated. In the general election of 1999, UMNO lost nearly a quarter of its parliamentary seats, including key seats in Muslim majority areas. Opposition to UMNO policy, which continued after the elections, increasingly made Daim a liability to Mahathir. Eventually Daim was removed from his special economic advisory position in April 2001 and Mahathir pledged to root out corruption from the political system.[16] In June 2001, Daim was also forced to resign as Finance Minister, with Mahathir himself assuming the finance portfolio.

Since then, the operational independence enjoyed by BNM appears to have increased, though it remains somewhat at the mercy of shifting government policy preferences. In 2002, for example, BNM was unable to enforce limits it had earlier imposed on individual holdings of bank stocks.[17] Proposals for a prompt corrective action framework that would require automatic regulatory responses to specified kinds of bank under-performance were floated by BNM in 2001, but a formal PCA framework was still under discussion in 2003 (BNM 2003, 120).

BNM's continuing political subordination has been most in evidence in the area of banking sector consolidation. The Financial Sector Master Plan of 2001 envisaged the creation of a small number of large and sufficiently strong financial institutions that would no longer rely on the periodic government bailouts of the past. The initial list of six government-designated "anchor banks" threatened the position of some existing bank owners, both bumiputera and Chinese (Hamilton-Hart 2002, 165). Subsequently, the government backed down by announcing an increase in the number of anchor banks to ten. There have also been rumors of political interference in bank mergers. Multipurpose Bank, a relatively small bank chosen as one of the initial six anchor banks able to take over others, was controlled by an ally of Daim, then the Finance Minister.[18] As recently as March 2006, the government forced Southern Bank to accept a takeover bid from the larger, state-controlled Bumiputra Commerce Holdings (BCH), by blocking bids from other banks. The chief executive of BCH was the brother of the deputy prime minister.[19]

Rules on Capital Adequacy, Loan Classification, and Provisioning

Malaysia adopted the minimum Basle capital adequacy ratio of 8 percent in the early 1990s, applied on a consolidated basis from March 1998 (IMF 1999b, 70). Unlike Indonesia, BNM had no need to depart from this minimum international capitalization standard after 1997. Furthermore, BNM generally follows Basle-consistent capital definitions and tends to adopt a more conservative stance than some other Asian countries.[20] There is also evidence that the regulatory authorities in practice have encouraged banks to maintain CARs well in excess of the Basle minimum. For example, Danamodal recapitalization aimed to bring intervened banks up to a minimum CAR of 14 percent, after an assessment by an American investment bank and BNM's regulatory department (IMF 1999b, 65). As figure 5.1 suggests, average banking sector CARs have been consistently above 10 percent and smoothly rising since 1997, an unusual outcome among the crisis-hit countries.

However, below the surface of this apparently strict policy and improving bank capitalization outlook there is evidence of a discretionary relaxation of capital definitions during the crisis that allowed banks to maintain reported CARs at these relatively high levels. For example, although banks sold NPLs to Danaharta at prices determined by independent auditors, they were allowed to amortize the implied loss (of 54 percent on average) over five years, hence spreading out its negative effect on income and capital. Furthermore, from November 2000, banks were allowed to recognize audited half-yearly profits in their calculation of total capital. This reversed an earlier January 1997 decision to prevent banks from doing so, which at the time was aimed at slowing the rapid pace of credit expansion (BNM 2000, chap. 4).

Most important, loan classification rules were relaxed at a crucial point in the crisis. On 18 October 1997, loan classification rules had been tightened from a 6-month delinquency standard to the more internationally recognized 3-month standard then being adopted across the region. Then, on 23 September 1998, after Anwar's sacking, BNM reverted to the former 6-month delinquency standard to allow banks "breathing space" (Koh and Soon 2004, 12). Substandard loans were defined as those in default for 6–9 months, doubtful loans for 9–12 months, and loss greater than 12 months. All of these definitions were much less stringent than minimum international best practice. The criteria for reclassifying rescheduled loans as performing were also loosened, and banks were given minimum lending

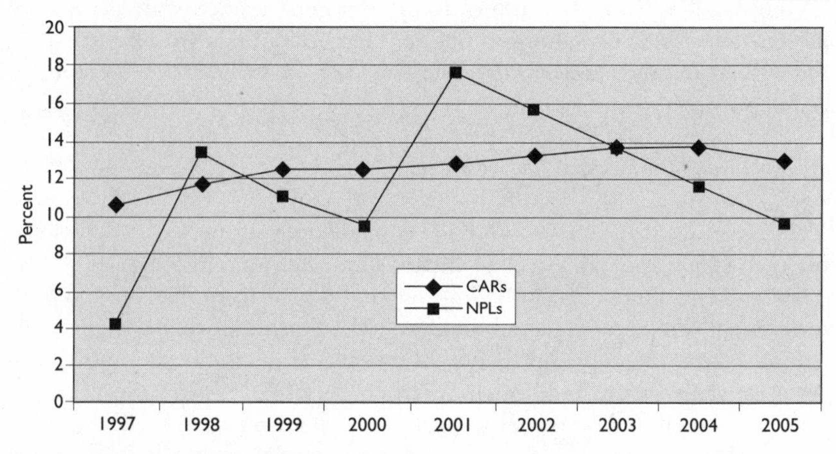

Figure 5.1. Malaysia: CARs and NPLs, 1997–2005

Sources: IMF, *Global Financial Stability Report,* various issues.
Note: Figures are banking sector averages. CARs are Tier I and II capital as a percentage of total risk-adjusted assets. NPLs are nonperforming loans as a percentage of total loans. NPL figures exclude NPLs transferred to Danaharta but are calculated using the standard 3-month in arrears method.

targets in order to promote growth. This policy relaxation was explicitly (and reasonably) justified by Prime Minister Mahathir as necessary to promote economic recovery:

> Shortening the period for NPLs when the Ringgit and share market were fast depreciating and under repeated attacks by speculators, in a regime of high interest rates was unwise as due consideration was not given to the potential negative effects that could occur. The amount of additional loan-loss provisions that had to be made by banking institutions to comply with the 3-month NPL period and 20 percent specific provision policy was approximately ringgit 7 billion.... There was really no reason to tighten the NPL since the banking system had more than adequate provision for bad loans.[21]

In the first year after this relaxation, only 21 of 78 financial institutions (representing 46 percent of total loans) continued to use the 3-month NPL classification standard, which did remain an option (IMF 1999b, 68–69). Interestingly, BNM continued to publish NPLs on its website on both 3-month and 6-month bases, although major banks have converged upon the stricter 3-month definition in recent years. As of 2006, there was no sign of the adoption of international best-practice methods in the form of FLC loan accounting, though BNM is actively planning for the adoption of the

Basle II regime and IFRS 39, which will entail major changes in this area by January 2008.

Even using the stricter 3-month definition, BNM's NPL figures need to be treated with some caution, as methods of calculation changed in December 1997 with the effect of reducing "headline" NPLs. Hence, in figure 5.1, internationally comparable methods of calculation are used.[22] Malaysia's rapid recovery in 1999 helped to reduce reported NPLs, but this reduction was also partly due to further forbearance, whereby BNM allowed banks to classify as performing some loans to large firms in difficulty (Fitch Ratings 2001, 6). NPLs rose again over 2000–2001 on account of slowing growth and a re-tightening of the rules relating to loan classification in cases of large corporate restructuring. Somewhat surprisingly, Malaysian NPLs remained above Indonesia's level for some years after 2001 in spite of Malaysia's shallower crisis, faster economic recovery, and its much more effective bankruptcy regime.[23] Although we need to be cautious in comparing NPLs across countries, it is consistent with the interpretation that Malaysia's 3-month loan classification criteria have been relatively conservative, despite the government's efforts to present a rosier picture and to relieve pressure on banks in the early post-crisis years.

As for provisioning rules, the Malaysian system is slightly different to that elsewhere in the region as the special mention category is omitted, though it is not necessarily less stringent. General provisioning requirements are 1.5 percent and specific provisioning requirements for uncollateralized portions are 20 percent, 50 percent, and 100 percent for substandard, doubtful, and loss respectively. In January 1998, the provisioning requirement on the uncollateralized portion of substandard loans was increased to 20 percent from 0 percent previously. Then, on 23 September 1998, along with the other measures mentioned above, this 20 percent provisioning requirement for substandard loans was made optional in an effort to reduce pressure on banks. At the same time, NPLs that had been restructured or rescheduled could be reclassified as performing when the repayments under the rescheduled terms were complied with for a continuous period of 6 months, instead of 12 months as before.[24]

As elsewhere in Asia, collateral values (which must have been obtained within the last 12 months from an independent valuer) may be used to reduce the specific provisioning requirement after an appropriate "haircut." Also, unlike in Singapore but as in Indonesia, if cash or cash-equivalent collateral exists, this can reduce the severity of the classification (Song 2002, 19–20). This practice can be a potential source of regulatory laxity and of vulnerability. For example, in 1997–98 the collapse of real estate and equity markets led to a substantial reduction in the value of collateral attached to bank loans in Malaysia, requiring much higher provisions on existing NPLs. Continuing economic recovery more recently allowed the authorities to tighten provisioning rules by requiring collateral to be valued on a forced sale basis. In addition, only 50 percent of this value may be used to offset the provisioning requirement on NPLs in arrears for more than five years, and none for NPLs in arrears for more than seven years.[25]

In sum, the Malaysian capitalization, loan classification, and provisioning regime is more stringent than in many Asian countries, but still less stringent than in Korea or the United States. The government's decision to relax these regulations explicitly in September 1998 and to depart from international best practice was not very different to Indonesia's move to require its banks to meet only a 4 percent minimum CAR after early 1998. As in Indonesia and Thailand, a few years of regulatory relaxation were followed by re-tightening and convergence upon international minimum standards once growth recovered. Pressure was also put on BNM to engage in forbearance policies with regard to loan classification until 2001. Since then, however, the authorities have reasserted their former reputation for relatively strict supervisory practice in these areas by tightening most of the standards relaxed during the crisis years. Certainly, by 2003 bank analysts rated the average financial strength of Malaysian banking institutions as slightly better than that in the other crisis-hit countries, though this would be expected, given the lower level of economic distress in the Malaysian economy after the crisis.[26] Moody's and other international ratings agencies continued to rate the financial strength of Malaysian banks as higher than that of banks in the other crisis-hit countries over 2005–6.

Other Prudential Rules

After the Asian crisis, most other prudential rules in Malaysia were brought into conformity with international standards, and there is less evidence of post-1997 forbearance in these areas. On 25 March 1998, BNM reduced the single lending limit (for single and group borrowers) from 30 percent of capital to 25 percent of capital, consistent with the Basle standard.[27] The 1989 BAFIA already prohibited loans to directors, staff, and their associated companies. In November 1999, BNM expanded this prohibition to include lending to controlling and/or influential shareholders (Koh and Soon 2004, 6), a much stricter rule than in Indonesia.

Before the crisis, BNM also regulated and monitored banks' net foreign currency open positions as well as the external liabilities of the corporate sector. Offshore borrowing, particularly by the corporate sector, was substantial in Malaysia before the crisis, but much lower than in Indonesia. Malaysia's foreign exchange reserves more than covered the short-term element (DFAT 1999, 40). From December 1994, residents could borrow a maximum of ringgit 5 million equivalent in foreign currency from any source (Meesook et al. 2001, 4, 51). This seems to have effectively limited the exposure of the private sector to offshore borrowing. Generally, the enforcement of such regulations appears to have been relatively effective—in marked contrast to the other crisis-hit countries (Jomo and Hamilton-Hart 2001).

Compliance with International Standards of Corporate Governance

Formally, Malaysia's approach to corporate governance has been closer to the Anglo-Saxon model than that of most of its neighbors. The legacy of British common law and stock market practices and the activism of the Kuala Lumpur Stock Exchange (KLSE)[28] have enabled Malaysia to obtain a relatively good reputation in corporate governance today. However, as I argue in section 3, the political priorities and relationships that have dominated economic policymaking in Malaysia since the 1970s have often resulted in a significant gap between appearance and reality. Below, I assess corporate governance in the areas of board independence, other board committees, minority shareholder rights and disclosure, and corporate governance in the banking sector. Before doing so, I briefly outline corporate governance practices before the crisis.

Corporate Governance before the Crisis

Malaysia's reputation for relatively good corporate governance before the crisis was better than that of most of its neighbors (DFAT 2002, 2:133; Capulong et al. 2000, 1:3). Besides Singapore, Malaysia was the only Asian developing country to have required listed companies to have both independent directors and audit committees before the crisis (Barton, Coombes, and Wong 2004). The KLSE also endorsed the 1992 UK Cadbury Report on corporate governance and adopted rules to strengthen the role of boards, though there was no corporate governance code as such. All listed companies' audit committees were required to have an independent chair and at least one member with membership of the Malaysian Institute of Accountants or other relevant accounting experience (DFAT 2002, 2:145). This reputation may account for the government's decision to complete and to publish a ROSC on corporate governance in 1999, which was updated in 2005 (World Bank 1999, 2005c).[29]

However, important aspects of corporate governance in Malaysia had much in common with other Asian countries. Family ownership is widespread, similar to the levels in Thailand. Among listed firms, the use of cross-shareholdings and pyramid structures to maintain control is also substantial (Claessens, Djankov, and Lang 1999; DFAT 2002, 2:134–35). The use of nominee accounts by both domestic and foreign investors to hide ultimate ownership was also extensive in the past. On average, nominees were the most important of the top five shareholders for all listed companies at the end of 1997, owning 45 percent of all companies (World Bank 1999, s.2).

Moreover, as in Singapore, the government and government-controlled funds and investment vehicles are major investors and hold controlling stakes in some major firms. Connections between government and business generally were (and remain) extensive and are a key factor affecting corporate governance outcomes (Gomez 2004). The Industrial Coordination Act of 1975, a key plank of the NEP, positively discriminated in favor of ethnic Malays by, among other things, setting a target (for 1990) of a minimum quota of 30 percent equity participation and employment for bumiputeras in companies with at least RM100,000 in share capital and 25 workers. Increased bumiputera participation came mainly at the expense of foreign shareholders, who dominated the economy in the early post-colonial period (Khoo 2001, 185–86; Gomez 2004, 121). State ownership of previously foreign-owned assets also grew rapidly, and these were often used to benefit well-connected bumiputera entrepreneurs. Over time, Chinese business interests were also disadvantaged as the UMNO coalition consolidated Malay control over the key economic ministries from 1974.[30] UMNO itself came to control substantial corporate assets, entrusting many of them to individuals closely associated with UMNO and the NEP project. Through his dominance over the instruments of political power, Mahathir used his privatization policy to transfer such assets permanently into the hands of bumiputera business allies (Searle 1999; Gomez 2004).

The core tension in corporate governance in Malaysia, then, has been between the relatively open and rules-based regulatory framework and the discriminatory principles of the NEP. At the formal level, Malaysia's regulatory framework was strong, and efforts were underway before the crisis to improve it. However, substantive compliance lagged as the relationship between Malay business interests and the ruling political elite became increasingly close, and regulatory enforcement became correspondingly ad hoc (Gomez 2004).

Post-Crisis Reforms in Corporate Governance

As in banking regulation, the government took a series of initiatives on corporate governance very soon after the crisis began. The KLSE undertook a survey with PricewaterhouseCoopers, which reported, contrary to the official line, that institutional investors saw corporate governance in Malaysia as only marginally better than in China, the Philippines, Indonesia, and Thailand—and well below those of Singapore, Japan, and Hong Kong (KLSE 1998). In March 1998, the government established a High-Level

Finance Committee on Corporate Governance and approved its recommendations in February 1999 (Finance Committee on Corporate Governance 1999). The resulting Malaysian "Code of Corporate Governance"—approved by the main regulatory agency, the Securities Commission (SC), in March 2000—elaborates voluntary best-practice principles (Finance Committee on Corporate Governance 2000). As of the end of 2005, only 43 percent of the Finance Committee's recommendations had been implemented, and the rest were still in progress—this figure had not changed since 2003, indicating that reform has stalled in recent years.[31]

The SC's implementation record is better than its equivalent in Thailand, but the slow pace of adoption is an important constraint on full compliance. The KLSE incorporated the corporate governance code into its listing rules in 2001, but these requirements are only legally binding when approved by the SC (Nathan, Lin, and Fong 2000, 3). Listed companies are required to disclose in their annual reports how they comply with the code. In addition, the Malaysian Institute of Corporate Governance (MICG) was created in March 1998 to improve awareness of corporate governance issues and to train directors. The new listing rules required all directors to undertake such training, which is ongoing.[32] In the wake of these initiatives, Malaysia's formal standards were said to rival those of Hong Kong and Singapore (DFAT 2002, 2:134; PricewaterhouseCoopers 2002). Key aspects of this framework are summarized below and compared with regional best practice (table 5.1). In the following sections, I discuss outcomes in the areas of board independence, other board committees, shareholder rights and disclosure, and corporate governance in the banking sector in more detail.

Board Independence

The Malaysian "Code of Corporate Governance" and KLSE listing requirements suggest that one third of all directors or two directors, whichever is highest, should be independent of management. "Independence" means that such directors cannot be linked by family ties or substantive business relationships to senior management or major shareholders. Levels of compliance with this requirement are reasonable, though the standard itself lags international best practice. In 2002, 69 percent of listed companies had more than the minimum requirement of independent directors, but in only 14 percent of the top 50 listed companies did independent directors constitute at least half of the board, the current NYSE requirement (Standard & Poor's 2004b, 8). The code requires no minimum number of board meetings but suggests that they meet "regularly" and favors disclosure of their frequency (Finance Committee on Corporate Governance 2000, 11). The code also strongly recommends but does not require that the chairman and CEO roles are separated. Again, compliance with this recommendation

TABLE 5.1
Selected corporate governance rules: Malaysia and Asian best practice, 2003–4

	Malaysia	Asian best practice standard
Boards		
Cumulative voting for board members permitted?	No	Pakistan (mandatory)
Limit on how many company boards an individual may serve?	Yes: 25 (10 listed; 15 unlisted)	Korea (2 for non-executives)
Minimum number of board meetings per year	None, though favors disclosure of number of meetings	Thailand
Fit and proper test for directors?	Yes	Yes
Legal responsibility of board for financial statements	Collective	Hong Kong (fully liable)
Company prohibited from indemnifying directors?	In cases of negligence, default, breach of duty/trust	Malaysia
Continuing training required for directors?	Yes (KLSE rule)	Malaysia
Legally required separation of chairman and CEO?	Recommended by CG code	Malaysia
Independent directors required?	Yes (minimum of 2 or 1/3 of board, whichever is higher)	Korea (majority for banks and large companies)
Audit committees required?	Yes	Yes
Audit committees: minimum number of independent directors required	Majority, incl. one with expertise	Thailand
Remuneration and nomination committees required?	No, but recommended	Philippines (Yes)
Disclosure		
Quarterly and annual reporting	Yes	Yes
Consolidated financial reporting?	Yes	Yes
Annual reports provide information on CG and any divergence from codes	Yes	Yes
Shareholder participation		
Can shareholders vote to remove directors?	Yes (>50% of votes)	Malaysia

TABLE 5.1—cont.

	Malaysia	Asian best practice standard
Do shareholders vote on issuing capital?	Yes (>50% of votes)	Thailand
Do shareholders vote on board remuneration?	No	Thailand
Do shareholders vote on major corporate transactions (acquisitions, disposals, etc.)?	Yes (>50% of votes), if transaction >25% of NTA (or net profits, equity shares, etc.)	Malaysia
Minimum % shareholder votes required to call an extraordinary shareholder meeting	10%	Korea (3%)
Minimum % shareholder votes required to place issue on shareholder meeting agenda	5%	Korea (1%)
Corporate control		
Notification threshold in event of substantial acquisition of shares	5%	5%
Threshold for mandatory offer for all shares	33%	Taiwan (20%)
Shareholder redress		
Derivative action	Yes	Yes (Hong Kong, India, Korea, Singapore, etc.)
Class action	No	Yes (Hong Kong, India, Singapore, etc.)
Related party transactions		
Disclosure of related party transactions	Yes	Yes
Shareholder approval of related party transactions?	Yes (>50% of votes), if transaction value>5% of NTA (or net profits, equity shares, etc.); interested party must abstain	Thailand

Sources: OECD (2003, Appendix A); Nam and Nam (2004, table 1).
Note: NTA=net tangible assets.

is generally good. In only 12–15 percent of companies was this not the case. Board members must have relevant professional experience and the KLSE requires all directors to attend a mandatory, one-off training program; continuing training is also required (PricewaterhouseCoopers 2002, 3–4, 6). Most large firms in Malaysia also provide additional training opportunities for directors (Nam and Nam 2004, 77). The maximum number of company boards on which a director may sit is 25 (10 listed and 15 unlisted), which is very high. Reporting of directors' attendance at board meetings is now required (World Bank 2005c, 28).

But more important, are Malaysia's corporate boards independent of management in practice? Surveys of director opinions generally suggest that real board independence in Malaysia is significantly higher than in the other crisis-hit countries (e.g., Nam and Nam 2004, 67, 78–84). Even so, it is clear that a significant real compliance gap remains. Most Malaysian firms remain closely held, either by families or the state. Controlling owners still dominate board elections in some cases and appoint "shadow directors" who undermine board independence. One survey found that 43 percent of Malaysian directors said it was "unthinkable" that director candidates proposed by management could be rejected; only 10 percent thought it could happen "sometimes" (Nam and Nam 2004, 67). Malaysia, like Australia and Korea, has instituted "attribution rules" to impose fiduciary responsibilities and liability upon such shadow directors, but it is difficult to make such laws effective (OECD 2003, 53).

Audit and Other Board Committees

KLSE listing rules require company boards to elect an audit committee consisting of a majority of independent directors, at least one of whom should have relevant expertise. Audit committees must nominate auditors, evaluate internal control systems, review the audit report, and, among other things, review any related party and conflict of interest transactions for noncompliance (KLSE 2005, s.15.13). Levels of compliance with this committee composition rule are reasonable: about 80 percent of major firms meet these standards. Audit committees also typically met more frequently than other board committees (Standard & Poor's 2004b, 14). However, most Malaysian firms do not meet the international best-practice standard of a fully independent audit-committee membership (Pricewaterhouse Coopers 2002, 3; Nam and Nam 2004, 73, 76).

In 1999, the World Bank ROSC reported that Malaysian audit committees, as elsewhere, were often ineffective because of lack of expertise or information (World Bank 1999, s.5.4). More recently, a survey suggested that Malaysian directors were relatively confident about the effectiveness of audit committees, though such judgments may be self-serving (Nam and Nam 2004, 73–74). As has been clear from the United States and other developed countries in recent years, ensuring that audit committees effectively perform their functions remains extraordinarily difficult, so it would be surprising if oversight failures were unusual in Malaysia.

As in Thailand, remuneration and nomination committees are only recommended, not required by the KLSE listing rules. Again, this lags international best practice (e.g., the current U.S. rule requires fully independent compensation and nomination committees). Nevertheless, by 2002, about three quarters of all listed Malaysian company boards had such committees, compared to less than one quarter in 2001 (PricewaterhouseCoopers 2002, 3). By 2002–3, 64 percent of the top 50 listed companies had nomination committees in which independent directors constituted a majority; the equivalent figure for remuneration committees was 46 percent (Standard & Poor's 2004b, 11–12). These figures are much higher than in Thailand, though of course this does not necessarily mean that such committees always play a central role in proposing and scrutinizing senior company appointments and their compensation. Credible evidence in this area is very difficult to obtain.

Shareholder Rights and Disclosure

In formal terms, shareholder rights are well protected in Malaysia, though of course this is also true of Thailand. As in other countries where family ownership is high, a key issue is the potential for exploitation of outside shareholders. Most major listed companies in Malaysia are controlled by block shareholders, and about a third of CEOs of such companies are from the founding family (Nam and Nam 2004, 51). The Malaysian Accounting Standards Board (MASB) has adopted IAS 24, which requires Malaysian companies to disclose a range of specified data on related party transactions. All such significant transactions (involving 5 percent or more of assets, profits, share capital, etc) must be announced immediately to the KLSE and must be approved by at least 50 percent of shareholders; interested parties must abstain. Given the high concentration of ownership in Malaysia, this threshold (lower than Thailand's 75 percent) may still not be sufficient to prevent the abuse of minority shareholders.[33] However, there are additional checks. Minority shareholders must approve inter-group loans. An independent advisor must be appointed to judge whether the transaction is fair to all shareholders and audit committees must scrutinize it (KLSE 2005, s.10–08). A Minority Shareholder Watchdog Group was also established in 2002 under the auspices of the EPF.

Listed companies must provide quarterly financial reports to investors according to accounting standards set by the independent MASB, which was established in June 1997. In 1999, MASB undertook a review of all Malaysian accounting standards to ensure their consistency with IAS (Nathan, Lin and Fong 2000, 13). MASB policy is to adopt, mostly word-for-word,

IASB standards with a view to full harmonization in the near future. However, it reviews each standard and reserves the right to delay adoption or to provide a domestic alternative. As of 2003, Malaysia had adopted all but five IAS/IFRS (World Bank 2005, 23).

What of substantive compliance in these areas? Various enforcement mechanisms exist. The SC is responsible for the enforcement of rules for listed companies and BNM for financial institutions. Under the Companies Act and Securities Commission Act, shareholders may sue companies that provide misleading information and directors that fail to discharge their fiduciary responsibilities. In August 1998, the KLSE and the SC issued various measures aimed at restoring confidence in the stock market by improving transparency, including the disclosure of beneficiaries of nominee shareholding accounts.[34] Compliance with this rule seems to be good (DFAT 2002, 2:144). The KLSE and the SC may also undertake actions against companies and their directors who breach listing requirements or impose losses on shareholders (Nathan 2001, 9–10). These provisions are more robust than in Thailand, for example.

Even so, problems with outside shareholder exploitation continue to arise. As noted above, controlling shareholders still tend to dominate elections to corporate boards. There is no provision for cumulative voting for directors in Malaysia, in contrast to Thailand and Korea. The hurdle to remove directors is a modest 50 percent (the same percentage required to appoint directors), but gathering sufficient votes remains difficult in most cases. Derivative actions are possible, including by the SC on behalf of shareholders, to claim compensation for losses incurred. But these are difficult to enforce in the courts, and any damages awarded accrue to the company (Koh and Soon 2004, 30; World Bank 2005c, 7). There are also various practical obstacles to shareholders undertaking legal actions against companies or directors, notably that each shareholder must bring his own action to establish damage and to obtain compensation, since class action suits are unavailable (Nathan 2001, 9; OECD 2003, 21; World Bank 1999, s.4.3).

As elsewhere in Asia, the practical difficulties of individual shareholder action means that enforcement is largely in the hands of the state. The SC is financially independent of government, funded by market levies, and has a board on which a mix of private and public sector representatives sit (the latter being in a minority). It has a reputation as an effective regulator, though some argue that its subordination to the Minister of Finance raises questions about its independence (World Bank 1999, 2.2; 2005c, 12–13). The SC has wide administrative autonomy, but it lacks judicial powers. The finance minister appoints the chairman and the board of the SC, and the chairman and four board members of the KLSE; he may dismiss them at any time.

In fact, unevenness of enforcement has been a major problem in Malaysia, with politically connected companies and bumiputera entrepreneurs gaining preferential treatment. After Anwar fell from grace in September 1998, Anwar-connected officers at some major companies were replaced with associates of his successor, Daim Zainuddin (Gomez 2004, 125). As Gomez notes:

> ...the rights of shareholders appear seldom to be respected while company directors remain accountable only to the Prime Minister and not to the investors in the companies they lead....Control appears ultimately to be in the hands of political elites to whom these businessmen are closely linked. (Gomez 2004, 133)

The incidence of weak enforcement against connected firms and individuals peaked in the aftermath of the crisis, when a number of politically connected companies sought and obtained substantial government assistance. The long-running Renong-UEM saga visibly demonstrated the importance of political connections in limiting compliance pressure for new corporate governance rules. Renong, the UMNO holding company and the country's largest conglomerate, was run by a Daim associate, Halim Saad. Heavily indebted when the crisis broke, Renong's failure would have been politically disastrous for the ruling party, so the government undertook a series of maneuvers to keep it afloat. In November 1997, UEM, Renong's engineering subsidiary, was permitted to take over 32.6 percent of its parent's stock without making the standard disclosures required under KLSE rules. Moreover, UEM was granted a waiver from having to make a mandatory general offer for all remaining shares, despite an announcement by Finance Minister Anwar to the contrary (an associated company, Time Engineering, owned another large stake in Renong). Nor was the approval of UEM shareholders sought, as required for all substantial acquisitions, even though Renong was UEM's controlling shareholder. UEM's share price fell 46 percent in the week following the announcement, the common perception being that Renong was being bailed out at UEM's expense and that of its minority shareholders (Nathan, Lin and Fong 2000, 8). Halim Saad was also relieved by UEM of a put option he had offered to UEM shareholders on their Renong stock, without reprimand or fine from the regulators.

These and other abuses gradually sapped political support for the government, particularly as Anwar's sacking had mobilized a growing anticorruption movement. Eventually, in September 2001, after Daim's removal, the government took control of both Renong and UEM.[35] Since then, some commentators see enforcement as having improved (e.g., CLSA Emerging Markets 2002, 65, 2005, 61; DFAT 2002, 2:147). Some of the most visible links between government and business were dismantled (Case 2005:295).

In January 2003, the KLSE suspended trading of the stocks of 67 companies for breaches of rules on related party transactions; 16 were de-listed.[36] However, there is no visible upward trend in the number of actual enforcement actions taken by the SC since 1999, when these peaked (World Bank 2005c, 32). Generally, the quality of enforcement of corporate governance regulations in Malaysia remains dependent upon the attitude of the political leaders. The key recommendation of the Finance Committee in 1999 "[t]hat regulators should have sufficient autonomy to enforce laws without interference or fear or favour" still had not been implemented as of end 2005, despite Mahathir's retirement from politics.[37] As Gomez (2004, 134) remarks, "regulatory institutions can—and usually do—act independently, but they are also used as a tool by powerful politicians for vested interests." On average, this means that shareholder rights are better protected in Malaysia than in many Asian countries,[38] but there continue to be important exceptions to this generalization.

Corporate Governance in the Banking Sector

As noted, BNM is responsible for enforcing regulations relating to financial institutions, and it also requires them to adhere to additional corporate governance guidelines. The 1989 Banking and Financial Institutions Act (BAFIA) called for boards of banks to include some nonexecutive directors, but otherwise it was largely silent on the issue. Since the crisis, BNM has been proactive in this area. New BNM guidelines were issued in 1999 to extend the prohibition on lending to connected shareholders or their associated companies. BNM's *Guidelines on Directorship in Banking Institutions* (BNM/GP1) were also revised in July 2001 and replaced by the *Guidelines on Corporate Governance for Licensed Institutions* in 2005 (BNM 2001, 116, 2005, 133). The number of directorships held by CEOs of banks is now limited to five, though the limit excludes directorships in statutory institutions and government-owned companies.

In June 2003, BNM required banks to establish remuneration, nomination, and risk-management committees, and in each case specified a series of tasks. The risk-management committee must be wholly composed of nonexecutive directors. Banks are also encouraged to make public disclosures on board committee membership, qualifications, responsibilities, and director attendance at meetings (Koh and Soon 2004, 26). Minimum qualifications and training for directors of banks were also specified in addition to existing "fit and proper" criteria. Persons holding political office may not act as directors of financial institutions. BNM supervisors assess management and director performance in these areas, among others (BNM 2003, 116, 120). In August 2003, BNM required the rotation of bank auditors every five years, audit committee approval of the provision of non-audit services by auditors, and BNM approval of auditor reappointment, in line with U.S. Sarbanes-Oxley requirements (BNM 2003, 123). Auditors were already required under the 1989 BAFIA to inform BNM of any discovery of dishonesty or fraud, whether relating to under-capitalization or other irregularities (this is not the case in Thailand, for example). The new 2005 *Guidelines* require separation between CEOs and board Chairmen and between shareholders and management (BNM 2005, 133–34).

In addition to BNM's role in this area, Danamodal was also tasked with improving risk management and corporate governance in those banks in which it had become a strategic shareholder. This was primarily to be achieved through its influence over senior management and the boards of such banks. The Financial Sector Master Plan also included various corporate governance objectives. The effect of the series of mergers that followed did not, however, alter the ownership structure of the industry, in which families, the government, and corporations remain key shareholders in most major financial groups. As of early 2004, only three of the ten groups had reasonably widely dispersed ownership (Koh and Soon 2004, 16).

Nevertheless, most studies suggest that corporate governance in Malaysian banks has improved considerably since the crisis. Those banks best known for serious governance failures before the crisis, notably Bank Bumiputera and Sime Bank, were merged with others and management was replaced. In CLSA's 2000 survey of corporate governance in Asia (CLSA Emerging Markets 2001), the samples of large Malaysian and Thai companies had approximately the same average corporate governance score (55 out of 100). The average score of Malaysian banks (62) was higher than that of Malaysian nonbanks (54), though this difference was not great.[39] Since then, the quality of corporate governance in banking has remained above average, but the continuing dominance of domestically owned and state banks in Malaysia has meant that this sectoral "outperformance" has been less marked than in Thailand and Indonesia, where foreign ownership levels in the banking sector are now much higher. Conspicuously among the other crisis-hit countries, Malaysia did not raise its preexisting foreign ownership limit for banks of 30 percent of total shares.

To summarize, Malaysia's degree of formal compliance with international corporate governance standards has been very high. In CLSA's 2002 survey of corporate governance in Asia, Malaysia stood out in having the best score of all Asian countries on the quality of corporate governance rules and regulations, exceeding those of Singapore and Hong Kong. However, it also received a conspicuously low score on enforcement and also on the political/regulatory environment of corporate governance (table 4.2, chapter 4). During the early post-crisis years, a series of corporate scandals highlighted the close relationships between political and business elites. In these cases, regulatory independence and outside shareholder interests were conspicuously sacrificed. The overall result was a reasonably good average quality of compliance marred by very poor levels of compliance in politically sensitive cases.

Has the situation improved since 2001, as some have claimed (e.g., CLSA Emerging Markets 2005, 61–62)? Certainly, the number of scandals involving politically connected companies has fallen since Daim's sacking in 2001, which removed one of the most important links between government and business. However, despite some new initiatives, the adoption of the reforms recommended by the 2000 Finance Committee on Corporate Governance has actually stalled since 2001. In addition, as noted earlier, enforcement measures taken by the SC did not increase from this time. Other surveys agree with this mixed judgment. Researchers from Standard & Poor's and the National University of Singapore gave a mean corporate governance disclosure score of 65 for the top 50 listed Malaysian companies, well above those for Indonesia and Thailand, but below that for Singapore companies (81). The degree of variance was relatively low for Malaysian firms.[40] There are always exceptions to such generalizations.[41] However, even the very best corporate governance performers in Malaysia lag international best practice in a range of areas (Standard & Poor's 2004b, 16–17).

Explaining Compliance Outcomes

Which theories of compliance best fit the outcomes described above? Consistent with our expectation, Malaysia committed itself to compliance with SDDS in 1996 and was judged by the IMF to be fully compliant by September 2000. By contrast, the level of formal and substantive compliance with banking supervision and corporate governance standards was markedly lower after the crisis. This is consistent with the argument that large domestic compliance costs in these areas were the main cause of compliance failures. The Malaysian government initially committed itself to full compliance in both areas at the beginning of the crisis but soon found that the domestic economic and political costs of doing so were unsustainable. Mahathir's sacking of Anwar in September 1998 was the moment when the political contradictions of Anwar's policy reached a peak. Mahathir explicitly justified significant departures from international banking supervision standards on the grounds that regulatory tightening in the midst of economic crisis made no sense, though it was also clear that tighter compliance would have entailed unsustainably large costs for business interests close to UMNO and the whole NEP strategy.

Behind the scenes, there were more hidden forms of regulatory forbearance, including forbearance on loan classification rules by BNM. However, the balance between formal and substantive compliance was different in

Malaysia than in the other crisis-hit countries. From September 1998, the Malaysian government was more willing to question openly the desirability of full compliance with international banking standards at that point in time. This policy shift might be explained, as MacIntyre (2003) has argued, by reference to Malaysia's relatively centralized political system, producing policy outcomes that are volatile and dependent on the attitudes of the political leadership. However, as we have seen, the Malaysian government's policies in these areas have actually been less volatile and more orthodox than this interpretation would suggest. Even in September 1998, Mahathir was arguing for only a *temporary* departure from international banking standards, suggesting that the external pressures for formal compliance at least remained strong. Anwar's policy of relatively rapid compliance with stringent international standards of banking supervision was itself unsustainable in the circumstances and would necessarily have required substantial regulatory forbearance behind the scenes. After September 1998, the level of regulatory forbearance in Malaysia was similar to that in the other crisis-hit countries; it was just more explicit, possibly because of the absence of the IMF and the greater freedom of political maneuver enjoyed by Mahathir.

In the area of corporate governance, the government was considerably less radical and formal policy was quite stable; indeed, it has been very orthodox from the outset. In marked contrast to politically decentralized Thailand (until 2001), improvements in corporate governance have not been delayed by legislative gridlock. There were important revisions to legislation, notably the Securities Commission Act (2000 and thereafter), the Securities Industry Regulations Acts (1998, 1999), the new Companies Commission Act (2001), the Anti-Money Laundering Act (2001), the Development Financial Institutions Act (2002), and the Payment Systems Act (2003). The existing Central Bank and Companies Acts already gave significant powers to regulators (and in the latter case to shareholders, including substantial voting rights). The new Malaysian Corporate Governance Code was quickly revised to bring it up to current international standards and was adopted by the KLSE.

The fall in UMNO's vote in 1999 among the Malay community was a reaction to perceived high levels of corruption within the ruling party, particularly among those Muslim voters who saw Anwar as a martyr to Mahathir's political venality (Case 2005, 294). This arguably made it more difficult for Mahathir to depart explicitly from the good corporate governance agenda, especially after his commitment to root out corruption in politics. However, with Daim in control of economic policy until mid-2001, this commitment could only be skin deep. Continuing abuses and weak enforcement were evident when the corporate governance rules conflicted with UMNO's political priorities and business interests. Bailouts of connected companies continued (Haggard 2000, 166–71). Hence, in corporate governance, the degree of mock compliance has been greater than in banking supervision.

Consistent with our theory, economic recovery from 2002 brought with it an increase in the quality of compliance in banking supervision, though somewhat less in corporate governance. Some saw Daim's departure as heralding a new, positive, pro-enforcement approach by Mahathir to corporate governance in 2001. However, as noted earlier, the actual record of enforcement by the SC showed no upward trend at all from 2001–4. This suggests that the political and legal constraints on the SC's enforcement capacity remained largely in place, despite Daim's exit. Economic recovery did restore the fortunes of Malaysia's corporate sector, including the large firms that remained closely connected with UMNO, and this produced fewer large corporate governance scandals than over 1998–2000. However, the quality of corporate sector compliance in this area has shown no marked upward trend since 2001 (CLSA Emerging Markets 2005, 61–66).

Compliance costs remain high for many family-owned and state-connected firms. Concentrated ownership and the absence of large private institutional investors limit the impact of stock market pressure on companies to improve corporate governance. Nevertheless, the government's important ownership position in the Malaysian economy does give it potential influence. In the wake of Mahathir's departure, the new Badawi government used the large state-owned investment and pension companies to push through improvements in government-linked companies (World Bank 2005c, 10). Nevertheless, the reluctance of the political elite to underpin corporate governance standards with greater SC enforcement capacity revealed the limits to government intentions in this area.

This example also suggests that low exogenous institutional capacity has not been the major problem; rather, the major problem is the ability and periodic willingness of the government to subordinate supervisory agencies to political priorities. The key regulatory agencies in Malaysia, BNM and the SC, are, in fact, generally recognized to be relatively competent and effective institutions, along with the courts (Hamilton-Hart 2002; World Bank 2005c, 12–13). Often, the government has allowed these agencies considerable operational autonomy, and the results have been good. The record of financial restructuring after the crisis, for example, has been much better than in Indonesia and Thailand.

As for international forces affecting compliance, these have often been weak, as in the Indonesian and Thai cases. IFI conditionality has been irrelevant in Malaysia because of the government's ability and desire to avoid an IMF program. Even after its economic recovery, the Malaysian government has kept the IMF, in particular, at a distance, refusing to participate in the FSAP/ROSC program, with the sole exception of a ROSC in corporate governance. Even so, as I have argued, despite the Malaysian government's desire to avoid the IMF, it has remained relatively orthodox in formal policy terms regarding compliance with international standards.

Does this suggest that neoliberal ideas have influenced Malaysian government thinking in this area? This seems very doubtful. Dr. Mahathir, unlike Anwar, was more than willing to confront most of the orthodoxies supported by the IFIs in recent years. As argued in this chapter, it is more likely that overt resistance to Western-style corporate governance policies was avoided because of pre-existing institutional legacies and because Mahathir perceived this to be incompatible with his pledge to eliminate corruption in politics and business in and after the 1999 elections. Prime Minister Badawi may be temperamentally more disposed to neoliberal reforms, and has produced some important new initiatives in the state-controlled sector, but he too has recognized the need to compromise with the forces of political patronage in his party (Case 2005, 301–7).

As for market forces, these may have played a role in encouraging the Malaysian government's formal policy on standards to be fairly orthodox. However, the concentration of ownership in listed companies, few of which list abroad, and the important role of government in the Malaysian economy substantially limit the impact of market pressure on compliance at the corporate level. At the level of substantive compliance, market forces have probably been no greater, and possibly less strong, than in Indonesia and Thailand. Malaysia's lower level of indebtedness than the other crisis-hit countries meant that it was less vulnerable to creditor pressure, even assuming that this existed. Mahathir's willingness to use stringent capital controls to defend the currency suggested he was not too concerned about upsetting international investors. International equity investors, as we have seen in the cases of Indonesia and Thailand, have not in any case generally punished companies with worse corporate governance records.[42] Finally, the relatively limited role of foreign banks in Malaysia has been another factor that sets it apart from the other crisis-hit countries.

The High Politics of Compliance

It was almost a matter of principle for the Mahathir government to resist external, especially "Western," pressure for reform. Anwar became seen as the domestic vanguard of this external pressure and a threat to Mahathir's own political position. This attitude was linked to Malaysia's colonial history and the NEP, seen as a vital pillar of the country's social and political stability. However, the domestic reform movement gained considerable strength after Anwar's removal and encouraged the government to accept the need for change. This largely grass-roots movement has been important in a country in which neoliberal reformers have not generally been welcomed by the political leadership and in which the independent press, private institutional investors, and NGOs have also been weak. Eventually, therefore, the domestic political costs of outright noncompliance with international standards became too high even for the Mahathir government. However, it would be wrong to conclude that external forces promoting formal compliance were wholly unimportant in the Malaysian case, since domestic opposition was fueled in part by Mahathir's perceived resistance to a regional reform trend.

It should be emphasized that Malaysia's pre-crisis framework in corporate governance and banking regulation was already superior to most in the region and so the extent of reform required was less. Furthermore, in spite of Mahathir's rhetoric, post-crisis policy in these areas was often more orthodox than is commonly assumed. This is not to say that the level of formal compliance with international standards was perfect. In fact, in banking regulation, in particular, there were clear departures from international best-practice principles, notably in the areas of supervisory agency independence and loan classification standards. However, with the exception of agency independence, the long-term goal of the government was always to comply fully with the main international standards.

A series of reform bills brought Malaysia even closer to international best practice in these areas, demonstrating that parliamentary ratification was not a serious obstacle to compliance, as it was in Thailand. Major regulatory institutions like the stock exchange, the SC, and BNM were given considerable authority both to adopt international best-practice standards and to enforce them. The level of bureaucratic corruption was also relatively low and competence relatively high. Thus, as domestic pressure for greater transparency and for an end to the cronyistic relationships between UMNO and major bumiputera business interests grew, the quality of compliance with corporate governance rules rose. In the area of banking regulation, the government's self-interest in promoting greater financial stability after a series of very expensive rescues combined with fairly competent regulatory agencies to produce much better outcomes than in Indonesia. This also allowed Malaysia to avoid ceding control of domestic banks to foreign investors.

Nevertheless, given the depth of the crisis in 1998, as elsewhere in Asia, something had to give. The nature of mock compliance in Malaysia varied somewhat between banking supervision and corporate governance. Perhaps because of BNM's reputation for relatively good, technocratic supervision, the Mahathir government felt compelled to engage in explicit regulatory forbearance by relaxing rules relating to loan classification and provisioning in late 1998. In the area of corporate governance, enforcement was weak for politically connected companies over 1998–2000. Even since then, the SC's enforcement record did not change markedly as the economy improved;

nor has the average quality of corporate governance shown much improvement. Most commentators attribute this to the continuing importance of family and state ownership in the Malaysian political economy. The Badawi government's new initiative relating to government-linked companies suggests that the quality of compliance may improve gradually. Nevertheless, the government's continued unwillingness to grant key regulatory agencies independence and its intention to retain an important role for state ownership in the economy means that the potential for ad hoc political interference in regulation remains significant.

6

Banking Supervision, Corporate Governance, and Financial Disclosure in Korea

In this chapter, I complete the assessment of compliance with international standards in the largest of the four main crisis-hit Asian economies, South Korea. I extend the scope of assessment even wider than in the previous chapter to include standards in banking supervision, corporate governance, and accounting.

More than any of the other countries after the crisis, Korea was most vigorously committed to compliance with international financial standards and to convergence upon regulatory neoliberalism. A new government headed by Kim Dae-Jung put together an economic reform team whose neoliberal credentials were strong and which enjoyed greater political support than in any of the other countries. In 2003, the government claimed that Korea had achieved or exceeded international best practice in most important respects. However, since Korea was also in many ways the exemplar of the Asian developmental state, this case also exhibits the tensions and difficulties that emerged in this transition project. As we shall see, as elsewhere in Asia, mock compliance was also evident in Korea in the early post-crisis years, both at the level of policy and in the private sector. Although there has been a considerable shrinkage of the real compliance gap in banking supervision more recently, compliance failures continue in some areas, particularly in corporate governance, indicating that noncyclical factors remain important constraints. Once again, we find that family ownership is a key constraint upon compliance in this area.

Crisis and Compliance in Korea

The Korean crisis produced an apparently deep-seated shift in official attitudes toward regulation. The old regulatory system was accepted by most in government as having allowed or even encouraged the poor financial and corporate decision-making that helped to cause the 1997 crisis. Much of the blame was put on developmentalism itself. As a Ministry of Finance and the Economy (MOFE) publication of 2002 put it,

> The origins of the 1997 Korean financial crisis can be traced to structural weaknesses in the national economy that were accumulated in more than three decades of rapid "government-led" development.... As though that were not enough, government-led economic development had made moral hazards endemic, as indicated by the widespread belief that chaebol conglomerates and financial institutions could not possibly fail regardless of what they did, so long as they were large enough. Corruption had become pervasive and the cozy relationship between political and business circles had nearly made transparency and accountability foreign concepts in Korea.... The national consensus regarding the need to eliminate the accumulation of structural defects was so clear-cut and determined the Government could not postpone economic reform any longer. The goal and objective was to dismantle a government-led system of economic growth and replace it with a more advanced and efficient system based on market principles.[1]

The IMF or U.S. Treasury could hardly have put the case for a shift from developmentalism to neoliberalism more boldly than this. Both the diagnosis and policy prescription eminently suited the purposes of the new government in Seoul. President Kim Dae-Jung, elected on 18 December 1997, only weeks into the crisis, was determined to use the opportunity it presented to reduce permanently the political and economic power of the large chaebol (family-controlled conglomerates). Consistent with Kahler's (1990) "orthodox paradox," the shift toward neoliberalism entailed an increase in the power of the state (Hundt 2005). A number of economic reformers joined the new administration and filled key positions in the government and bureaucracy, though the President's own center-left party never controlled Parliament. However, unlike in Thailand, the authority accorded to the Korean presidency allowed Kim to make extensive use of extra-legal degrees to push through reform (Woo-Cumings 2003, 213–14). Furthermore, political support for this project was considerable, as the rising economic and political influence of the chaebol was widely seen as the cause of Korea's problems (Graham 2003; Weiss and Hobson 2000; Yoon 2000). By the end of 1997, the top 30 chaebol accounted for 50 percent of total corporate debt (and the top five one-third); many had debt-equity ratios above 400 percent. Hanbo Steel's collapse in January 1997 had already highlighted the close relationship between major firms and politicians, though many more corruption scandals followed (Chopra et al. 2001, 10).

The idea of fundamental regulatory reform and even a shift toward neoliberalism was not new in Korea. The Kim Young Sam administration's (1993–97) *Segyehwa* policy sought to prepare Korea for competition in the new age of globalization (Thurbon 2003, 350). This policy aimed to transform Korea into a market-based economy and to reduce the power of conservative ministries such as the MOF (in this case, by merging it with the former pilot agency, the Economic Planning Board [EPB], to create the MOFE in 1994). It was also a means of distancing the state from the increasingly powerful chaebol, the offspring of developmentalism (Weiss 2003, 250–51). These reforms accelerated the withdrawal of the state from its former role of allocating finance to preferred sectors and firms.

Nevertheless, the prioritization of growth over prudential regulation continued after 1994 and calls for regulatory reform grew. Eventually, the President agreed to establish the Presidential Commission on Financial Reform in January 1997, with a mandate to review and recommend reforms to the financial regulatory and supervisory structure in Korea. In contrast to previous such commissions, MOFE was neither consulted about the Commission's composition nor included in its membership. Some Commission members privately referred to it as the "death to the banks committee," reflecting their view that chronic regulatory forbearance, aided and abetted by MOFE, had created weak banks and endemic moral hazard in the financial and corporate sectors.[2] The Commission made a series of recommendations, including that the four separate financial regulatory agencies be merged into a single unified and independent financial regulator. Besides proposing to raise regulatory standards to international best-practice levels, the Commission also argued for automatic PCA-style regulatory triggers to reduce the scope for supervisory discretion. In short, regulatory neoliberalism had reached Korea before the crisis hit.

Draft legislation reflecting these recommendations was submitted to the National Assembly on 23 August 1997, before the Korean crisis, but opposition from major chaebol, the Bank of Korea (BOK), and MOFE ensured that it stalled. This situation persisted even as the foreign exchange situation deteriorated dramatically in November, forcing the government to request financial assistance from the IMF (IEO 2003, 36). Korea's first LOI to the IMF included a specific commitment to hold a special session of the National Assembly after the presidential elections to pass the bill to establish a single financial supervisory agency, a plan the IMF was happy to endorse.[3] More generally, the first LOI stated that:

> The government is convinced of the need not only to address the immediate problems of the financial system, but more fundamentally to set the basis

> for a strong domestic financial system. To do this, efforts will be made to increase market discipline, strengthen prudential supervision, and regulation in accordance with international best practice standards, increase the manpower needed for effective supervision, and strengthen the legal framework. Accounting standards and disclosure rules will be strengthened according to institutional best practices. Financial statements of large financial institutions will be audited by internationally recognized firms. Prudential standards will be upgraded to meet Basle core principles. Financial institutions will be encouraged to refine their risk assessment and pricing procedures, and to strengthen loan recovery; actions in these areas will be reviewed as part of prudential supervision.[4]

MOFE, as the most powerful ministry with ultimate responsibility for financial sector supervision, was widely blamed for the crisis and hence had no effective voice in the reform debate in late 1997.[5] The chaebol were also politically weakened, though their lobby group, the Federation of Korean Industries (FKI), attempted to argue that IMF intervention represented a takeover of the Korean economy by Wall Street.[6] The incoming government's sidelining of MOFE and chaebol views and its strong commitment to reform was crucial in stabilizing the situation, in stark contrast to Indonesia (IEO 2003, 36). On 24 December, Korea's major creditor banks announced they would roll over their Korean loans. Then, on 29 December 1997, Parliament passed a bill to establish the integrated financial regulator envisaged earlier by the Presidential Commission.

In line with the commitments to the IMF, regulatory reform accelerated in 1998. The national shame of the crisis was used by reformers to push through the adoption of international standards. In April 1998 the government established a new Regulation Reform Committee under the office of the President with the task of revising "every regulation to fit international standards" (Choi 2001). The co-chair of the committee was the Prime Minister, with six other ministers (including MOFE) and representatives from industry and academia, including an American lawyer.[7] The government explicitly replaced the previously dominant Japanese governance benchmark with a global benchmark that looked more to the United States and the United Kingdom.[8] Hence, although IMF pressure for reform was important until August 2000 when Korea repaid its IMF loans, key figures in the government and bureaucracy essentially agreed with its prescriptions.

By 2002, the prevailing sentiment in official Korean circles was that the job of bringing Korea's financial regulatory framework up to international best-practice levels was mostly complete.[9] The formal regulatory framework had been transformed, the financial sector had undergone massive restructuring, foreign ownership of listed shares and banks had increased dramatically, economic recovery was solid, and NPLs in the banking sector had been reduced to levels well below that of other Asian countries, including

Japan. The degree of transformation that has been achieved in Korea is undoubtedly remarkable. However, as I demonstrate below, the quality of compliance has been less good than this official view allows, particularly in the early post-crisis years.

Korean Compliance with International Banking Supervision Standards

Before assessing Korea's post-crisis compliance with international banking standards, we first need to consider Korean banking regulation and supervision before the crisis. The Korean government adopted the BIS capital ratios for guidance purposes in the July 1992 Banking Act. The primary objective was to facilitate the overseas expansion of Korean banks and to reduce their foreign borrowing costs (Chey 2006, chap. 6). Targets for bank capital of 7.25 percent and 8 percent of risk-weighted assets were set for the end of 1993 and the end of 1994, respectively. Only from the end of 1995 did these targets become mandatory (FSS 2000, 52). Korean banks nevertheless maintained official average CARs that exceeded the Basle minimum from 1992, with the sole exception of 1997 (figure 6.1).

The reliability of the pre-1998 official figures on CARs and NPLs is very doubtful. The profitability of domestic banks and many of their borrowers was poor and worsening from the early 1990s (Hahm and Mishkin 2000). Risk weightings were largely in line with the flexible Basle rules, but tier 2 capital included all loan loss provisions (Basle rules only allow the inclusion of general provisions: BCBS 1988, 5).[10] Even greater laxity was evident in loan classification and provisioning rules. Before 1998, substandard NPLs and below were defined as loans on which the repayment of interest or principal was at least six months overdue, compared to the three-month international standard. Classification was also dependent upon the assumed value of attached collateral, and only NPLs not covered by collateral were reported (a mere 0.8 percent of total loans in 1996: Balino and Ubide 1999, 17). Loans in arrears up to six months could be defined as precautionary, on which provisions of only 1 percent were required. This category included loans to borrowers in debt workout programs or on "early warning lists" and made up the bulk of the total. Furthermore, banks often simply avoided reporting NPLs by "evergreening" (rolling over problem loans when they became due). Banks had strong incentives to do this because provisions in excess of 2 percent of total loans were not tax deductible; the regulatory assumption was that loan losses in any year would not exceed this amount. In practice, average provisions fell short of this (Balino and Ubide 1999, 18). A tightened provisioning framework was introduced in 1994, but MOFE granted a grace period for implementation until the end of 1998

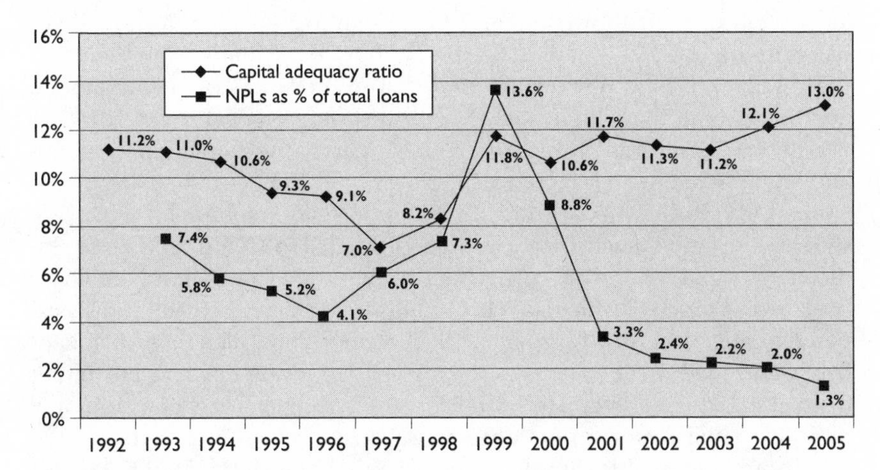

Figure 6.1. Korean domestic commercial banks: Average CARs and NPLs, official estimates, 1992–2005

Sources: FSS website, Baliño and Ubide (1999).
Note: Figures are end of period. CARs are Basle definition, simple average for all banks. NPLs are substandard loans and below. Definitions of CARs and NPLs changed over this period (see text).

out of concern that bank CARs and profitability were under pressure (Chey 2006, chap. 6). Overall, NPLs were considerably underestimated, provisions were very low, and CARs were highly inflated.

There are different explanations for this regulatory laxity. Korean reformers tended to see MOFE as having been captured by the banks and chaebol who opposed stricter regulatory standards. A system similar to Japanese *amakudari* operated, whereby experienced MOFE supervisors obtained retirement positions in financial institutions and helped them to hide problems from regulatory agencies (Chey 2006, chap. 6). Others argue that capacity problems were to blame: the pre-crisis Korean regulatory structure was highly fragmented, disorganized, and sometimes poorly staffed, in part due to the EPB-MOF merger (Chopra et al. 2001, 7; Thurbon 2003, 354–55). However, it is difficult to believe that had the organizational structure of financial regulation been better before 1997, MOFE would have undertaken much stricter regulation and supervision. Even when regulatory tightening did occur, long grace periods were often granted to financial firms. For example, new rules limiting bank exposure to single borrowers to 20 percent of capital for loans and 40 percent for guarantees were introduced in the 1991 revised General Banking Act, but with a generous three year phase-in period. This was re-extended in 1994 and again in 1997. Single total exposure limits to the top 30 chaebol were also tightened to

45 percent of capital for commercial banks and 150 percent for merchant banks in August 1997, but these were well above Basle limits. Even then, neither banks, chaebol, nor regulators had an interest in strict enforcement, and breaches of these limits were common (Lindgren et al. 1999, 70).

The key reason for lax regulation and supervision was the government's and MOFE's dominant preference for growth.[11] The Office of Banking Supervision (OBS) in the Bank of Korea (BOK) was formally responsible for banking supervision, but in practice both were subordinated to MOFE. MOFE was also directly responsible for the supervision of the rapidly expanding merchant bank sector, much of which was chronically under-capitalized and heavily exposed to single or group borrowers. Chaebol often controlled these merchant banks and used them to circumvent the restrictions on offshore borrowing by banks (Lindgren et al. 1999, 67–78). MOFE assigned only one employee to regulate this sector, an endogenous capacity problem that reflected the low priority the ministry attached to prudential supervision. MOFE was also responsible for the specialized government-owned banks, including the largest, Korea Development Bank (KDB), which provided long-term loans to the chaebol and was a key tool of developmentalism. The adoption of Basle standards itself was driven not by a desire for prudential tightening but because of the concern that non-adherence would reduce Korean banks' creditworthiness and ability to borrow abroad, thereby jeopardizing growth.

The same was true for the Kim Young Sam government's five-year "blueprint" for gradual financial liberalization, associated with its bid to join the OECD. Pressure from the corporate sector to access foreign capital to facilitate heavy investment programs favored capital account opening (Pirie 2005, 30). The resulting combination of regulatory laxity and partial financial liberalization that encouraged heavy short-term offshore borrowing proved highly destabilizing (Cho 2001; OECD 1999b, 30). It was precisely this systemic bias against strict prudential regulation and supervision that the new Kim Dae-Jung government pledged to eliminate.

In turning to post-crisis compliance, I assess the nature and quality of Korean compliance with international banking standards in the areas addressed in earlier chapters: independence of regulators; rules on capital adequacy, loan classification and provisioning; and other prudential rules.[12]

Independence of Regulators

The Korean government lost little time in reorganizing its regulatory framework along Western lines. A new financial regulatory authority, the Financial Supervisory Commission (FSC), was established in April 1998. The FSC was granted significant new powers to deal with the crisis, including supervisory responsibility for the whole financial sector and powers to promote corporate restructuring. The FSC's executive wing, the Financial Supervisory Service (FSS), was established at the beginning of 1999; by the end of that year it had assumed the duties of the four regulatory agencies it had subsumed. FSC is a policymaking body and formally responsible for supervising FSS, which is responsible for implementation, including on-site and off-site supervision. The Securities and Futures Commission (SFC) was also established to oversee market practices, and, like FSC, has the right to issue orders to FSS. BOK and the Korea Deposit Insurance Corporation (KDIC) also have the right to require the FSS to examine banks or to demand that their employees participate in joint examinations.[13]

The government position is that the FSC/FSS is in practice more independent than, say, the United Kingdom's FSA.[14] However, it would be wrong to take this view at face value, as do some observers (e.g., Pirie 2005, 5). The IMF's Independent Evaluation Office notes that the new framework was "not entirely in keeping with the preferences of the IMF and World Bank" (IEO 2003, 183). The IMF itself notes a widespread perception of insufficient regulatory independence and inadequate legal protection for FSC, FSS, and SFC staff against lawsuits (IMF 2003a, 5, 24).[15] Regulatory capacity in Korea is relatively good, though the IMF (2003a, 35) criticizes "the lack of adequate examination staffing resources [in FSS] to carry out supervision duties."

Concerns about insufficient independence arise because the FSC and FSS are formally part of the president's office and under the supervision of the prime minister, in contrast to the United Kingdom's FSA. There are many ways in which the government, including MOFE, continues to control the appointment of senior regulators. The FSC Chairman concurrently holds the position of FSS Governor and is a cabinet minister. The FSS Governor in turn recommends up to four Deputy Governors and up to nine Assistant Governors. Terms of office are three years, once renewable; dismissal is only allowed for incapacitation or misconduct. The FSC itself has nine members who are appointed by the President on the recommendation of the Cabinet Council. The vice-chairman, appointed by the President on the recommendation of the MOFE Minister, is concurrently chairman of the SFC. MOFE, BOK, and KDIC all have ex-officio representation (FSS 2000, 38). MOFE is also able to appoint another nonstanding member of the FSC. Furthermore, all legislation relating to the financial sector must be drafted and submitted by MOFE, in consultation with FSC. A recent comparative study concluded that for these reasons, Korea's new financial regulator was only slightly more independent of government than its predecessor, and was much less independent than most other countries surveyed (Quintyn, Ramirez, and Taylor 2007).

More direct evidence that the FSC/FSS have been subject to a substantially higher degree of political subordination compared to the United

Kingdom's FSA can be found in the high turnover rate of governors. By December 2002, there had already been three chairmen of the FSC since its establishment, with new appointments arising from cabinet reshuffles in January 2001 and again in August 2001. Some in the FSC itself also thought that the chairmanship had become politicized, reducing its independence.[16] This politicization stemmed from the conflict between the FSC's dual responsibilities for financial supervision and corporate restructuring, which sometimes put it at loggerheads with the most powerful chaebol.

In the first two years or so after the crisis, many feared the consequences of a bankruptcy of another highly leveraged major chaebol, notably Daewoo or Hyundai. In the case of Daewoo, the country's second-largest chaebol, FSC/FSS and MOFE knew the depth of Daewoo's problems before it collapsed in late 1999, but did not act out of fear of sparking a renewed financial crisis.[17] Moreover, regulators permitted banks to classify much Daewoo debt as normal or precautionary until its collapse, even though the group was deeply distressed from 1997 (Graham 2003, 130–36; IMF 2001b, 95). It is fairly clear that pressure to stave off Daewoo's collapse came directly from the government. Contrary to its political rhetoric about the end of the "too big to fail" policy, the government offered guarantees to some of Daewoo's domestic bank creditors to roll over credits, asked foreign banks to do the same without guarantees, and asked nationalized banks to grant new credits to Daewoo in August 1999—all of which proved to be in vain (Noland 2000b, 238–43). However, Daewoo's position was weakened by its chairman's antagonistic relationship with the government. Creditor pressure led to the unraveling of Daewoo group after August 1999 (Graham 2003, 134–35).[18]

Political concerns that Hyundai's collapse might also be imminent were deeper, partly because Hyundai's chairman was closely associated with Kim Dae-Jung's "sunshine policy" of accommodation with North Korea and partly because parts of the group were among Korea's industrial jewels. Hyundai's semiconductor business, Hynix, created by a merger of Hyundai's and LG's semiconductor subsidiaries under the government-sponsored "Big Deal," continued to have financial difficulties after 1998.[19] Allegations persisted that the government pressured banks, including foreign-controlled ones, to roll over loans to Hynix and to other parts of the distressed Hyundai group after 2000. The state-owned KDB alone underwrote nearly 3 trillion won of Hynix bonds in 2001. From May 2000 to June 2002, Korean financial institutions, mostly state-controlled, provided large amounts of new loans, equity swaps, bond purchases, debt extensions, and write-offs to Hyundai group.[20] About half of this assistance went to Hynix, even though it was then uncreditworthy (U.S. ITA 2003, 18).[21] As in the Daewoo case, Hynix loans were also often classified through late 2001 as normal or precautionary, though Korean banks were later required to write down substantial values of these loans (Fitch Ratings 2002, 2–3). In September 2004, when Hynix's economic fortunes had recovered, its senior management and auditors were indicted for a series of fraudulent accounts over the whole period 1996–2003.

The Daewoo and Hynix cases suggest that less had changed in the immediate aftermath of the Korean crisis than some have argued.[22] Without the role played by regulatory forbearance and new loans from state-controlled banks in keeping them afloat, it is likely both would have collapsed much earlier. As the President's office explained in response to queries about government support for Hyundai group in 2002, "[w]e are doing what is deemed necessary to save companies leading the country's strategic industries."[23] In the process, financial supervisory agency independence was undermined. Below, I provide further evidence that the government continued to intervene in financial regulation after 1998, in spite of claims to the contrary.

Rules on Capital Adequacy, Loan Classification, and Provisioning

After the crisis, minimum CARs for Korean banks continued to be the standard 8 percent, but the authorities indicated their intention to strengthen capitalization by instructing banks to meet an unofficial target of 10 percent by the end of 2001.[24] Recapitalizations and purchases of banks' NPLs with public funds aimed to ensure that banks achieved these targets (Kim 2001, 114–20).[25] A new PCA framework was adopted in April 1998 which automatically required banks to submit restructuring plans to the authorities within two months if their CAR fell below specified thresholds or if their CAMELS rating deteriorated (FSS 2000, 62–67). The introduction of "combined" accounting for the top 30 chaebol (see below) in 2000 put more pressure on banks' CARs, and six banks were required to submit new rehabilitation plans.[26]

In many other ways, capitalization standards were tightened to make them consistent with international standards on the advice of the IMF (FSS 2000, 52). From January 1999, banks could no longer include special provisions for substandard loans and below as Tier 2 capital (general provisions continued to be eligible up to 1.25 percent of risk-weighted assets). Assets in trust accounts with guarantees were weighted at 100 percent from January 2000 (instead of 10 percent). From January 2002, the FSS/FSC also required 10 major banks (and 17 foreign bank branches) to take into account market risk in setting their CARs, consistent with the 1996 amendment to the Basle Accord (FSS 2003a, 14).

However, as in the other crisis-hit countries, there was also some formal noncompliance in the five years after 1997, reflecting the depth of financial distress produced by the crisis. First, under the January 1999 rules, special provisions on precautionary loans could still be included as tier 2 capital, which is not Basle-consistent. Second, grace periods to adopt the new capitalization rules were granted that extended well beyond 1999, particularly for regional and domestic banks without international operations (Chey 2006, chap. 8). Third, in November 1998 the new PCA rules were relaxed, allowing supervisors to postpone the issuance of an improvement order for banks failing to meet minimum CARs (FSS 2004, s.37). As the economy slowed again over 2000–2001, the authorities also temporarily lowered the target CAR from 10 percent to 8 percent, and to 6 percent for non-international banks. The FSC also announced that banks would not be penalized for failure to meet required CARs during the post-Daewoo round of financial restructuring when the government injected more funds into the banking sector (Chey 2006, chap. 8). Finally, after the SK Global crisis in 2003, the authorities reduced the minimum CAR once again for "first class" banks from 10 percent to 9 percent (IMF 2004c, 17).

This mixture of regulatory tightening and ad hoc relaxation/forbearance over the five years from 1997 can also be seen in the loan classification and provisioning regime. In July 1998, the authorities tightened loan classification rules to define substandard (and below) loans as those with arrears of 90 days or more, bringing Korea into line with the minimum global standard. Minimum provisions on precautionary loans were also raised from 1 percent to 2 percent.[27] However, loan classification practice remained relatively lax through 1999 as Daewoo's problems escalated. In August 1999, the head of the FSC even described HSBC's intention to apply international loan classification standards to Seoul Bank (which it wished to purchase) as "irrational" (Noland 2000b, 236). The government also successfully persuaded the IMF in 1999 to classify loans to companies in debt workout programs as precautionary rather than substandard, considerably reducing banks' provisioning requirements (Chey 2006, chap. 6).

From December 1999, with economic recovery still robust, banks were required to employ a stricter U.S.-style FLC system for loan classification, applied in principle to all categories of borrowers.[28] In formal terms, this system arguably represents best practice in Asia and globally. It uses discounted cash flow (DCF) analysis and management assessments to assess the true value of impaired loans, rather than the traditional backward-looking method (FSS 2000, 53).[29] A backward-looking element in loan classification was retained to ensure that the new FLC standards did not result in lower provisioning levels (column 2, table 6.1). Under this new system, collateral could no longer be used directly to reduce the provisioning requirement (as in Indonesia, Japan, Malaysia, Singapore and Thailand).[30]

After the introduction of FLC, many loans previously categorized as precautionary were reclassified as substandard or below, leading to a large

TABLE 6.1
Asset classification standards and provisioning requirements for Korean banks

Asset classification	FLC description (customers) from 1999	Minimum required provision*
Normal	No risk to full collection of principal and interest	0.5%
Precautionary	Potential weaknesses in near future but no immediate risk to collection; or arrears > 1 month and < 3 months	2%*
Substandard	Considerable risk to collection of assets; amount expected from customers with credit arrears ≥ 3 months, or in default, liquidation or bankruptcy, or from doubtful and estimated loss customers	20%
Doubtful	Portion of assets in excess of amount expected to be collected from customers with a considerably weakened capacity to repay, or with credit arrears ≥ 3 months but < 12 months	50%*
Estimated loss	Portion of assets in excess of amount expected to be collected from customers from which collection is not probable, or with credit arrears > 12 months	100%

Source: FSS (2000, 54–55).

Note: The above classifications and provisioning applied from 1994, but there was a grace period of five years for their implementation. In July 1998 the provisioning requirement on precautionary loans was increased from 1% to 2%, and that on doubtful loans was reduced from 100% to 50%.

increase in official NPLs and a doubling of required provisions in Korean banks (figure 6.1; IMF 2001b, 96; Kim 2001, 121). By September 2000, average provisioning across the banking sector was about 40 percent of all subnormal loans, more than double the pre-crisis level.[31] Despite this, there was a sustained recovery in bank profits since the nadir of 1998 (figures 6.2, 6.3).

Again, this demonstrates that Korean ambitions in terms of compliance with international banking standards have been more ambitious than almost any other country in Asia since 1997. Even so, continuing difficulties in the corporate sector have constrained these ambitions in practice. The Hynix saga revealed that even after the adoption of the FLC system, loan classification and provisioning by Korean banks was less conservative and more politically influenced than the official view claimed. Continuing difficulties in the SME sector also suggested that reported NPLs, which fell rapidly from 2001 (figure 6.1), still underestimated the true level of bad loans as late as 2003. The BOK itself showed that in 2003, as in 2000, three

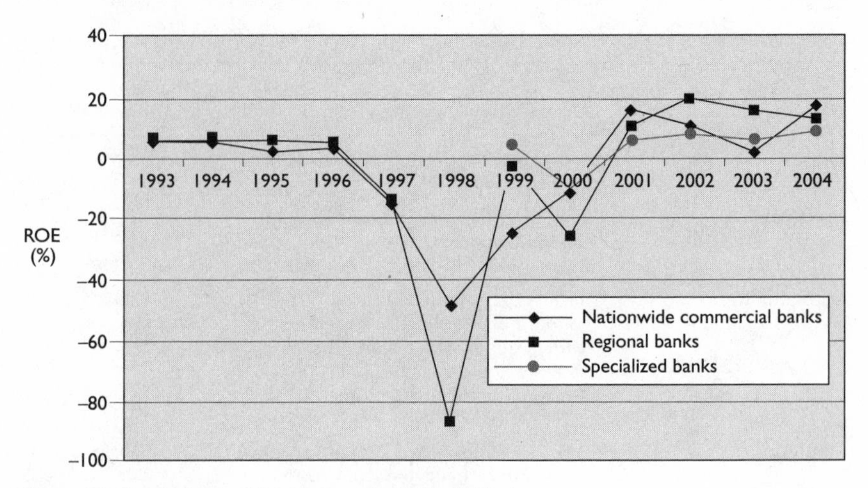

Figure 6.2. Korean banks: Return on equity, 1993–2004

Source: FSS website
Note: No data are available for specialized banks before 1999.

out of ten Korean firms still had debt interest coverage ratios of less than 100 percent, indicating substantial lingering financial distress, particularly in the SME sector (BOK 2004, 561).[32]

Other Prudential Rules

Credit concentration and connected lending limits, which were tightened but poorly enforced just before the crisis, were tightened again in the revision to the Banking Act and the Regulations on Banking Supervision of May 1999. Crucially, limits on exposures to single and group borrowers were significantly reduced (table 6.2). The new limit of 20 percent for single and 25 percent for group exposures brought Korea into compliance with BCP 9, though the former is still higher than the U.S. limit of 15 percent. The new limits apply not only to loans and guarantees, as under the old system, but to all forms of credit risk. The credit ceiling on loans to large shareholders remains unchanged, though the definition of a large borrower was tightened.

New rules designed to address the pre-crisis maturity and currency mismatch problems were also adopted. The won liquidity ratio (short term assets—those with maturities of less than 3 months—to short term liabilities) must exceed 100 percent (FSS 2000, 58). The regulators also require financial institutions to report their observance of foreign exchange position

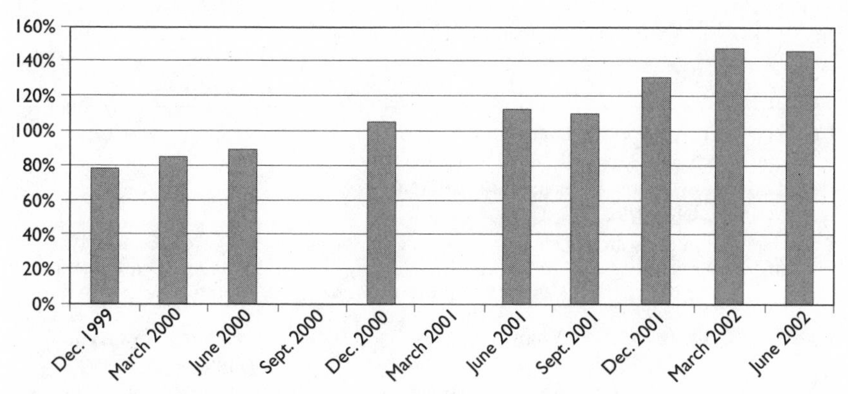

Figure 6.3. Korean banks: Provisions on substandard and below loans (SBLs) as % of total SBLs, 1999–2002

Source: FSS Press Releases.
Note: No data available for September 2000 and March 2001.

limits on a daily basis. Since June 2000, the foreign currency asset to liabilities ratio for maturities of up to 90 days, including assets and liabilities of overseas subsidiaries and offshore accounts, must be at least 80 percent (FSS 2000, 58). Stricter "gap ratios" have applied to very short-term foreign currency assets and liabilities since January 1999.[33] At least 50 percent of foreign currency loans of 3 years or longer must be financed by foreign currency borrowings of 3 years or longer. Since April 1999, country exposure limits are imposed according to each country's credit rating, and additional limits are placed on total lending to countries with below investment grade ratings. There is no evidence that the FSS has not enforced these regulations.

There was some slippage on the new lending limit rules, mirroring the pattern noted earlier in capitalization and loan classification. The new LLLs were introduced more slowly than initially promised to the IMF (FSS 2000, 56–57; IEO 2003, 183). The revised credit ceiling for single borrowers of up to 25 percent of bank capital was phased in, effective from 1 January 2000. Even then, an interim period exemption until end-2002 was given to banks that exceeded the ceiling for "unavoidable reasons," connected with the government's "Fast Track Program" in 2001 to refinance major firms' maturing bonds (IEO 2003, 183). State-owned KDB, the single biggest lender to the chaebol, was given until end-2004 to comply with the new group lending limit, a deadline that was not met.[34] With these important exceptions, the new limits appear to have been enforced (figure 6.4). On average, banks have substantially reduced lending to the corporate sector since 1998. Bank lending to chaebol as a percentage of total loans fell from 25 percent to 14 percent

TABLE 6.2
Revised Korean credit ceiling regulations

	Before May 1999	After May 1999
Credit ceilings on single borrowers	Loans: 15% Payment guarantees: 30%	20%
Credit ceilings on group borrowers (chaebol)	Loans and payment guarantees: 45%	25%
Credit ceiling on the sum of large exposures	Loans or payment guarantees of above 15% of equity to single borrowers or single groups should not exceed 500% of a bank's equity capital.	Credits greater than 10% of a bank's equity capital to single and group borrowers should not exceed 500% of a bank's equity capital.
Credit ceiling on large shareholders	The smaller of 25% of bank equity and the percentage shareholding in bank equity capital of the borrower	The smaller of 25% of bank equity and the percentage shareholding in bank equity capital of the borrower

Source: FSS (2000, 57).
Note: An "enterprise group" is defined as "a group of companies whose businesses are substantially controlled by the same person."

over 2000 to mid-2002, as foreign ownership in the banking sector increased and as most banks focused on more profitable consumer lending.

Undoubtedly, there has been substantial upgrading of Korea's regulatory and supervisory framework since 1997. In some areas, notably loan classification and provisioning, Korea has gone further than all the other crisis-hit countries in emulating stricter U.S. banking supervision standards. With the exception of the state-owned development banks, the close links between banks and the chaebol have been considerably reduced. The initial effect of the crisis was to bring many commercial banks back under state control, but the privatization program that followed actively discriminated in favor of foreign and widely spread ownership of banks and against chaebol ownership (FSS 2003b, 30–32). This policy has had powerful consequences. By mid-2005, three of eight nationwide commercial banks were under foreign control and most of the rest were reasonably widely held by institutional and strategic investors. There are also dozens of foreign branches of international banks, mostly in Seoul. Over time this has increased the quality of compliance with international standards, notably regarding bank capitalization and LLLs, in part by encouraging the introduction of new risk management techniques across the sector and by lowering the aggregate importance of chaebol lending.

These positive longer run effects of the crisis on Korean compliance must be set against the short and medium term effects, which pushed in

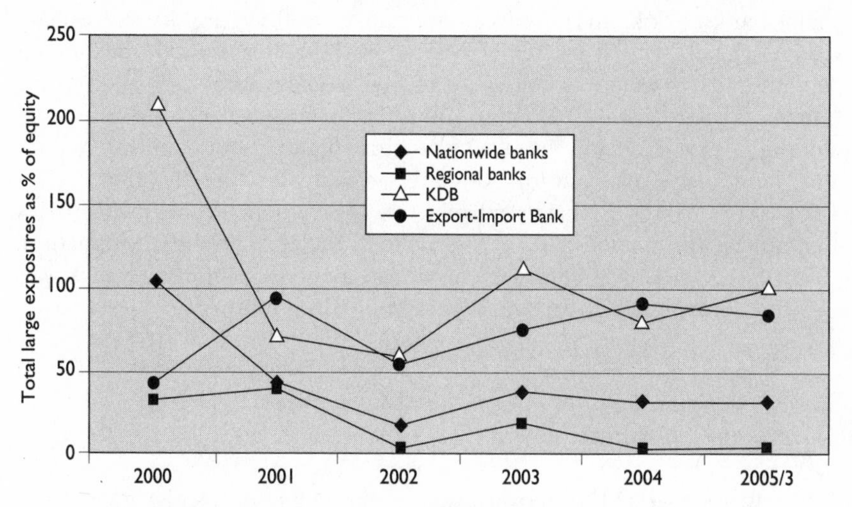

Figure 6.4. Korean banks: Large exposure ratio, 2000–2005

Source: FSS website

Note: Large exposures are defined as credits to single or group borrowers that exceed 10% of bank capital. Figures are for end of period.

the other direction. In 2003, the IMF's FSSA team (IMF 2003a, 5) judged Korea's observance of international standards and codes as "high" and the problem of NPLs and insolvency in the banking sector as "largely addressed." However, like many FSSAs and ROSCs, this report arguably reflects the political constraints on IFI assessments of compliance. As we have seen, there was continuing evidence of forbearance on loan classification in 2003. Indeed, elsewhere in the FSSA report the widespread skepticism of private analysts concerning Korean compliance in the banking and nonbank financial institution sectors is noted (IMF 2003a, 24).

The government and the regulatory authorities were caught in a basic dilemma. They wanted to use the crisis to transform the Korean financial sector, but they also understandably wished to promote financial stability, economic growth, and employment. The rhetorical commitment to the rapid adoption of international standards threatened these latter objectives in the first five or so years after 1997. The FSC's dual responsibility for both financial supervision and chaebol restructuring meant that this dilemma was felt at the heart of the regulatory system, resulting in a series of explicit and more hidden departures from the rules that had been adopted in the wake of the crisis.

As the effects of the crisis have gradually worn off, the quality of compliance by major banks and the strength of the financial sector have both improved. The FSS has been visibly tough in recent cases of noncompliance by major banks. Kookmin, Korea's largest bank, was fined and its senior management given "severe disciplinary warnings" in September 2004 for (among other things) overstating the value of loan collateral and some other accounting irregularities.[35] Even so, noncyclical factors result in some continuing divergence from the ideal type of regulatory neoliberalism. Agency independence is relatively low compared to many developed and emerging market countries. This facilitated an active governmental role in the process of financial and corporate restructuring after the crisis, but its continuation, along with various regulatory exemptions for the development banks, creates the perception of lingering developmentalism in Korea.

Korean Compliance with International Corporate Governance Standards

Given the Kim Dae-Jung government's view that the over-leveraged and poorly managed chaebol bore much of the blame for the crisis, corporate governance reforms were a key part of the policy response in Korea over 1998–99. In this area, as in banking supervision, the stated policy was to force the chaebol to adopt Western standards of corporate governance through a combination of new regulation, supervisory enforcement, and market pressure (the latter facilitated by greater corporate transparency). Below, I assess Korean compliance with international standards in four main areas: board independence, board committees, shareholder rights, and corporate governance in the financial sector.

Before the crisis, Korea's pre-crisis corporate governance framework was rudimentary. Until the mid-1990s there was little discussion of the subject outside of a few academic and reform-minded circles.[36] Given the extraordinary success of the major chaebol, few took the view that the Korean corporate model was seriously flawed (Graham 2003, 11–87). The senior management of the chaebol, often dominated by founding families who achieved control through cross-shareholdings and pyramid structures, received little regulatory scrutiny. Just prior to the crisis, Korea's top 30 chaebol on average did business in 20 different industries with 27 different subsidiaries. By 1995, the largest, Hyundai Group, consisted of 46 companies, of which only 16 were publicly listed. By 1997, another nine companies were added to the group (Capulong et al. 2000, 2:70). The desire of controlling shareholders to maintain their position led to a strong preference for debt-financed expansion, much of it short term.[37]

Company boards were often very large, ineffective, and packed with controlling shareholders, their allies, and directors of affiliated companies. Hostile and foreign takeovers were not permitted (Jo 2001, 7–8). The misleading form of consolidated financial reporting in existence in Korea since

1993 and the poor quality of disclosure (see section 3) made it extremely difficult for regulators and banks to comprehend and monitor companies' financial positions, as the Daewoo scandal among others would later demonstrate. Unconstrained over-investment and diversification meant that much of the corporate sector was unprofitable by the mid-1990s (Capulong et al. 2: chap. 2; Jo 2001). However, high investment rates also produced rapid growth, which suited the purposes of successive governments.

Some ineffectual reforms were tried before the crisis. Amendments to the 1980 Monopoly Regulation and Fair Trade Act in 1986 and 1990 prohibited holding companies and placed limits on cross-shareholdings (Capulong et al. 2000, 2:93). "Operating" holding companies were permitted, defined as companies whose investments in others did not exceed 50 percent of total assets. However, major shareholders still managed to exercise control through pyramid structures. The fiduciary responsibility of management to all shareholders was not clearly established in law. Of all the major Asian economies, the divergence between cash flow rights and dominant shareholders' control rights was greatest in Korea (Claessens, Djankov, and Lang 1999; Shin 2001).[38] Cross-guarantees of debt between members of chaebol groups remained common, transferring wealth from healthy to weaker companies within groups. Outside shareholders, typically in a large numerical majority, were often exploited.

In 1994, the existing system of requiring investors wishing to purchase more than 10 percent of a company's equity to obtain prior regulatory approval was dropped. In principle, this would free up the market for corporate control, but hostile takeovers remained rare because of the dominant position of controlling shareholders (Capulong et al. 2000, 2:109–10). In January 1997, bank boards were required to include at least 50 percent outside (independent) directors to strengthen the monitoring of management. Before this rule could be implemented, however, the crisis hit Korea and forced more extensive reforms.

The first Korean LOI of 3 December 1997 included only a general commitment to corporate governance reform.[39] Subsequent revisions provided for more specific commitments, including the appointment of outside directors to company boards, the strengthening of shareholder rights, and various provisions on corporate disclosure.[40] These Anglo-Saxon style reforms appealed to Kim Dae-Jung because of his desire to reduce the economic and political power of the chaebol. As Kap-Soo Oh, Deputy Governor of the FSS argued:

> [W]hat we set out to do in essence was to completely transform the old rules and cultures into a transparent corporate governance system broadly based on effective checks and balances, high fiduciary standards and genuine

accountability of directors and executives, a culture of self-policing, and responsiveness to the interests of shareholders and investors.[41]

After the meeting between President Kim and the owners of the major chaebol on 13 January 1998, the "five principles for corporate reform" were promulgated, committing the chaebol to specific improvements in corporate governance over 1998 to 2000. Measures to increase board independence had to be adopted from February 1998, consolidated financial statements had to be produced from 1999, cross-debt guarantees had to be eliminated by March 2000, and debt-equity ratios reduced below 200 percent by December 1999.

In March 1999, the government established a Committee on Corporate Governance to recommend further reforms, which produced a nonbinding "Code of Best Practice for Corporate Governance" in September (KCCG 1999). The report gives shareholder rights pride of place, though like the OECD's PCG it also discusses stakeholder rights. The government also commissioned in 1999 a foreign consultancy report on the country's corporate governance framework, funded by the World Bank and led by Bernard Black of the Stanford Law School. Unsurprisingly, the Black report of May 2000 argued strongly for a shift toward an Anglo-Saxon system of corporate governance emphasizing shareholder rights and adopting bolder recommendations than the KCCG report (Black et al. 2001). Various new domestic NGO groups that favored good corporate governance, notably the People's Solidarity for Participatory Democracy (PSPD), actively supported this line.

As the Black report suggested, achieving this goal in a political economy in which the chaebol were firmly entrenched would be difficult, as the main compliance costs would fall squarely on the large chaebol and their influential controlling shareholders (Black et al. 2001, 539). A paradoxical effect of the government-promoted mergers was to strengthen the market position of the major chaebol in key sectors. The major chaebol also provided campaign funding for politicians and parties, especially the conservative opposition parties (the largest of which was the New Korea Party, which later became the Grand National Party). Business organizations such as the Federation of Korean Industries (FKI), the Korean Employers' Federation (KEF) and the Korean Chamber of Commerce and Industry (KCCI) were well organized and remained politically influential, despite Kim Dae-Jung's attacks on their position. Chaebol-owned think tanks propagated their views in policy circles, while the newspaper industry remained very dependent upon chaebol advertising revenues. Through such mechanisms, the chaebol launched a major counter-offensive against corporate governance reform in 1998, claiming that a coalition of the IMF, foreign investors, and international companies were using such reforms to undermine Korea's international competitiveness.[42] The conservative opposition party echoed a pro-chaebol line and, given the government's lack of control of Parliament, could sometimes delay and obstruct the government's corporate governance agenda. This political opposition to reform, as we shall see, was in marked contrast to the relative consensus on banking sector reform.

Board Independence

Despite chaebol opposition, the Commercial Code was modified in December 1998 so as to define more clearly the nature and responsibilities of directors, to establish their fiduciary duties and to increase the penalties for dereliction of duty. "De facto" or shadow directors, those who acted for major shareholders, were subjected to the same legal obligations as elected directors. In 1999, the KCCG adopted a fairly weak recommendation that required companies to appoint a minimum of 25 percent of independent directors to their boards. This fell well short of U.S. standards and the minimum requirement of 50 percent for Korean banks that was in place since January 1997. Gradually, however, rules for listed firms were tightened. From 2000, the 50 percent minimum outside director requirement was extended from banks to all financial institutions. From 2001, the Korean Stock Exchange (KSE) required large listed companies to adopt the same rule.[43]

In line with these changes, the proportion of independent directors on Korean corporate boards has increased substantially since 1997. Most listed companies have achieved formal compliance with the regulations, mainly by reducing the numbers of inside directors and the average board size (Jang and Kim 2001, 3). The problem remains, as elsewhere, that formally independent directors are rarely truly independent in behavioral terms.[44] Indeed, Korea often scores worse in this area in corporate governance surveys than other Asian countries (Nam and Nam 2004, 75). Family shareholders generally dominate the appointment of directors, who are often former executives of related companies (Jang and Kim 2001). Independent directors are often deprived of important company information. Furthermore, the chairman and CEO positions are typically combined, reinforcing family shareholder control (Nam and Nam 2004, 2). Local institutional shareholders are mostly passive and controlled by chaebol, and proxy voting procedures are complex and costly (Jang 2001; Standard & Poor's 2004d, 3).

A KSE survey of 2000 found that supposedly independent directors voted with the management 99.3 percent of the time.[45] More recently, a survey of Korean directors found that over 60 percent thought it "unthinkable" that director candidates nominated by management could be rejected; another 38 percent thought it could happen only "rarely." Furthermore, 85 percent of respondents replied that independent directors disapproved of board agenda items "rarely" or "never" (Nam and Nam 2004, 67, 73). In practice, therefore, little seems to have changed in this area since the crisis.

Board Committees

The KCCG was also very timid in its recommendation on board committees: "[t]he Board may, if necessary, establish internal committees that perform specific functions and roles, such as the Audit, Operation and Remuneration Committees" (KCCG 1999, s.II.6.1). Large companies and banks were encouraged to establish audit committees, two-thirds of which, including the chair, should be made up of independent directors (KCCG 1999, s.III.1.1–2). In February 2000, the KSE made audit and nomination committees a requirement for large listed companies but not for others, consistent with the KCCG recommendations (KSE 2003, s.46–6). At least one audit committee member is required to have professional knowledge and experience of corporate accounting, as in the United States and the United Kingdom.

The result of these reforms has been the very partial adoption of board committees. Over 75 percent of respondents in a 2003 survey of Korean directors said that their companies had no audit committee; similar proportions had no compensation or nomination committee (Nam and Nam 2004, 73). Moreover, even where such committees exist, many doubt their effectiveness because of the shortage of truly independent directors (IMF 2003a, 6, 63; Standard & Poor's 2004d, 5). As in many countries, independent directors often lack the specific expertise and information necessary to challenge management in areas such as accounting and executive remuneration. In Korea, nominations committees have also not prevented family owner-managers from grooming their offspring to succeed senior management, as illustrated in the cases of Hyundai and Samsung.

Shareholder Rights

Various formal improvements have also been made in the area of shareholder rights, which were notoriously weak before 1998. In some areas such as rights to call shareholder meetings, Korean rules are now among the strictest in Asia (table 4.1). Once again, however, the practical results have been limited. The issue of cumulative voting for directors is an example. Government proposals to introduce mandatory cumulative voting for board members, also recommended by the Black report, ran into powerful opposition from the business community and in Parliament. The result was that cumulative voting rules became optional for Korean companies from December 1998 (KCC 382–82). From July 1999, the minimum shareholding requirement for requesting cumulative voting for directors was reduced from 3 percent to 1 percent, unless it is disallowed under the company's articles of incorporation.[46] The government justified the voluntary nature of the rules by arguing that cumulative voting was not a dominant practice in the major Western countries. This is true, though arguably cumulative voting might be necessary in Korea so as to achieve compliance with other international standards in this area.[47] The practical result has been that cumulative voting is rarely used. As of early 2003, more than 80 percent of Korean listed companies had explicitly revoked it in their articles of incorporation (IMF 2003a, 62).

The lack of board independence has compounded the problem of promoting outside shareholder rights. Most shareholder meetings continue to be short and perfunctory in comparison to, for example, those in Malaysia (Nam and Nam 2004, 65). Boards of directors, rather than shareholders, are required to give approval of related party transactions larger than 1 percent of revenues or assets, a rule that clearly lags international standards and practice elsewhere in the region. In February 1999, directors of Samsung SDS issued bonds with warrants to the chairman's son at a price far below the market level and also approved Samsung group purchases of shares owned by him in four money-losing companies. The board of Samsung Electronics even approved a guarantee of the chairman's own personal debts to creditor banks. All of these actions occurred despite their significant negative effect on Samsung companies' stock prices and despite Samsung's reputation as one of Korea's best managed and governed chaebol.[48] In March 2001, outside shareholder efforts to increase their influence on Samsung's board were defeated. PSPD nominated an outsider candidate for the board of Samsung Electronics, who received 16.07 percent of the vote. Most support came from foreign institutional investors, though several large Korean public pension funds also voted in favor of the candidate. Only one private Korean institutional investor backed the candidate; all the others voted with management, which delivered victory to the latter.

To overcome such problems, the government proposed to enhance the ability of outside shareholders to sue companies and directors against strong chaebol opposition.[49] The KCCG report of 1999 was typically cautious in this area, emphasizing the potential costs of "excessive claims" (KCCG 1999, recommendation 4). Nevertheless, thresholds for initiating actions against directors, managers, and auditors have been reduced dramatically. In December 1998 an amendment to the Commercial Code reduced the minimum requirement for a lawsuit against a majority shareholder of a listed company from 1 percent to 0.01 percent of total shares. In October 2000, following a recommendation of the Black report, the government announced its intention to introduce the U.S. system of class action suits.[50] Business lobbies strenuously resisted class action legislation in the National Assembly on the grounds that it would encourage frivolous shareholder actions and disrupt efficient management.[51] Eventually, a watered-down version of the bill passed that allowed class action suits from January 2005 for the largest companies and from January 2007 for all listed companies (Woo Yun Kang Jeong & Han 2004, 7).

Whether these changes will have significant effects on the treatment of outside shareholders remains to be seen. Derivative suits are allowed, though these are costly for shareholders to undertake (awards are paid to the company) and have been very rarely used (IMF 2003a, 32). Moreover, Korea is a relatively nonlitigious society and anti–director suits have not yet significantly multiplied. Furthermore, many Korean directors remained unaware of their new fiduciary duties (Nam and Nam 2004, 24, 86).

However, this is certainly not true for foreign institutional investors, whose ownership of Korean listed companies has increased considerably since 1997. Foreign ownership of Korean listed firms reached 40 percent on average by the end of 2003 (FSS 2003c, 12). These investors may use the new class action laws in the future to insist on fairer treatment of outside shareholders. Domestic investor rights activists working through groups such as the Citizens' Coalition for Economic Justice and the PSPD have also attempted to use the new corporate governance rules to improve the treatment of outside shareholders, though with limited success so far.[52] There are some signs of greater board respect of shareholder rights (CLSA Emerging Markets 2005, 55). However, except in the most egregious cases of outside shareholder exploitation, it can be difficult to use legal rights to enforce better treatment. The concentration of control rights means that it is still almost impossible for outside shareholders to remove directors who are not performing their duties. One example was the long-running failure of Sovereign Asset Management, a Dubai-based institutional investor holding a 14.8 percent stake in SK Corp until July 2005, to remove SK Corp's fraud-convicted chairman.[53]

Corporate Governance in the Financial Sector

After the crisis, the government imposed stricter standards of corporate governance on banks than upon nonbanks, in part to encourage bank monitoring of borrowers. As noted above, this included the requirement that independent directors constitute at least 50 percent of the board. In practice, the average figure for commercial banks at the end of 2003 was 61 percent, implying a good level of formal compliance (Park 2004, 48).

Audit committees with at least two-thirds independent directors have also been required for all commercial banks since January 2000, in contrast to nonfinancial companies. Again, this requirement is met in practice (Park 2004, 49). Banks' boards must also appoint an independent compliance officer elected by two-thirds of the board members (FSS 2003b, 50). The

FSS also applies a fit and proper test to major shareholders, directors, and management of banks (FSS 2003b, 29). This test ensures that bankrupts and those convicted and imprisoned within the previous five years are excluded from these roles. Those punished for financial misdemeanors are also barred from 2–5 years, depending upon the gravity of the offense. Members of the boards of directors of banks must be experienced in banking and finance. These rules appear to have been reasonably well enforced since 1998.

Since 1982, ownership limits have been in place for banks aimed at limiting chaebol control. Individual shareholders may not own more than 10 percent (increased from 4 percent pre-crisis) of the total shares of a bank, though there are exceptions to this rule. After the crisis, the Korean government and KDIC were exempted to allow them to inject funds in the restructuring and recapitalization process (FSS 2000, 48). Other exceptions to these ownership limits are for regional banks, where the limit is 15 percent, converted banks (8 percent), and, crucially, joint venture and foreign-owned banks. Nonfinancial firms owning up to 10 percent of a bank could not exercise voting rights greater than 4 percent of total shares. Banks cannot lend to large shareholders more than the lesser of 25 percent of their capital or the shareholder's capital contribution to the bank, and large credits (over 0.1 percent of the bank's equity capital or five billion won) must be unanimously approved by the board (FSS 2003b, 30–32).

Both the government's focus on raising financial sector corporate governance and the higher level of foreign ownership have produced improvements in banks' corporate governance practices. Foreign ownership generally is positively associated with better corporate governance in Korea (Nam and Nam 2004, 106). Large surveys of corporate governance by company such as CLSA's (2002) suggest that in Korea, as elsewhere, the average corporate governance score of banks (51) is higher than that of nonbanks (44). Even so, this score for Korean banks remained significantly below the average corporate sector score for Hong Kong, India, Malaysia, Singapore, Taiwan, and Thailand. This disappointing outcome may have been partly due to government attempts over the previous two years to pressure banks to lend to distressed large chaebol such as Hyundai, in breach of new risk-management guidelines. By 2004, the BOK argued that rising foreign ownership in the Korean banking was having positive effects on the quality of corporate governance.[54] In 2005, CLSA also ranked three widely held banks with substantial foreign institutional investor participation—Hana, Kookmin, and Shinhan—in the top quartile of corporate governance.

Contrary to the government's intentions, improving corporate governance in the banking sector has had limited spillover effects on the corporate sector generally. The ability of the major chaebol to tap the capital markets for external finance limits the ability of banks to act as general monitors of corporate governance. In addition, corporate governance in the state-owned banks remains very weak. For these banks, independent directors are a small minority on their boards (Park 2004, 48).

To summarize, concerted efforts by the Kim Dae-Jung and the successor Roh Moo-hyun administrations to improve compliance with corporate governance standards met with more concerted business sector resistance than in banking supervision.[55] In formal terms, Korean corporate governance rules have been significantly upgraded since the crisis. However, these rules are rarely among the strictest in Asia, indicating that even in terms of formal compliance Korea has lagged considerably. Moreover, these formal rules have hardly constrained the ability of families to continue to exercise controlling influence over Korea's largest companies, often to the detriment of outside shareholder interests. Independent surveys of the quality of corporate governance in Korean companies consistently demonstrate modest results, even compared to other developing Asian countries (CLSA Emerging Markets 2003, 2005; IIF 2003; IMF 2003a, 32; Nam and Nam 2004, 52).

Growing foreign ownership of some companies has in some cases improved the quality of corporate governance. High levels of foreign institutional investor ownership of shares in companies like Samsung Electronics, Kookmin Bank, and POSCO have been associated with relatively strong corporate governance (CLSA Emerging Markets 2005, 57). More has also been possible in the banking sector, where business resistance has been much less strong and foreign ownership levels higher. However, the best-known Korean company, Samsung, also exhibits the persistence of family ownership and only a gradual improvement in corporate governance outcomes. Overall, family control via cross-shareholdings of the top ten chaebol actually increased from 1997 to 2002, despite a large increase in foreign ownership levels (IIF 2003, 4; see also Graham 2003, 124–25).

The chaebol have successfully played on themes of nationalist resistance to foreign control (which must be distinguished from foreign investment). This has been made easier by the way in which foreign "vulture" funds who invested in major banks have been seen to have profited excessively from the crisis and subsequent recovery. New restrictions (from April 2005) on the intra-group voting rights of the financial units of large chaebol met with considerable resistance. Samsung group openly refused to implement this rule and challenged it in the courts, claiming with other chaebol that it would leave them open to hostile, potentially foreign, takeover.[56] Even if the old days of government-directed investment are long gone in Korea, a general reluctance to dilute national control of the commanding industrial heights of the economy remains widespread.

Korean Compliance with International Accounting Standards

As the Deputy Governor of the FSS noted in December 2002, "there was a general understanding among the regulators, the investing public, and the accounting profession that Korea's accounting standards were inadequate and lagged behind the best international accounting practices."[57] Convergence upon IAS was a key part of the Korean government's post-crisis strategy to improve financial sector stability and corporate governance.[58] Improved disclosure by public companies would in theory facilitate greater transparency and outside shareholder influence over corporate decisions.

Before the 1997 crisis, the simplicity of Korea Financial Accounting Standards (KFAS) left them open to wide variations in interpretation and accounting practice. Areas of weakness included: deferrals of foreign exchange gains or losses on long-term foreign currency assets and liabilities; incomplete adoption of present value accounting; loose criteria for the classification of leases; incomplete application of the equity method of accounting; accounting for financial instruments; deferral of research and development costs; de facto exclusion of the purchase method in accounting for business combinations; nondisclosure of segment information; and poor loan loss accounting and provisioning standards in the financial sector. Compliance even with these lax standards was poor, as was regulatory enforcement (Kim 2000, 8–9).

Part of the problem was the lack of independence of the accounting standard setter. MOF/MOFE dominated the process of setting KFAS and had little interest in strict enforcement or in the principle of corporate transparency, given the dominance of industrial policy and growth objectives (Kim 2000, 8–9). From 1958, MOF was responsible for setting Korean accounting standards, though its interpretations were formally issued by the Korean Institute of Certified Public Accountants (KICPA) from 1974. From 1981, the Securities Supervisory Board became formally responsible for promulgating KFAS, but MOF/MOFE retained a key role in standard setting (KAI-KASB 2000, 2). Although an Advisory Committee constituted of academics and professionals advised the government on accounting issues, international comparability was not a priority before 1997.

Most crucially, although consolidated group accounting was required of listed companies since 1993, this often gave a very misleading picture. The high ownership threshold for consolidation of group companies and the absence of a requirement to disclose intra-group guarantees made chaebol accounts before the crisis highly misleading. The true level of chaebol indebtedness only became apparent after the crisis broke, as dramatically exposed in the Daewoo case.

In a survey of accounting disclosure by the largest banks and companies in various East Asian countries in 1997 (i.e., using pre-crisis accounting standards), Rahman (1999) found major divergences between KFAS and both IAS and U.S. GAAP. The degree of divergence from international standards was often worse for Korean companies than for Indonesian, Malaysian, and Thai companies. Of 28 major IAS benchmarks, all of the Korean banks and nonfinancial companies surveyed by Rahman complied fully with only one (the disclosure of foreign currency debt in local currency equivalent). In important areas such as the reporting of related party lending and borrowing, segment information, and off-balance sheet financing commitments, none of the banks or companies surveyed provided any financial information at all (though half acknowledged the existence of related party transactions). No bank or company followed IAS guidelines for reporting foreign currency translation gains and losses (Rahman 2000, 4). Effectively, it was impossible for outsiders to know the true financial position of major Korean companies. Nevertheless, as was often the case throughout Asia in the early 1990s, many international investors still provided substantial funds to these very nontransparent companies, facilitating continued divergence rather than convergence upon international standards.

The new Kim Dae-Jung government saw the upgrading of Korean accounting standards as a crucial step toward restoring international investor confidence after the crisis.[59] The outgoing Kim Young-Sam government had already made a commitment to improving domestic accounting standards, including the production and auditing of consolidated accounts in the financial and corporate sectors, in the 3 December 1997 LOI. In the 2 May 1998 LOI, accounting reform was included as one of the structural performance criteria, which required "listed companies to publish half-yearly financial statements prepared and reviewed by external auditors in accordance with international standards" by September 1998.[60] A month before the deadline, half-yearly audited statements were released, but it is doubtful they were wholly in accordance with international standards. Below, I address post-crisis Korean standard setting and the quality of compliance with international accounting standards.

Institutional Reform: Accounting Standard Setting

The government's and IMF's deadlines for accounting reform proved overly ambitious given the scale of the task and the desire to adopt the standard international procedure of issuing public exposure drafts of new accounting standards and soliciting responses before issuing final versions. The FSC, which became formally responsible for issuing Korean accounting standards, organized a Special Committee on Accounting Reform to make proposals, which first met in May 1998. It suggested a series of reforms in the second half of 1998, using IAS and U.S. GAAP as benchmarks.[61] After releasing exposure drafts for public comment, the FSC and SFC issued a set of substantially revised KFAS on 11 December 1998, applicable from fiscal year 1999.

Even before the crisis, reformers had proposed delegating accounting standard setting to an independent private sector body. In October 1998, the government, in consultation with the World Bank, established the Korea Accounting Standards Board (KASB), part of the Korea Accounting Institute (KAI). KASB began operation in July 2000 and aimed to "harmonize" KFAS with IAS and U.S. GAAP (KAI-KASB 2001, 2). However, in contrast to Singapore and Hong Kong, but similarly to the other three crisis-hit countries, Korea does not allow listed domestic companies to report directly using IAS/IFRS. Rather, listed companies are required to report on the basis of KFAS, which themselves are devised on the basis of IAS/IFRS and U.S. GAAP. From January 2006, foreign companies listed in Korea are allowed to report using IFRS or U.S. GAAP, but as of that date there were no such listings in Korea. In March 2007, the authorities announced an intention to move toward the full adoption of IFRS for listed companies from 2011.[62]

This new system is more transparent than its predecessors, though the FSC retains the right to direct KAI to revise standards where necessary to protect stakeholder interests and ensure IAS consistency (Kim 2000, 10). Furthermore, although the membership of the KAI is very broad, it does include chaebol lobby groups like FKI. However, whether this affects the work of the KASB is unclear, since it is dominated by accounting academics and professionals. KAI also enjoys financial independence from other government agencies, including FSC and MOFE.

Korean Compliance with International Accounting Standards

In practice, KASB has ensured that Korean standards are "largely consistent" with IFRS (World Bank 2004b, 1, 11). The revised accounting standards of December 1998 required, among other things, Korean companies to recognize impairment losses for most tangible assets using a fair value method (articles 55–75), and to detail foreign currency assets and liabilities and related gains/losses (article 68), segment information (article 87) and related party transactions (article 87) in the footnotes. The definition of related parties is comprehensive and close to that in IAS 24. Companies must divulge the names of related parties and any significant transactions with them, including sales and purchases, short-term and long-term accounts payable and receivable, and collateral and guarantees provided by and for the company. These new standards removed some of the most important gaps in Korean standards that existed until December 1998 and brought Korea closer to IAS. Penalties for fraudulent audit reports were also increased significantly (Kim 2000).

Crucially, on 21 October 1998, the securities regulator issued the requirement (Article 6) that large chaebol needed to implement "combined" accounting for fiscal years beginning on or after 1 January 1999.[63] From that point, consolidated accounting was mandatory for smaller chaebol, requiring the consolidation of accounts of subsidiaries in which parent companies have a direct or indirect stake of 30 percent or more. Combined accounting was considered a more stringent standard, requiring chaebol to include all companies under their effective control in a single set of accounts, whether or not they have a direct equity interest in them.[64] This closed a major loophole in the existing Korean financial reporting system. Along with the prohibition on intra-group guarantees by March 2000, it was a major step in the direction of greater transparency of financial accounting in Korea.

Since 2001, KAI-KASB has continued to revise Korean accounting standards in line with IFRS. Consistent with the U.S. Sarbanes-Oxley Act of August 2002, CEOs and CFOs are now also required to certify the completeness and accuracy of the company's financial statements. As in many other countries, Korea tightened rules relating to auditor independence in 2002, including requiring the disclosure of payments to auditors for non-audit services (FSS 2003a, 15).

Although the gap between international and Korean accounting standards is today much smaller than before the crisis, it is not negligible. An October 2001 benchmarking study found that, in contrast to IAS/IFRS, there were no specific rules in Korea on the measurement of value in use relating to impairment losses (IAS 36.5), the de-recognition of financial assets (IAS 39.35), the disclosure of the fair values of financial assets and liabilities (IAS 32.77), the fair values of investment properties (IAS 40.69), or segment liabilities (IAS 14.56; Nobes 2001, 78–79). Differences also exist on consolidated accounting, where some entities (such as special purpose vehicles) are not consolidated under Korean rules, though Korean standards are arguably more specific. As discussed below, Korean accounting standards for banks also remained significantly less stringent in some areas than in the United States. Only some of these gaps have been closed in recent years (World Bank 2004b, 11, 14). In announcing in March 2007 that Korea would converge fully on IFRS from 2011, the Korean authorities accepted that there was a widespread perception of continuing differences between domestic and international standards.

To give a rough estimate how much Korean accounting practices have converged toward IFRS since the crisis, I investigated the extent to which some major Korean companies met IFRS requirements in their 2003 financial statements. I focused on areas of poorest quality disclosure before the crisis, choosing six of the top seven Korean listed companies, all of which provide financial statements in English.[65] These companies are subject to untypical pressure from their foreign investors and from domestic regulators to improve financial disclosure and so should give a fair indication of best practice in Korea in 2003–4.

The results in table 6.3 suggest that compliance with IFRS has dramatically improved in these key areas since 1997, with some exceptions. However, Korean firms tended not to provide detailed segment information by geographic area or on the outstanding fair value of derivative contracts. These results are similar to those of the World Bank (2004b, 12–13), which found evidence of considerable noncompliance with Korean GAAP in areas such as foreign exchange accounting, disclosure of contingent liabilities (including outstanding litigations), and accounting for marketable securities and fixed assets. Both these results, and those reported later for Korean banks, suggest that Korea has made major strides toward formal convergence, but that disclosure in some areas remains lower than that in the major Western economies. The poor compliance with Korean GAAP in a few areas also suggests continuing weaknesses in the internal and external audit process, as well as in SFC sanctions of violations.

Of course, table 6.3 says little about the quality of the information provided, even where there is complete formal compliance with Korean GAAP and IFRS. To what extent have Korean companies complied with the spirit of the new standards? Evidence of this kind is more difficult to find. Certainly, Korea has moved up the global accounting quality ladder since 1997, but it remains a long way from the top. In its annual executive survey of the quality of accounting and auditing standards, the World Economic Forum has consistently ranked Korea at the global mean from 2002 through 2006, showing no trend toward improvement over this period. Given that this survey takes into account the quality of auditing as well as formal accounting standards, it implies a continuing compliance gap with international best-practice standards of financial reporting.[66] Consistent with this evidence, the World Bank ROSC found also that the quality of disclosure was sometimes still poor in Korea, particularly in the important area of related party transactions (World Bank 2004b, 11).

The FSSA report argued that "a shortage of properly trained accountants, auditors and corporate finance officers" were "a major impediment to complete implementation of Korean GAAP" (IMF 2003a, 6, 35, 46). The World Bank also pointed to capacity constraints as a problem (World Bank 2004b, 1). However, the evidence also suggests that disclosure remains a problem in areas that go to the heart of corporate governance conflicts in Korea, notably related party transactions. In this case, the ultimate source of

TABLE 6.3
Major Korean companies: Selected areas of formal IAS compliance, 2003 financial statements

Reporting category	Relevant IAS	Samsung Electronics	Posco	SK Telecom	Kepco	Hyundai Motors	LG Electronics	Percentage compliance
Related party lending and borrowing	1, 24	Y	Y	Y	Y	Y	Y	100%
Foreign currency debt	21, 32	Y	Y	Y	Y	Y	Y	100%
Foreign currency debt: short and long term	21, 32	Y	Y	Y	Y	Y	Y	100%
Foreign currency debt (won): gain or loss	21, 32	Y	Y	Y	Y	Y	Y	100%
Derivative instruments: fair value and gains/losses	32	N	N	N	Y	N	N	17%
Segment information (revenues, results, assets): countries	14	N	N	N	N	Y	N	17%
Segment information (revenues, results, assets): industries	14	Y	Y	Y	Y	Y	Y	100%
Contingent liabilities	10	Y	Y	N	Y	Y	Y	83%
Average compliance across standards		75%	75%	63%	88%	88%	75%	77%

Sources: Company audited financial statements, English language versions (notes).

continued compliance failures is the reluctance of controlling shareholders to disclose fully such transactions. As noted earlier, audit committees are only mandatory for the largest companies and in any case have been generally ineffective in constraining owner-managers.

It would be wrong to suggest that there has been no improvement in the enforcement of financial disclosure rules in recent years. In March 2003, one of the biggest chaebol, SK, was indicted for accounting fraud. MOFE admitted in response to this case that accounting quality still lagged well behind that in other advanced countries.[67] In September 2004, Kookmin Bank and Hynix Semiconductor were both also subject to penalties for financial misreporting.[68] Before the crisis, such vigorous enforcement measures would never have been undertaken against major Korean companies, suggesting that much has changed. Nevertheless, the evidence provided above also suggests that enforcement actions against less egregious forms of financial misreporting have been less effective.

As elsewhere, the quality of compliance in financial reporting is heavily dependent upon the internal and especially the external auditing processes. There is a widespread perception that the quality of external audits is much higher for the Big Four international audit firms than that for domestic Korean auditors, though Big Four audits did not prevent the accounting frauds at Kookmin and Hynix.[69] FSS reviews of company audits over 1998–2002 suggested that many were substandard (World Bank 2004b, 9, 13). Since 1998, there have been many reprimands and fines of companies and auditors when the FSS and SFC have determined that negligence has occurred. For example, in 2003, the FSS conducted an audit review of 93 companies (79 of which were randomly selected) and found accounting violations in 17 of these. In the latter cases, both the companies and the auditors were reprimanded; some auditors were banned from doing further audit work (FSS 2003c, 64). The SFC also has the power to replace auditors and to designate auditors for companies that are highly leveraged, with substantial related party transactions, with substantial CEO control rights (25 percent for listed companies), or who are in breach of various rules (World Bank 2004b, 4). From 2006, auditors must be rotated every six years and audit staff must be rotated every three years, consistent with the new U.S. rules. Auditors are now also prohibited from providing audit clients with various kinds of non-audit services. Auditors are required to report violations of accounting standards to shareholders and to internal auditors or audit committees. However, "[t]his requirement has seldom been fulfilled in practice" (World Bank 2004b, 8, 10).

Disclosure Requirements for Financial Institutions

The FSC announced substantially revised accounting standards for financial institutions in December 1998, broadly based upon IAS 30 ("Disclosures in the Financial Statements of Banks and Similar Financial Institutions"). In addition to their monthly reports on regulatory compliance to the FSS, the authorities required banks to file quarterly financial reports to shareholders from September 1999. Financial institutions were also obliged to comply with IAS regarding off-balance sheet transactions, including derivatives, asset classification, and contingent liabilities (Kim 2000).

Financial disclosure by Korean banks has also improved dramatically since the crisis, but by 2002–3 they were still some way behind Basle standards and the more detailed U.S. disclosure requirements. Table 6.4 provides an indication of how four of the top five Korean banks' disclosure measured up against 14 of the most important BCBS (1999a) standards for 2002–3.[70] Since the largest banks tend to be subject to the most intensive compliance pressure by regulators, domestic and international investors, and counterparties, this should provide an indication of best practice in Korea.

The results show that three of the four banks comply with about three-quarters of the main Basle standards, while another falls substantially short. Note that U.S.-listed banks are legally required to meet all 14 of these standards in their annual financial reports to U.S. authorities. Thus, Kookmin Bank, which also provides annual accounts in U.S. GAAP in accordance with its sponsored ADR listing, meets 100 percent of the disclosure requirements in its U.S. financial reports. Interestingly, however, it provides less information in its Korean GAAP accounts. Korean rules do not require, for example, banks to make substantive disclosures relating to geographic information, concentrations of credit risk, accrued interest cessation, or recourse arrangements.[71] Some of these standards are less important than others, but it demonstrates that Korean disclosure standards continued to lag U.S. standards.[72] In one case the level of compliance was very low. This evidence also suggests that although market pressure on Korean banks to improve disclosure may be significant, it is far from fully effective. With the exception of Woori, foreign ownership levels are significant, suggesting this may be a factor in better disclosure. However, in general, even though banks could provide more information than is strictly required by national regulatory standards, they tend not to do so, even when (as with Kookmin) they provide such information in their U.S. reports or when (as with KEB) they are foreign-controlled.

Korean accounting standards have been transformed since the crisis, with substantially new standards in most of the key areas of weakness that existed before the crisis. As in banking supervision, the transfer of responsibility for standard setting from MOFE to the FSC and later KAI-KASB has been important, though MOFE itself has publicly supported convergence upon international standards. New rules on combined accounting for the major chaebol and on reporting of related party transactions, to name two of the

TABLE 6.4
Major Korean banks: Scores on BCBS 1999 sound financial disclosure standards

		2002–3 annual (Korean GAAP) reports			
Sound Practice No.	Disclosure of:	Hana Bank	Kookmin Bank	Korea Exchange Bank	Woori Finance
2	System for recognizing loan impairment	1	1	1	1
14	Policies and methods used to determine specific & general allowances	1	1	1	1
15	Credit risk management system	1	1	1	1
16	Loans by major categories of borrower	1	1	1	1
17	Loans by geographic area	1	1	1	0
18	Significant concentrations of credit risk	0	1	0	0
19	Summary info about recourse arrangement & expected losses	1	1	0	0
20	Impaired loans by major categories of borrower	1	1	1	0
20	Amounts of specific & general allowances against each category	1	1	1	0
21	Impaired loans by geographic area	0	0	0	0
21	Amounts of specific & general allowances by geographic area	0	0	0	0
22	Reconciliation of changes in loan allowances	1	1	1	1
23	Balances of loans on which accrual of interest has ceased due to deterioration	0	0	1	0
24	Summary info re troubled loans restructured during the year	1	1	1	0
Total		10	11	10	5
% score		71%	79%	71%	36%

Sources: BCBS 1999a; bank annual reports, 2002 or 2003.

most important, have provided for financial disclosure where previously none existed.

Two generalizations can also be made. First, the high costs of compliance with IAS/IFRS for the chaebol have meant that the process of formal convergence has been very gradual, as for outcomes in banking supervision and corporate governance. Listed Korean companies will be required to converge fully upon IFRS by 2011–13. Second, there continues to be a significant real compliance gap even between Korean GAAP and the quality of actual financial disclosure by Korean companies. Recent high-profile cases of financial misreporting highlight a continuing problem of low compliance with accounting and auditing standards by some large Korean companies, but they also demonstrate that enforcement has been considerably strengthened since 1997.

Explaining Compliance Outcomes

The results of the Korean case are largely consistent with the theory elaborated in chapter 2. The crisis galvanized the administration of the new Korean President, Kim Dae-Jung, to transform Korea's chaebol-dominated economy into an exemplar of regulatory neoliberalism in Asia. Although financial regulation has been transformed since 1998, the broader goal has not been attained. Many international standards have been imported into Korea's regulatory framework, but the quality of compliance with these standards varies considerably. SDDS compliance was achieved as early as November 1999, though improved compliance with the other standards considered here took much longer and remains incomplete.

Formal compliance with many international standards has been achieved. In contrast to Thailand, Korea did not consistently suffer from acute legislative blockage, despite the fact that President Kim Dae-Jung never enjoyed control of Parliament. In part, this was due to Kim's ability and willingness to employ his considerable emergency powers (Woo-Cumings 2003, 213–14). However, where political consensus was lacking, given deep opposition from the business sector, the conservative opposition parties were able to delay and obstruct the government's reform agenda. This is especially clear in the area of corporate governance reform, where major initiatives ground to a halt in Parliament or were substantially weakened. In the banking sector, private sector opposition was much less forceful because of the absence of chaebol control of banks and foreign control of three major banks. The other five major commercial banks, all with dispersed ownership, have also shared an interest in restoring their battered reputation among customers and investors by accepting enhanced prudential regulation. At the same time as improving their levels of compliance with international standards, the banking sector is now mostly profitable in spite of the credit card debacle of 2003–4 (Fitch Ratings 2004). All Korean banks also share a strong interest, along with the international banks operating in Korea, in the government's strategy of promoting Seoul as a regional "financial hub."[73]

Consistent with our theory, the quality of compliance was lowest in the immediate aftermath of the crisis and improved gradually as the economy and financial system recovered. The relatively efficient restructuring of the Korean banking system allowed compliance with international banking standards to improve most quickly. Even here, however, continuing financial distress in the corporate sector, including in some of the country's largest chaebol, led to a series of regulatory relaxations and ad hoc regulatory forbearance in the period up to 2004. Despite the Kim Dae-Jung government's rhetorical commitment to full compliance, a commitment continued by the Roh government since 2003, compliance has often taken second priority to the maintenance of economic growth. This is entirely reasonable, though it suggests that the Korean political economy has been less transformed than some have suggested. Regulatory agencies remain largely subordinate to political goals and have had to set aside their compliance goals when these have conflicted with growth objectives, both short and long term (the latter including the goal of maintaining Korea's position in strategic industrial sectors).

As in Malaysia and Thailand, there was considerably less improvement over time in the quality of compliance with corporate governance standards. Here, noncyclical factors, mainly continuing high levels of family control of nonfinancial companies, has meant that substantive compliance in this area has been resisted by many such shareholders. Corporate boards often remain rubber stamps for controlling shareholders who continue to run their businesses in the interest of their family members and who, as a consequence, have been willing to tolerate substantially higher costs of capital than international peers (the so-called "Korea Discount").[74] Precisely because Korea's competitiveness still depends so extensively upon the major chaebol, post-crisis governments have not wished entirely to dismantle the system that produced the Korean industrial miracle. On the contrary, despite their political distaste for chaebol influence, these governments have actually enhanced the domestic positions of the major chaebol and in some cases their associated families.

This continued concentration of family control in the major chaebol has generally trumped the growing internationalization of Korean corporations on other measures, including minority share ownership, export intensity, and foreign subsidiaries. Although foreign institutional investors have steadily built up considerable stakes in listed Korean companies, this has not generally translated into corporate control. Again, the main exception to this generalization is in private sector commercial banking, where foreign control in some cases and dispersed ownership in others have generally supported government objectives. However, even in this sector, heavy inward foreign investment has not yet resulted in full compliance with Western-style standards of corporate governance and financial disclosure.

Compared to the other countries considered in this book, exogenous administrative capacity constraints in Korea are least important in explaining compliance outcomes. High levels of technical competence and relatively large pools of skilled human resources have allowed the Korean bureaucracy to regulate efficiently and effectively in a range of areas. One possible exception is in the area of the enforcement of rules on financial disclosure, though even here it seems clear that the main source of continuing noncompliance lies in the attitudes of controlling shareholders and managers. Generally, however, variations in Korean compliance outcomes are better explained by the different levels of political opposition to compliance in the private sector.

As for the influence of the IFIs on compliance, it is uncontroversial that the IMF in particular played an important role in encouraging the government to commit itself to compliance with a range of specific international standards. Nevertheless, it is also true that key figures in the government and bureaucracy largely shared the IMF's objectives in this respect. The difference between the Korean, Indonesian, and Thai cases is that in Korea high level political support for the reform program was much stronger and the Korean President was able to push through the adoption of international standards. However, when the government's political priorities conflicted with the compliance agenda, as they did on a number of occasions in the post-crisis years, the IMF could do little about it. Furthermore, the IFIs had virtually no influence over the Korean private sector, which as we have seen was key to compliance outcomes.

What of the compliance effects of neoliberal ideas? These were arguably much more important than in any other of the cases. A neoliberal economic "change team" (cf. Williamson 1994) was empowered by the crisis and Kim Dae-Jung himself adopted the rhetoric of regulatory neoliberalism in an effort to transform fundamentally the Korean political economy (Hall 2003). However, it is possible that the apparent commitment to neoliberal reform on the part of Korean political elites was tactical rather than deep. Notably, in contrast to Indonesia, the new Korean government's neoliberal rhetoric probably played an important role in stabilizing the foreign exchange and loan markets at the beginning of 1998 (IEO 2003, 36). Moreover, as we have seen, the Kim government was more than willing to depart from a strict interpretation of neoliberalism when this conflicted with its broader priorities, notably growth. This, and the fact that compliance outcomes differ widely across standards, casts considerable doubt on the argument that ideational factors were of decisive importance.

Finally, what of the role of market forces in compliance? In the most basic sense, the market forces unleashed by the crisis, including capital flight, clearly did promote a shift toward regulatory neoliberalism. As noted above, international creditors may have been reassured by the government's explicit commitment to compliance with international standards in early 1998. Inward foreign portfolio and fixed investment also boomed in the early post-crisis years. This was due to the perception that there were major bargains to be had in Korea, but also because investors seemed to believe that the government's new policy direction would be maintained. When foreign investors have occasionally complained that Korean policy has shifted back to a more nationalistic stance, government officials have been quick to reassure them that Korea remains committed to openness and to best-practice regulation. In many ways, Korea offers the most compelling example of how a strong desire to promote inward investment fostered a strong initial commitment to compliance with international standards.

However, there is much less evidence to suggest that this post-1997 policy shift and the related significant increase in actual capital inflows have produced substantive compliance with international standards. In the areas of corporate governance and financial reporting, the quality of compliance has been less good, despite considerable increases in the level of foreign portfolio ownership of many Korean listed companies. The major chaebol have undertaken many corporate governance reforms since 1997, such as increasing the number of independent directors and reducing board size, but often these changes have placed few real constraints upon controlling family owner-managers. We also saw that in the case of the relatively few foreign-listed Korean companies, including banks, there appeared to be no strong effect of such listing on the quality of corporate governance and financial disclosure at home. This is perhaps most surprising in the area of financial reporting, where one might expect foreign institutional shareholders to be concerned about the quality of disclosure. The continuing difficulties facing shareholders in instigating litigation against firms and auditors for poor quality disclosure may help explain this. Once again, this case underlines the weakness of market forces in promoting substantive compliance and more stringent regulatory enforcement in such circumstances.

As in Indonesia and Thailand, a partial exception to this generalization needs to be made for the role of inward FDI. Significant increases in foreign investment have played a role in improving the general level of substantive compliance with international standards in the banking sector, where much of the FDI has been concentrated. Even so, as we saw, a high degree of foreign ownership does not necessarily guarantee that traditional problems of corporate fraud and governance scandals are eliminated, as the cases of Kookmin, Hyundai, and Samsung demonstrate. Thus, the national corporate governance and financial disclosure environment remains a very powerful determinant of firm-level compliance even in the presence of substantial transnational economic linkages.

The Domestic Political Limits of Regulatory Neoliberalism

The perceived costs of noncompliance with international regulatory standards were very high for the new Korean government that took office in the midst of the crisis. The government desperately needed to reassure international banks, with whom it immediately began negotiating, that it would both guarantee their Korean loans and resolve the regulatory failures that were seen as an important cause of the crisis. Korean nationalism also played an important role, both in strengthening the government's desire to recover lost national pride by committing the country to full convergence upon international best practice and in galvanizing public support for reform. As elsewhere, the perceived costs of outright noncompliance were at least as much domestic as international in origin. For President Kim, in particular, the international standards project could be used to achieve the deepening of Korean democratization by weakening the economic and political power of the major chaebol. More than in any other crisis-hit country, pro-compliance forces enjoyed direct access to and support from the highest echelons of the Korean government. Neoliberal economic technocrats, a handful of shareholder activists, many academics, and some NGOs all supported the President's agenda.

Domestic politics, as in the other crisis-hit countries, has been the most important factor in real compliance outcomes. Despite the apparent desire for wholesale reform on the part of the government, domestic opposition to substantive compliance soon regrouped. Formal ratification of legislative reforms in a range of areas was achieved in many areas, though not always as quickly as initially promised. In some areas of corporate governance, chaebol opposition was able to prevent ratification for some years after the crisis. In general, however, formal ratification failure was not the main source of compliance failure.

The broad influence of the economically dominant major chaebol, including in the media, meant that pro-compliance groups did not enjoy more than lukewarm public support. The competitiveness and continued success of Korea's best-known firms were important for jobs, growth, and for national prestige. The government itself soon found itself in the paradoxical position of acting to entrench the dominance of particular chaebol in key sectors. When some, such as Hynix, were threatened with collapse, strict compliance with new bank regulation and corporate governance standards was sacrificed to protect key industrial assets, jobs, and growth. In various areas, the initial goal of strict compliance was replaced by considerable regulatory forbearance. Such forbearance was more important than bureaucratic failure or blockage in producing mock compliance. Administrative capacity and competence were high by average regional standards and corruption was lower, even if far from negligible.

A second crucial source of mock compliance in the Korean case has been firm-level behavior. Again, this is clearest in the area of corporate governance and financial disclosure, where the chaebol have often sought to comply with the form but not the spirit of the new regulatory framework. In the banking sector, where levels of foreign control are higher and where the need to restore battered reputations was more pressing, behavior has been more compliant. Also, as the economy recovered and levels of distress in the banking sector fell, so did the costs of compliance for banks, allowing a gradual reduction in the levels of regulatory forbearance in this sector. By contrast, the level of compliance with international corporate governance standards by the chaebol-dominated nonfinancial sector has remained poor. The quality of compliance with international accounting standards has also continued to lag that in other major developed countries. This pattern of firm-level mock compliance demonstrates the difficulty faced by even the most committed governments in promoting substantive compliance in the face of concerted private sector opposition. Once again, high and concentrated private sector compliance costs and the difficulty for outsiders of monitoring corporate and bureaucratic behavior combined to produce mock compliance outcomes.

7

Practical and Theoretical Implications

This study began by asking three main questions. These are: To what extent do Asian countries comply with international regulatory standards? What explains compliance and noncompliance? And to what extent is mock compliance a sustainable strategy for developing countries and private sector actors? In this chapter, I provide answers to these questions by drawing on the detailed assessment of compliance outcomes in four crisis-hit Asian countries that is provided in the main body of this book.

Post-Crisis Compliance with International Standards in Asia

The empirical chapters demonstrated that in Indonesia, Korea, Malaysia, and Thailand there has been a transition toward regulatory neoliberalism since 1997. In all cases, the crisis reinforced more tentative pre-crisis policy shifts toward stricter financial regulation, but which (with the partial exception of Malaysia) had generally failed to affect substantially both public regulation and private sector behavior. In the wake of the 1997–98 crisis, governments in all four countries publicly committed themselves, often within the context of IMF conditionality, to the overhaul of their frameworks of financial regulation in line with international best practice standards. Although this proved politically controversial in all countries, by mid-1998 there was surprisingly little open rhetorical deviation by governments from this agenda.

Since 1998, all four governments imported international standards of many kinds into domestic legislation and administrative frameworks, notably

SDDS in the area of macroeconomic data transparency, but also in banking supervision, corporate governance, and accounting standards, among others. In most cases these international standards were drawn directly from those promulgated by the main international standard-setting bodies, including the IMF, Basle Committee, OECD, and IASB. Sometimes, because these international standards were often fairly general, governments and the IFIs also drew upon more specific financial regulations in place in the major Western countries, above all the United States and sometimes the United Kingdom. Formerly obscure concepts such as Prompt Corrective Action, Forward-Looking Criteria, Tier 1 capital, independent directors, and IFRS found their way into government policy speeches and documents, private sector press releases, and the news media in Asia.

As a result, the broad framework of financial regulation and supervision has changed markedly in most Asian countries since 1997, including the four investigated in detail here. The chronic failures of regulatory oversight and enforcement that were evident in countries like Korea and Indonesia before 1997 appear to be much less extensive today. The formerly widespread abuses of legal lending limits by many Asian banks and the nonexistent levels of disclosure of key information in much corporate financial reporting in the region appears also to be a thing of the past.

However, despite this clear movement in the direction of regulatory neoliberalism, the quality of compliance with international standards since the crisis has varied considerably over time, across standards, and across countries. Over time, a pattern emerged whereby formal compliance was often easier to achieve than substantive, behavioral compliance. This is not to say that the formal adoption of international standards was always easy. Indeed, there was also a clear tendency for governments and the IFIs to be excessively optimistic about even formal compliance prospects at the outset of the crisis. In Thailand, notably, formal compliance with international standards has proven very difficult to achieve due to parliamentary opposition. Even in Indonesia, Malaysia, and Korea, early optimism that stringent new standards of bank capitalization and loan classification could be rapidly adopted soon led to backtracking as it became clear that this would exacerbate private sector financial problems and jeopardize economic recovery. Such "temporary" departures from international standards continued as late as 2003–4.

In other words, there was a tradeoff between the extent of formal compliance and the ability of governments to avoid reneging on compliance commitments either through regulatory forbearance or selective enforcement. When formal compliance was relatively high, as in Korean banking supervision by 1999, the government subsequently employed considerable regulatory forbearance once it became clear that substantive compliance would have imposed unacceptably high costs on the private sector and the government. By contrast, when formal compliance was low, as in Thailand generally, the need for regulatory forbearance was also lower. Even here, when international standards were imported by the stock exchange into the Thai regulatory framework, enforcement was often poor.

Across all countries, failure of parliamentary ratification was much more likely in the area of corporate governance standards than in banking supervision. This appears to be because the crisis had the effect of increasing government control over the banking sector, thereby concentrating private sector opposition to compliance in the nonbank corporate sector. Even so, the ability of such private sector opposition to block legislation importing international standards into domestic law was considerably greater in the Thai case than in the other three. In the case of accounting standards, none of the four governments allowed domestic firms the simple option of using IFRS or U.S. GAAP for financial reporting, preferring instead to set up domestic accounting standard setters that would vet IFRS, delay their adoption and in some areas modify them to suit domestic circumstances.

Even in cases where legislative hurdles were overcome and formal compliance achieved, substantive compliance in all countries was a work in progress, especially when the private sector costs of compliance were high. All four countries have been fully compliant with SDDS, as judged by the IMF, since 2001. Although some criticize the SDDS as insufficient and outdated (e.g., IIF 2006), in the absence of a stricter, well-established set of data standards, it remains the key benchmark for macroeconomic data transparency. It is also worth noting that most developing countries today are not compliant with SDDS.

By comparison with SDDS, compliance with international financial standards with higher private sector compliance costs and lower levels of transparency has lagged considerably. Over time, as the level of financial distress diminished with economic recovery, regulatory and supervisory authorities were often able to tighten the rules and move toward stricter supervision and enforcement. However, the improvement over time in the area of banking supervision has been much clearer than that in corporate governance and financial disclosure by listed companies.

Finally, the average quality of compliance has also differed perceptibly across countries, though this varies by issue area. Table 7.1 provides a rough summary of this variation by country and standard in 2005. It should be stressed that if a similar table were to be constructed for 2000 or 2002, most countries would be in the Low category and none would be in the High category for all non-SDDS standards. As a result, the table does not show the gradualism of the compliance process over time.

I have already noted that even the United States and the United Kingdom depart in certain areas from the ideal type of regulatory neoliberalism, so the rankings above can only be relative as well as very approximate. What seems

TABLE 7.1
Substantive compliance, circa 2005

	SDDS	Banking supervision	Corporate governance	Accounting
High	Indonesia Korea Malaysia Thailand	Korea		Malaysia
Medium		Indonesia Malaysia Thailand	Malaysia	Korea Thailand
Low			Indonesia Korea Thailand	Indonesia

Sources: SDDS: IMF DSBB; Banking supervision: various IMF reports; Corporate governance: CLSA Emerging Markets (2005); Accounting: World Economic Forum (2006); and author's estimates in all areas.

Note: Relative compliance quality is judged against best performers in Asia (Singapore and Hong Kong).

clear is that many East Asian countries remain further away from the ideal type of regulatory neoliberalism than is often assumed, and further away from it than the major Anglo-Saxon countries. None of the financial regulatory agencies in the Asian countries considered here enjoy levels of political autonomy comparable to the UK's Financial Services Authority, for example. Even in Indonesia, where a very independent central bank has sometimes conspicuously resisted government pressure, politics intruded into the regulatory process via parliamentary oversight committees, the bank restructuring agency (IBRA), and corruption. In Korea, a new financial regulatory agency enjoys a much greater degree of autonomy than did regulators before the crisis, but it remains relatively subordinate to the political executive. Most conspicuously in Malaysia and Thailand, there are few provisions for regulatory independence, even if regulators often enjoy considerable autonomy in routine matters. (The same is true, incidentally, of Hong Kong and Singapore, often seen as the exemplars of regulatory neoliberalism in Asia). In general, however, the key difference between the major Anglo-Saxon countries and the countries investigated here has less to do with their formal regulatory frameworks than their actual behavioral outcomes.

What Explains Compliance Outcomes?

The empirical evidence provided in chapters 3–6 support a core prediction of the theory of compliance elaborated in chapter 2, that deep economic crises have a paradoxical effect on compliance. In the short term, such crises increase the likelihood of formal compliance with international regulatory standards, but as they also raise compliance costs for much of the business sector, they favor mock compliance strategies on the part of government and the private sector. Where these costs can be socialized and where noncompliant behavior is more visible, as for the macroeconomic data standards, compliance tends to be both easier and more likely. This explains why compliance with SDDS has been higher across all four countries and why it came at an earlier point in the process. It is also consistent with this prediction that in other areas where these conditions did not apply, substantive compliance lagged and only gradually improved with economic recovery. The degree of improvement was greatest in Korea and Malaysia where economic recovery was more robust, although even here slowdowns in 2000–2001 retarded the compliance effort.

The financial crises of the late 1990s had the effect of empowering both domestic proponents of reform and international forces that favored compliance. Although economic reform and compliance with international standards were not equivalents, for many domestic and international critics the latter was a key test of governments' reform intentions. This coalition was sufficiently strong in most cases to extract official commitments from Asian governments to adopt international standards as benchmarks for regulatory reform. Generally, however, without support from key domestic groups for the international standards project, such formal commitments might not have been forthcoming, despite international pressure—not least since such external pressure was often seen as illegitimate and heavy-handed even by pro-reform domestic groups. This was particularly clear in Malaysia, where external pressures were weakest. Even in Korea, where external pressure was much stronger, neoliberal reformers used the crisis to strengthen their hand. The IMF was very dependent upon this group of reformers to achieve many of its own goals. A similar if less productive alliance existed in the other crisis-hit countries.

It is very difficult to quantify how high the costs of outright noncompliance were in each case. However, given that it is difficult to find an example of a government willing to adopt an explicit strategy of noncompliance, including those that were relatively unaffected by the crisis, it seems clear that governments generally perceived these costs to be high. For the three IMF countries in the midst of the crisis, a rejection of international standards might have jeopardized important relationships with Washington and with international banks to which large amounts of debt were owed. There was also an initial concern in all four cases that the G7 and IFI emphasis on international standards had sensitized skeptical international investors and creditors to the importance of country compliance. However, these concerns faded when foreign capital began flowing again to Asian countries and firms despite widespread doubts about the quality of compliance.

Ultimately, it was the domestic political costs of outright noncompliance that were often decisive. As we saw, even unorthodox and IMF-avoiding Malaysia was surprisingly conformist when it came to international regulatory standards. In this case, it was domestic political pressure on the government in the early post-crisis years and the fear of loss of office that was most important in producing this result. For pro-reform governments in Thailand and Korea, compliance with international standards was part of an electoral strategy of signaling their determination to deal with the causes of the crisis and to differentiate themselves from their corrupt and incompetent predecessors and opponents. This was even true to some extent for President Habibie and his successors in Indonesia, who were engaged in a constant struggle for their political survival.

Once governments had made formal political commitments to compliance, domestic politics took over. In this second stage of the compliance game, domestic pro-compliance forces, such as neoliberal technocrats and NGOs, were often isolated and weak, compared to the private sector actors on whom the costs of compliance largely fell. Interestingly, with the exceptions of Thailand in general and the specific area of corporate governance in most countries, opponents of compliance were often unable to block formal ratification and adoption of regulatory reforms. Hence, the bulk of this second-stage game was played out in the shadows: in the regulatory agencies and within regulated banks and firms themselves. This process excluded many pro-compliance actors and was to a considerable extent invisible to NGOs, neoliberal reformers, and institutional investors. In these shadows, a varying combination of regulatory forbearance, administrative blockage, and private sector noncompliance could flourish. The result was mock compliance: a combination of considerable formal compliance with international standards and behavioral departure from their prescriptions.

If crises were the only factor producing mock compliance with international standards, substantive compliance with all international standards would be largely achieved by now in all four countries. Since 2003–4, many Asian economies have once again achieved high growth rates. The persistence of mock compliance outcomes in some areas shows that other noncyclical factors are also at work. I have stressed the role of ownership structures in explaining why substantive compliance often remains highly costly for those who control many Asian companies.

Outside of the banking sector, family ownership has continued to be the dominant form of corporate ownership and control and has reduced the quality of compliance. This is because controlling families, whose control over cash-flow rights often substantially exceeds their control over share ownership, often have much to lose from the adoption of international corporate governance and financial disclosure standards. The theoretically positive impact of very high levels of ownership concentration in terms of aligning the incentives of inside and outside investors seems generally to be swamped by the negative effects of concentration. For the corporate families who still dominate much of the Asian nonbank private sector, mock compliance had the advantage of blunting the demands of the pro-compliance lobbies while conceding little in practice to outside shareholders.

In the banking sector, governments generally socialized a large proportion of the private costs of compliance through large public capital injections. Furthermore, this often had the effect of removing family owners from banks. Given the desire to recoup the enormous costs of financial restructuring and to promote better management practices in the banking sector, governments in Indonesia, Korea, and Thailand were willing to allow foreign investors to take substantial stakes in many of these banks, including in some cases controlling stakes. In Indonesia, most of the major private banks are now in foreign hands as are about a third in Korea and Thailand. These foreign investors have generally supported governments' compliance objectives and have often raised average sectoral standards of risk management, financial disclosure, and corporate governance. This has helped to produce a more positive relationship between economic recovery and the quality of compliance with international banking standards than in other areas.

Nevertheless, there are limits to the extent to which foreign ownership can transform compliance outcomes, even in banking. Most Asian financial systems remain "bank-based" by comparison with those of the major Western countries, as noted in the introduction. As we saw in the Korean case, at certain junctures this led the government to pressure even foreign-controlled banks to continue lending to major industrial companies that were threatened with insolvency. Many restructured banks have focused on increased lending to retail customers rather than to firms since the late 1990s, which has weakened the linkages between the banking and corporate sectors in Asia. However, many Asian companies remain very dependent upon bank finance and still turn to major state-owned banks for loans. Such state-owned banks often still lag considerably in the quality of compliance with international standards of all types.

Also, what is important in the banking sector is foreign control rather than foreign ownership per se. For example, levels of foreign ownership of some of the major Korean firms hit by financial scandals in recent years (Kookmin, Hynix, SK) have been very high. Since the crisis, there have been large increases in the average level of foreign institutional ownership of listed corporations in some countries, notably Korea. Undoubtedly, this has encouraged many of the major chaebol to improve their standards of corporate governance and transparency. However, international institutional investors in the major chaebol have not generally wrested ultimate control of these firms from family owner-managers or prevented some notable abuses of outside shareholders from continuing. By contrast, when foreign investors have taken controlling stakes in domestic firms, mostly in the banking sector, levels of compliance have been noticeably better. At the limit, if all of a country's firms are branches or subsidiaries of parent firms from high compliance countries, this might obviate the need for high quality domestic regulation entirely.

Of course, there are substantial political limits to the process of internationalization of the banking sector, though these have been reached at lower levels in some countries than in others. Malaysia, whose financial sector crisis was less deep, largely avoided selling its banks to foreigners (and without significant observable disadvantages). In Korea, it is rumored that the authorities delayed the privatization of Woori financial group because of the desire not to let another large bank fall into foreign hands and the difficulty of finding a large enough domestic investor apart from the existing banks or chaebol (Fitch Ratings 2006, 2). In Thailand, a new military government announced at the end of 2006 that it would seek to reduce foreign ownership across the board to ensure Thai control of key sectors. Hence, although one general effect of the crisis might be said to have been to encourage governments to think of the financial sector as crucial "infrastructure" for economic development, the older view that finance should remain under national control remains strong in some quarters.

How does this explanation of compliance outcomes compare with other theories? It should be emphasized that it is broadly in agreement with a range of theories that stress the importance of domestic political and institutional factors in regulatory outcomes (e.g., Amyx 2004; Barth, Caprio, and Levine 2006; Haggard 2000; Hamilton-Hart 2002; MacIntyre 2003). Nevertheless, there are a few differences of emphasis that are worthwhile pointing out.

MacIntyre (2003) argues that post-crisis policy outcomes across countries can be broadly explained by varying degrees of political centralization. Although this theory helps to explain the greater prevalence of ratification failure in politically decentralized Thailand (before 2001), it is inconsistent with the finding that substantive compliance was generally poor across all countries in the early post-crisis years. Also, in contrast to MacIntyre's argument that high political centralization produces policy volatility, we have seen that formal policy outcomes relating to standards compliance have been relatively stable even in countries with higher political centralization. For example, despite the dramatic macroeconomic policy shift that occurred after Anwar's sacking in Malaysia in September 1998, formal regulatory policy remained more stable. This was especially true in the area of corporate governance policy, which remained fairly orthodox throughout the period from 1997. Of course, there were departures from orthodoxy behind the scenes in the form of mock compliance strategies on the part of government, regulators and the private sector, but this is true for all our country cases, not just Malaysia. Certainly, Prime Minister Mahathir was more willing than other leaders to depart explicitly from international standards of banking supervision, but this departure was temporary and more recently behavioral compliance has been better than in Indonesia or Thailand. More important than the degree of political centralization, then, seems to be the level of private sector compliance costs and the extent to which these translate into political costs for the incumbent government. In all four cases, these costs were unbearably high during and immediately after the crisis, necessitating considerable departures from substantive compliance.

I have also placed less emphasis than Hamilton-Hart (2002) on variations in the level of administrative capacity. I do not deny that this factor is often important and varies across the region from the relatively low levels of Indonesia to the relatively high levels of Malaysia and Korea. However, I have argued that the level of regulatory capacity is often politically endogenous, dependent on such factors as the willingness of the government to allow free reign to potentially over-zealous supervisors and the level of public sector corruption. To give one example, putting only one MOFE official in charge of NBFI regulation in Korea before the crisis demonstrated the low priority given to prudential regulation and the high public and private sector compliance costs that greater "capacity" would have entailed. After the crisis, although most regulatory agencies have significantly expanded staff and supervisor training, some governments have been reluctant or unable to provide supervisors with significantly increased enforcement powers (e.g., Thailand's Securities Commission). In Indonesia, Malaysia, and Thailand, the still very close linkages between government and business have often made enforcement agencies hesitate to use those formal powers that they do possess.

I have also argued that international forces have considerably less impact on compliance than is often argued (e.g., Ho 2001; Jayasuriya 2005; Pirie 2005; Simmons 2001; Soederberg 2003). Even as regards formal compliance, these authors have often overlooked the pattern of initial overcommitment and subsequent backtracking by governments highlighted in this study. More importantly, the ability of anti-compliance forces to block substantive compliance after formal adoption has taken place has often been underestimated.

Many theories exaggerate the potential for global market forces to promote compliance and convergence (Gill 1995; Hansmann and Kraakman 2000; Soederberg 2003; Soederberg, Menz and Cerny 2005). The evidence presented here consistently demonstrated that market forces, particularly after crises, often did promote formal compliance with international standards. However, as argued above, domestic pro-compliance forces were probably more important in securing political commitments to international standards. Furthermore, market forces were much less powerful when it came to substantive, behavioral compliance. The main reason for this is that market actors often find it difficult to discern the true level of compliance with international standards, with the clear exception of SDDS (where compliance outcomes are better). This difficulty of third party monitoring applies even to relatively sophisticated market players. One of my interviewees in Japan, a widely respected banking sector analyst employed by a major international bank, told me that UFJ Bank had one of the best management teams and good prospects for rapid recovery. Within less than two years, special inspections by Japanese regulators uncovered huge amounts of hidden NPLs at UFJ, leading to the subsequent removal of its management and its takeover by a larger domestic rival. If highly paid specialists do not always get it right, it is unsurprising that most market actors often fail to do so.

There are other reasons why market forces can favor mock compliance outcomes. As we have seen, ratings agencies such as Fitch and Moody's often provided very critical analyses of Asian banking reforms to the markets and widely publicized the view that official statements and statistics were often untrustworthy. However, despite the ratings agencies assigning very low stand-alone financial strength ratings to many Asian banks, investors and other creditors did not react by withdrawing funds from these banks. The reason is simple: such creditors take into account that national authorities almost always effectively guarantee the liabilities of *formally* compliant banks. Consequently, creditors care little about stand-alone financial strength ratings. As the World Bank noted in the case of Thailand's notoriously weak banks, "[t]he market does not discipline the financially weak Thai banks because of the implicit government guarantee of all deposits and because there is regulatory forbearance in respect of recognizing loan losses" (World Bank 2003, 20).[1] Thus, too-big-to-fail assumptions can short-circuit market pressure for substantive compliance with international standards. Market forces are, however, likely to sanction formal noncompliance by banks because visibly noncompliant banks tend to be placed under onerous supervisory controls and may even face outright nationalization (Moody's Investor Services 1999, 37).

More generally, investors often overlook low quality compliance if they perceive this to have little impact on their returns. "Push" factors such as the level of liquidity in major developed markets often dominate capital flows to emerging market, as opposed to local market and firm-level factors (IMF 2001a, 40–41). In periods of buoyant capital flows to emerging markets, as in recent years, the equity prices of companies with *lower* quality corporate governance have outperformed those of companies with higher quality governance (CLSA Emerging Markets 2005, 4). The consequence has been that many firms have not felt a need to undertake independent and transparent assessments of the quality of their corporate governance. Standard & Poor's, another credit ratings agency, announced in 2002 that it would offer corporate governance ratings to companies based on the OECD principles, but few companies have proven willing to pay for this service (Standard & Poor's 2002).[2] This evidence is consistent with my argument that market pressure for formal compliance will be greater in bad times, particularly in the wake of crises when regional peers are also adopting formal compliance strategies. However, even if companies did believe that they would be systematically punished for low quality corporate governance (a belief for which there is little evidence), controlling owners may simply be unwilling to comply if the costs for them of doing so are very high.

In some cases, market forces can have a positive impact on substantive compliance. As we have seen, rising levels of foreign ownership in the domestic banking sector in Indonesia, Korea, and Thailand have improved the quality of compliance with international standards in this sector. Even so, it is governments that made decisions to open their domestic banking market to foreign entry; hence, this factor is only in part a "market" force. As countries' financial sectors have recovered from the crisis, some governments have taken steps to impose new limits on foreign participation in this sector.

Other theories stress the compliance effects of neoliberal ideas. Hall (2003, 73), for example, argues that new (pro-compliance) "discursive practices generate narrative structures that have a constitutive effect on the subsequent discursive and economic practices of these actors." Stripped of jargon, this amounts to the claim that discourse constrains behavior. However, this simply overlooks the often large gap between the post-crisis rhetoric of Asian officials and companies and their actual behavior. These actors are more innovative than this argument implies, especially when compliance costs are high and when actors believe they can hide mock compliance from third parties. It also overlooks how governments have competing objectives that work against substantive compliance. In most countries considered here, objectives of shielding particular companies or economic sectors or of promoting growth and employment sometimes led leaders who were otherwise apparently committed to compliance to opt instead for regulatory forbearance. Another way of putting this is that although new ideas can help to bring political entrepreneurs into positions of importance, at the level of specific rules and supervisory practices, interest group politics tends to dominate regulatory outcomes when it matters.

Hall's argument is unconvincing in the Korean case upon which he focuses, but it also travels badly when applied to other country cases. In the Thai and Indonesian[3] cases, the governments also "talked the talk" of compliance with international standards but few would argue that there was not a large gap between words and deeds in both countries. Paradoxically, in the case of Malaysia, where the government was more than willing to take a conspicuously anti-Western, anti-Washington Consensus rhetorical stance, compliance outcomes were in practice often as good as in Indonesia or Thailand, and in some respects better.

Finally, the argument that hegemonic states working through international institutions can promote compliance and convergence has some merit. As we saw in chapter 1, the United States, in particular, used both coercion and persuasion to promote an idealized version of its own regulatory practices as international standards. Even where this was less successful (as in corporate governance and accounting standard setting), the United States and the United Kingdom were both privileged as regulatory benchmarks by many governments and market actors. Nevertheless, like market forces, hegemonic states and the IFIs have enjoyed much less influence over the *quality* of compliance with international standards. Malaysian compliance was often better than in the other IMF countries, a finding consistent with other literature that has stressed the relatively weak compliance effects of IFI conditionality (IEO 2002; Kahler 1992, 1993; Killick 1996). Notably, we have seen that the FSAP process has been a very weak force for substantive compliance. Even when governments have agreed to participate and have allowed reports to be published (a relatively rare thing in Asia), they have usually been shorn of sensitive material. Many published FSSAs and ROSCs exhibit a reluctance to expose compliance failures, requiring much reading between the lines.

This calls into question the dual roles of the IFIs as both promoters and enforcers of the standards project. The United States and other G7 countries who dominate the executive boards of the IFIs have not to date wished to disrupt this delicate balancing act. In strategically important Indonesia, for example, the major countries have been unwilling (since 1999) to risk provoking further destabilization despite much evidence of poor progress on financial reform.

Is Mock Compliance Sustainable?

Since the overall quality of compliance in Asia has improved over time, the obvious question arises of whether the various compliance gaps we have identified will gradually be filled. Is substantive compliance just a matter of time? The implications of our argument for this question should be clear: further improvements in the quality of compliance are likely to be slow and often difficult for most countries. Aside from compliance with SDDS, we have argued that large compliance costs often persist for important private sector actors in emerging market economies. In Asia, the robustness of economic growth in recent years has removed most of the financial distress produced by the crisis from private sector balance sheets. However, the noncyclical factors emphasized above, such as persistent high levels of family and state ownership and control, are likely to mean that full compliance in areas like corporate governance and financial disclosure will remain elusive for some years to come.

This argument has implications for the ongoing debate about the present and future of the East Asian state (Hadiz and Robison 2005; Jayasuriya 2005; Pirie 2005; Underhill and Zhang 2005; Weiss 2003). Some argue that the crisis and its aftermath spelled the end of the developmental state. Pirie (2005, 38), writing about post-crisis Korea, argues that:

> Korea went, almost overnight, from having a system of financial and monetary governance that left all major decisions in the hands of politicians, to one in which all key day-to-day decisions are made by autonomous bureaucrats—or, to put it another way, from institutional structures that supported interventionist policies to new structures that seek to embed the principles of the contemporary neoliberal order deep within the Korean state.

My own position is very different from this. We should remember, first, that powerful bureaucratic pilot agencies (in the Korean case, the former EPB) were a key characteristic of the early developmental state rather than Asia on the eve of the crisis. More important, although Pirie is right that much has changed in Korea since the crisis, he underplays continuities. The detailed analysis of banking regulation in Korea demonstrated a still considerable element of political intervention in the regulatory process, especially when strict compliance with new international standards would have threatened the survival of national champions (e.g., Hynix) or the maintenance of growth and employment. In other areas, notably corporate governance, Korean practice remains very far from the Western ideal type. This is not to say that nothing has changed in Asia, but simply to argue that it is wrong to assume that East Asia has entered a new era in which regulatory practice has converged with the rhetoric of regulatory neoliberalism. Indeed, as the memories of the crisis have receded and Asian countries have regained confidence, there are as many signs of retreat from the rhetoric of neoliberalism as of relentless progression toward it. Recent displays of nationalist pique over the behavior of foreign investors in Korea and Thailand are but one example.[4]

Of course, it would also be misleading to claim that the developmental state is alive and well in Asia. Always something of an elusive entity, it suffered a near fatal ideological blow in 1997–98, as the Korean case exemplifies. Pirie (2005, 40) is right to suggest that the "dominant principles underpinning the mode of regulation" are now broadly neoliberal. This creates a tension between rhetoric and reality, but it is well to remember that this tension exists, even if to a lesser extent, in the "exemplars" of regulatory neoliberalism in the United States and the United Kingdom. Meanwhile, in Malaysia and Singapore, political elites continue to manage pragmatically the commanding heights of industry in much the same way as before the crisis.

Others might disagree with this argument on the grounds that compliance failures will be unsustainable in the long run because they will undermine regulatory effectiveness. However, we have seen that compliance with international standards is sometimes but not always associated with regulatory effectiveness.[5] In the case of Indonesia, for example, there is a reasonably close relationship between substantive compliance failures and regulatory and supervisory failures. In other cases, the relationship is much less close. Malaysia, Singapore, and Hong Kong all notably diverge from core tenets of regulatory neoliberalism, including agency independence and policy transparency. And yet, regulatory and supervisory outcomes in these three countries have been markedly better on average than in other Asian countries. There are many conceivable circumstances in which regulatory forbearance, rather than the enforcement of fixed rules, might best promote financial stability.[6] In the Korean case, forbearance allowed the government room to build a coalition of foreign-controlled and widely held domestic banks that supported its efforts to improve and tighten banking regulation after 1999. The jury is also still out on whether Anglo-Saxon style corporate governance standards produce better managed firms with better growth prospects. After the many corporate governance scandals in the United States over the past few years, it may reasonably be doubted whether most "independent" boards in Western countries significantly constrain management. Meanwhile, many Asian family-controlled companies are global leaders in their sectors.

This is not to say that noncompliance is necessarily good: this is self-evidently untrue in areas such as related lending and many other risk management standards. It is difficult to think of reasons why "high quality financial reporting" or "good corporate governance" could be public bads, though whether any of the current international standards on offer in these two areas actually promote these broad objectives is open to debate. What the argument does suggest is that effective regulation is certainly possible while diverging from some core standards of the current global financial architecture. Regulatory effectiveness is very difficult to define precisely, in part because its objectives are often very general and multiple, and because there are likely to be tradeoffs between them (e.g., excessively strict regulation may promote financial stability at the expense of efficiency and growth). What constitutes effective financial regulation and supervision is beyond the scope of this study, but it is likely to depend on the level of development, sophistication, and internationalization of the economy, as well as on the nature of corporate ownership and financing.

What we can say is that, in the long run, a coercive approach to the enforcement of strict regulatory standards is unlikely to produce high quality compliance. As we have seen, the ability of firms at the bottom of the compliance pyramid to engage in various forms of noncompliant behavior is likely to mean that a top-down approach is unlikely to succeed. Persuasion is generally the best approach to regulation, backed up by the threat of punishment if it fails. Without the voluntary acceptance of new regulations by most regulated firms, regulation must rely entirely upon coercion, and firms will inevitably seek ways to circumvent the spirit of the rules (Ayres and Braithwaite 1992, 25–27). This has parallels with more general arguments that successful economic reform requires governments to build alliances with pro-reform groups in the private sector (Evans 1992, 178–79; Haggard and Kaufman 1992, 18–19). Policymakers cannot hope to oppose all societal interests at all times. The neoliberal view that effective "arm's length" regulation requires substantial distance between government, regulators, and all regulated parties so as to avoid regulatory capture can therefore be misleading (Beck, Demirgüç-Kunt, and Levine 2003, 2–3). As the distance between these three parties increases, so too does the likelihood that regulation will be ill-informed, heavy-handed, and excessively punitive. As Ayres and Braithwaite (2003, chap. 3) suggest, the solution to this dilemma consists in ensuring that regulation is transparent, that information is effectively transferred between regulators and the regulated, and that public interest groups are able to sanction regulators that fail to regulate effectively.

The Future of the International Standards Project

What, finally, are the future prospects of the international standards project in Asia and developing countries more generally? We have seen that the proponents of the international standards project greatly underestimated the difficulty of promoting compliance in emerging market countries. This is not simply a product of underdevelopment and weak institutions, though these have been important obstacles to convergence. Politics has mattered much more in the cases we have examined, and there are no strong reasons to believe that circumstances will be very different in other developing countries.[7] Governments in many emerging market countries have not been willing to accept the full implications of regulatory neoliberalism; nor have large proportions of their corporate sectors accepted that full compliance is in their interests. Mock compliance has been the outcome.

Since regulatory improvements are essential in many emerging market countries, the argument presented here turns our attention back to the process of international standard setting. At present, the strong influence of major Western countries over international standard-setting outcomes may both reduce their legitimacy and increase the likelihood of compliance failure. At one point during the Basle II negotiation process, for example, Asian countries (including Australasia) felt that the major Western countries were so unwilling to listen to their concerns that they were close to establishing an alternative "Asian Basle" system. More than a few Asian regulators referred to BCBS "consultation" as mere lip-service and as reflecting a desire to achieve the perception of legitimacy without altering their basic position.[8]

Given the different features of Asian political economies, it might be better for them to devise explicit policy standards that are more appropriate to local circumstances. This would seem especially necessary in the area of corporate governance, where Western standards have worked poorly to improve outcomes in the Asian context. For example, Yoshitomi and his co-authors (2003) argue that it would be more appropriate to promote a corporate governance system in Asia that is bank-centered rather than based on Western-style independent directors. In other areas, such as banking regulation, it is unclear what "Asian-style" standards would look like, and whether they would be perceived as a credible alternative to existing international standards. In accounting, the rapid spread of foreign share listings and international investment provides a strong argument for a single set of rigorous global standards. However, for many small companies and developing countries, the costs of compliance with such standards will often be too high.

The difficulties of implementation and compliance are considerably increased by the dynamic nature of the standard-setting process. The Basle process has accelerated rapidly since the early 1990s. The many countries that have struggled to implement Basle I must now focus on the adoption of Basle II. In accounting, current best practice standards are always at risk of being undermined by the next scandal. The burden this has placed on developing countries is great.[9] Innovation in international standards has been constant in recent years and has posed the highest compliance costs for public and private sector actors in developing countries. Since the Asian crises, the Basle Committee has agreed a major revision to its capital adequacy framework (Basle II), the OECD has upgraded its corporate governance principles, and the IASB has issued a series of new accounting standards. In addition, regulators in the major developed countries have issued many new regulations relating to financial regulation, corporate governance, and disclosure. In the case of the highly detailed U.S. Sarbanes-Oxley legislation of 2002, aspects of which were widely copied in Asia, there is a growing concern that it has had negative effects on the competitiveness of U.S. markets and that it needs substantial revision. As Naim (1999, 6–7) has argued, with each successive crisis in the 1990s:

> [P]olicy makers in reforming countries saw how the bar defining success kept being lifted and how the changes they were expected to make became

increasingly complex and, sometimes, politically impossible. Presidents and finance ministers also saw how their apprehensions were denounced as evidence of their lack of "political will," while the changing requirements coming from Washington and Wall Street were presented as reasonable changes resulting from the incorporation of "the lessons of experience." Common wisdom was simply "evolving."

Not only does the international standards project risk being unrealistic, it also seems unfair for two reasons. First, it is by no means clear that the major Western countries themselves always adhere to the idealized version of regulatory neoliberalism that they have promoted internationally. The British FSA openly engaged in regulatory forbearance by relaxing solvency rules for UK insurers when they came under pressure only a few years ago. At the same time, dramatic failures of corporate governance occurred in the United States, notably in the WorldCom and Enron scandals of 2001–2. High rates of executive compensation in underperforming companies in the United States and the United Kingdom suggest serious problems with the Anglo-Saxon model. However, the effect of these accounting and governance scandals was not to dislodge the U.S. corporate governance and reporting model, but to tighten further the prevailing rules on audit committees and audit processes, with ripple effects across the world. Given these concerns, it calls into serious question the legitimacy of the attempt by the major Western countries, the IFIs, and many international banks and investors to use the crisis to fundamentally remodel the relationship between state and market in East Asia.

Second, the emphasis of the international standards project is unfair in that previous financial crises have been caused not only by domestic policy failures in developing countries, but also by the tendency toward herd behavior in international financial markets. Basle II may yet require international banks to be more cautious about developing country lending than in the past, but there are few signs that the potential for instability in international portfolio capital flows has reduced.

No doubt in the future, as countries grapple with the problems of domestic institutional reform, standard setters will add new preconditions for success that go beyond current international standards. Given their dependence upon capital inflows, developing countries will inevitably remain vulnerable to future financial crises. Since 1997, many crisis-hit countries have been encouraged to continue the process of financial liberalization but to put in place a best practice regulatory framework as soon as possible. If, however, the latter is more difficult to achieve than was initially thought, it puts in doubt the rationale for proceeding with rapid financial liberalization (Hamilton-Hart and Jomo 2003). Some Asian countries, notably China, have sensibly resisted rapid financial opening while their financial sectors remain fragile and their regulatory frameworks are weak.

Many Asian governments have also been hedging their bets by accumulating extremely large foreign exchange reserves as an insurance policy against future financial crisis. Such measures are very costly, but understandable given how much we know about the difficulty of achieving effective financial regulation and how little we know about what constitutes international "best practice."

Appendix: Key International Standards and Codes

Year of Adoption	Standard-Setter	Standard or Code and Official Objective
Macroeconomic Policy and Data Transparency Standards		
1996–97	IMF: develops and monitors international standards in areas of direct operational relevance to its mandate to carry out surveillance over the international monetary system.	Special Data Dissemination Standard, General Data Dissemination Standard: The SDDS serves to guide countries that have, or that might seek, access to international capital markets in the dissemination of comprehensive, timely, accessible and reliable economic, financial and socio-demographic data to the public. The GDDS serves to guide any member country in the provision to the public of such data.
1998	IMF	Code of Good Practices on Fiscal Transparency: contains transparency requirements to provide assurances to the public and to capital markets that a sufficiently complete picture of the structure and finances of government is available so as to allow the soundness of fiscal policy to be reliably assessed.
1999	IMF	Code of Good Practices on Transparency in Monetary and Financial Policies: identifies desirable transparency practices for central

Year of Adoption	Standard-Setter	Standard or Code and Official Objective
		banks in their conduct of monetary policy and for central banks and other financial agencies in their conduct of financial policies.
Institutional and Market Infrastructure Standards		
1990/2002	FATF (Financial Action Task Force on Money Laundering): established by the G7 Summit in Paris in 1989, FATF comprises 26 member countries and monitors implementation in member and non-member countries.	The Forty Recommendations of the Financial Action Task Force on Money Laundering: set out the basic framework for effective anti-money laundering policies. Special Recommendations on Terrorist Financing: set out the basic framework to detect, prevent, and suppress the financing of terrorism and terrorist acts. The Recommendations were updated in 1996 and again in February 2002 in the wake of the 11 September 2001 terrorist attacks against the U.S., when the 8 Special Recommendations were added to the original forty.
1999	OECD (Organisation for Economic Cooperation and Development): the OECD promotes policies designed to achieve sustained economic growth and employment in its member countries.	Principles of Corporate Governance: aimed at improving the legal, institutional, and regulatory framework for corporate governance in OECD and non-OECD countries. They were revised in April 2004.
2001	CPSS/IOSCO (Committee on Payments and Settlements Systems/International Organization of Securities Commissions) CPSS was established by the G10 Central Banks and coordinates issues related to payment and settlement systems. IOSCO is an organization of national regulators of securities and futures markets. It develops and promotes standards of securities regulation to maintain efficient and sound markets.	Core Principles for Systemically Important Payment Systems (CPSIPS), Recommendations for Securities Settlement Systems (RSSS): CPSIPS sets out core principles for the design and operation of systemically important payment systems. RSSS identifies minimum requirements that securities settlement systems should meet and the best practices that systems should strive for.
2002	IASB (International Accounting Standards Board): an independent, privately-funded accounting	International Financial Reporting Standards: set out principles to be observed in the preparation of financial statements. A total of

Year of Adoption	Standard-Setter	Standard or Code and Official Objective
	standard setter based in London, UK, with board members from nine countries.	41 IFRS were issued as of July 2003 (including, up to April 2001, the formerly titled 'International Accounting Standards'). Updating is ongoing.
2002	IFAC (International Federation of Accountants): an independent body working to improve the uniformity of auditing practices and related services globally.	International Standards on Auditing: ISAs contain basic principles of auditing and essential procedures together with related guidance in the form of explanatory and other material.
2001 draft, not yet agreed	World Bank: an international lending bank that promotes poverty reduction and higher living standards in the developing world.	Principles and Guidelines for Effective Insolvency and Creditor Rights: intended to help countries develop effective insolvency and creditor rights systems.
Financial Regulation and Supervision		
1997	IAIS (International Association of Insurance Supervisors): established in 1994, IAIS provides a forum for co-operation among insurance regulators and supervisors from more than 100 countries.	Insurance Core Principles: comprise essential principles designed to contribute to effective insurance supervision that promotes financial stability. They were revised in 2003.
1998	IOSCO	Objectives and Principles of Securities Regulation: designed to help governments to establish effective systems to regulate securities markets and to promote investor confidence.
1999	BCBS (Basle Committee on Banking Supervision): established by the G10 Central Banks, BCBS provides a forum for regular co-operation among its member countries on banking supervisory matters.	Core Principles for Effective Banking Supervision: intended to serve as a basic reference for bank supervisory and other public authorities in all countries and internationally. The 25 basic principles are considered essential for any bank supervisory system to be effective. Revised in 2006.

Sources: IMF and Financial Stability Forum websites; US GAO (2003, 53–55).

Notes

Introduction

1. Chapter 1 discusses developmental and regulatory state models. On the former, see Amsden (1989); Berger and Hsaio (1987); Haggard (1990); Wade (1990); Woo-Cumings (1999) (actual practice, of course, varied greatly across Asia). On the latter, see Jayasuriya (2000, 2005); Robison (2005).

2. On the general topic of delegation, see Majone (2005) and Thatcher and Stone Sweet (2002).

3. For a similar argument, see Robison's (2005) review of other recent literature on economic reform in developing countries: Weyland (2002), Schamis (2002) and van de Walle (2001). It is also broadly consistent with general arguments about the adaptation of international standards to the local political circumstances of East Asian countries in Weiss (2003) and Woo-Cumings (2003), if not with all of their details.

4. A similar conclusion about compliance outcomes was reached by a recent IMF staff study (IMF 2004d, 12–15).

5. Malaysia is somewhat exceptional in that unlike the other three countries it was not subject to an IMF program. Nevertheless, it too came under substantial international compliance pressure.

6. The IMF itself does not assess the quality of the macroeconomic data posted by SDDS subscribers, but there are various requirements for the dissemination of statistical methodology, as well as reconciliations and cross-checks built into the dissemination format that allow users to assess quality. Note that the private Institute of International Finance (IIF 2006) argues that, on a broader measure of data transparency practices and investor relations, the Asian countries perform moderately well to poorly.

7. Indeed, they were worst for Singapore, the least crisis-affected country. Since 2001, new SDDS subscribers have tended to collapse all three stages of SDDS compliance into one, which has lowered the total country average delay in adoption.

8. For similar distinctions, see Raustiala and Slaughter (2002), 539; Shelton (2003, 5); Weiss and Jacobsen (1998, 4).

9. See Garrett (1998); Hall and Soskice (2001). It is inconsistent with other literature that makes relatively strong claims about international forces for convergence (e.g., Soederberg, Menz, and Cerny 2005).

10. I have also undertaken quantitative tests of my theory of compliance, but the quantitative data on standards compliance is currently of poor quality and the results are therefore omitted. See Das, Quintyn, and Chenard (2004) and Podpiera (2004), who use data on compliance outcomes that are only available to IMF staff.

11. Strictly speaking, regulation is the activity of rule-setting, whereas supervision is the activity of monitoring actor behavior and enforcing rules. However, because the main international standard in this area refers only to "supervision," I use this term to include both activities.

1. The Asian Crisis

1. The FSF, established in April 1999, is based at the Bank for International Settlements (BIS) in Basle.

2. See the Appendix for more detail.

3. Strictly speaking, only since April 2001 has the IASB issued IFRS. At this time, the IASB adopted all existing International Accounting Standards (IAS) issued by its predecessor, the International Accounting Standards Committee (IASC).

4. In some cases, as in the "Basle II" agreement on capital adequacy of 2004, the BCBS has allowed for a menu of regulatory options, though with a clear hierarchy of best practice.

5. IOSCO is the International Organization of Securities Commissions.

6. Remarks by Mr. Charles Freeland, Deputy Secretary General, BCBS, in ADBI 2000, 6.

7. Author correspondence with IMF staff, 18 November 2004. The IMF Executive Board agreed to allow the voluntary publication of the FSSAs in early 2001 (IMF, *Public Information Notice*, no.01/11, 5 February 2001). Reports available at http://www.imf.org/external/np/fsap/fsap.asp#cp.

8. The U.S. Treasury supports mandatory participation (U.S. GAO 2003, 65). Surprisingly, nowhere in this GAO report is it remarked that the United States, with Germany, had itself failed to submit to a ROSC or FSSA review; however, as of March 2005, the U.S. Treasury had conducted self-assessments in eight areas. See http://www.ustreas.gov/offices/international-affairs/standards/standards.html (accessed 8 March 2005).

9. By one estimate, it would have required (from 2002) 8 years for the IMF and 23 years for the World Bank to extend minimal ROSC coverage to their entire membership (Schneider and Silva 2002, 3).

10. Confidential discussion with Bank of Thailand official, January 2001. A senior IMF official remarked in December 2004 that Thailand had completed an FSSA, as yet unpublished: "Can the East Asian Miracle Persist?," speech by Takatoshi Kato, Deputy Managing Director, IMF, 2 December 2004; http://www.imf.org/external/np/speeches/2004/120204.htm (accessed 8 December 2004). However, Thailand does not appear on a recent list of completed and planned FSAPs (IEO 2006, 124).

11. An exception was Diaz-Alejandro (1985), who argued that the Chilean crisis of the early 1980s was due to a combination of premature financial liberalization and lax prudential regulation.

12. McKinnon, still firmly in the gradualist camp, argued that big bang strategies were misguided (McKinnon 1993, 4–10). In chapter 7 of this book he discussed prudential supervision, but in line with the dominant view of the time he emphasized the macroeconomic sources of financial instability.

13. See the background paper issued before the summit, which included a section on "promoting financial stability in a globalized economy." http://www.library.utoronto.ca/g7/summit/1995halifax/financial/5.html (accessed 22 February 2006).

14. Ibid.

15. The General Data Dissemination Standard (GDDS) was agreed later and aimed at the least developed countries.

16. It should be noted, however, that none of these countries were then judged by the IMF to have met all SDDS specifications (see table I.1, page 4).

17. A broad study by Eichengreen and Mussa (1998) found that financial crises were caused more by poor banking supervision than by capital account liberalization.

18. "Apparently," because the stated fiscal position of many East Asian countries masked the large unfunded public sector liabilities represented by private sector NPLs, and because some governments (notably in Thailand and Korea) provided foreign exchange reserve statistics in 1997 that were misleading. Reforms to the SDDS reporting requirements for foreign exchange reserves after the crisis were a direct response to the latter. See G22 (1998a, 15–16) for details of the Thai and Korean foreign exchange accounting.

19. Remarks by Michel Camdessus at the IMF Seminar on Capital Account Liberalization, Washington, D.C., 9 March 1998. http://www.imf.org/external/np/speeches/1998/030998.htm (accessed 14 August 2003). Ironically, at the time the relative resilience of the major Latin American economies, such as Mexico and Argentina (and, for a time, Brazil), reinforced the view that East Asian crony capitalism was to blame. Horst Köhler, Camdessus's successor as IMF Managing Director, argued that "Argentina and Chile were better placed to resist contagion during the Asian crisis because they were known to have systems of banking supervision and capital adequacy that meet or exceed the Basel standards." (Remarks by IMF Managing Director Horst Köhler, IMF/World Bank Conference on International Standards and Codes, Washington, D.C., 7 March 2001.)

20. The Asian Policy Forum is hosted by the Asian Development Bank Institute in Japan. Its objective was to foster a specifically Asian response to post-crisis reform issues. In practice, the Forum's proposals tend to be supplementary to rather than in conflict with the dominant agenda. http://www.adbi.org/Default.htm.

21. See, generally, Goldstein (2001) and Kapur (2001).

22. Another option, considered but dropped, was to make the *price* of official finance dependent upon the observance of standards. The G7 Finance Ministers (1999) also argued that "the Basle Committee should link risk weights to compliance with international standards," to encourage international banks to raise the price of loans. The BCBS decided against this option, citing the difficulty of applying "non-observance" criteria objectively (FSF 2000b, 47). The IMF Executive Board did, however, include observance of macroeconomic data standards among factors taken into consideration in committing financing to a country under the unused and now-expired Contingent Credit Line (CCL) facility (Clark 2000, 168, fn.20).

23. See Pempel (1999, 139); Woo-Cumings (1999b, 1–2). For extensions of the model beyond Japan, see Amsden (1989); Berger and Hsaio (1987); Haggard (1990); Wade (1990); Woo-Cumings (1999a).

24. The developmental state literature had often emphasized the discretionary allocation of cheap finance to particular beneficiaries in the private sector as part of an active industrial policy, but it claimed this was compatible with broader developmental objectives (Chang 1999; Wade 1990; Woo-Cumings 1991). As Woo-Cumings (1999b, 11–13) later accepted, this system created considerable financial fragility in the Korean case.

25. By predatory, Johnson meant states controlled by particular interests whose main objective was to redistribute wealth toward themselves or their associates rather than to maximize total societal wealth. In Indonesia, for example, business interests closely related to the dominant Suharto family obtained state contracts and large amounts of cheap finance from state-owned banks (MacIntyre 1993; Robison and Hadiz 2004, chap. 3).

26. "Neoliberalism" is a broad church and has evolved over time. Regulatory neoliberalism, which emphasizes the need for strong and autonomous technocratic state agencies, is different or supplementary to earlier forms of neoliberalism that only emphasized the need for deregulation and marketization. However, both versions argue for the de-politicization of economic policy and economic life generally. For useful reviews, see Robison and Hewison (2005), and Beeson and Islam (2005).

27. Thatcher and Stone Sweet (2002, 14–15) argue that there is a tradeoff between the credibility gained from delegation and the extent to which governments constrain this zone of discretion. At the limit, there are no credibility gains from delegation to a wholly constrained regulator. Majone (2005, 145) emphasizes that it is impossible in practice for political principals to write complete contracts for regulators that encompass every possible future eventuality.

28. Singapore is but one example. See http://www.mas.gov.sg/masmcm/bin/pt1Governance_and_Management_Structure.htm (accessed 22 March 2005), and IMF (2004a, 47).

29. As various authors point out, the 1991 FDIC act reduced but did not eliminate the scope for regulatory discretion (e.g., Pike and Thomson 1992).

30. "About the Financial Stability Institute," BIS, Basle, http://www.bis.org/about/fsi.htm (accessed 31 January 2001).

31. The rapid rise of equity prices gave some cause for concern, but generally they were seen as confirmation of the U.S. economic miracle (Shiller 2005, 106–31).

32. Alan Greenspan, "Information, Productivity and Capital Investment," remarks before the Business Council, Boca Raton, Florida, 28 October 1999. http://www.federalreserve.gov/BOARDDOCS/SPEECHES/1999/199910282.htm (accessed 1 February 2003).

33. "World's Most Respected Companies—Overview," *FT.Com*, 13 December 2000.

34. Correspondence, senior BOJ official, 29 April 2005.

35. Interview, Mr. Eisuke Sakakibara, Tokyo, 19 June 2002.

36. The FSF was established in April 1999. Country membership was marginally widened in June 1999 to include a single representative each from Australia, Hong Kong, the Netherlands, and Singapore.

37. These countries were: Argentina, Australia, Brazil, Canada, China, France, Germany, Hong Kong SAR, India, Indonesia, Italy, Japan, Korea, Malaysia, Mexico, Poland, Russia, Singapore, South Africa, Thailand, United Kingdom, and the United States. See "Rubin Statement at Opening of G22 Meeting," *USIS*

Washington File, 17 April 1998. http://www.usis-australia.gov/hyper/WF980417/epf502.htm (accessed 22 January 2002).

38. In the end, 25 countries were represented in the three working groups on fostering transparency and accountability, strengthening financial systems, and managing international financial crises. Belgium, the Netherlands, and Sweden were included at a later stage to assuage European concerns about the G22 process. The three reports are available at http://www.imf.org/external/np/g22/ (accessed 22 January 2002).

39 See especially G22 (1998b, 7–9, 13, 16). Hostility to the IMF sometimes seemed greater in the United States itself. The perception that U.S. taxpayers' funds were being wasted by profligate governments and risk-blind investors led the U.S. Congress to require in the International Monetary Fund Appropriations Act of 1998, which authorized an additional $18 billion of funding for the IMF, the establishment of an International Financial Institution Advisory Commission. The "Meltzer Commission," as it became known, produced a majority report in March 2000 that argued for some radical reforms, including IMF lending only to countries that "pre-qualify" on the basis of various criteria. See http://www.house.gov/jec/imf/meltzer.htm (accessed 22 January 2002).

40. To the G22, the G33 added: Belgium, Chile, Côte d'Ivoire, Egypt, Morocco, the Netherlands, Saudi Arabia, Spain, Sweden, Switzerland, and Turkey.

41. There are currently 13 country members: Belgium, Canada, France, Germany, Italy, Japan, Luxembourg, the Netherlands, Spain, Sweden, Switzerland, United Kingdom, and the United States.

42. A "Core Principles Liaison Group" also provided for consultation with and input from regulators from other emerging market countries, namely Argentina, Brazil, Hungary, India, Indonesia, Korea, Malaysia, Poland, and Singapore (BCBS 1997, 1–2). The draft was also sent to all banking regulators worldwide for comment. As a result, the BCBS argues that the BCP are "the first truly joint G10/non-G10 joint product." (Daniele Nouy, Secretary General of the Basle Committee, presentation to World Bank workshop on "Implementing Financial Sector Standards," Versailles, 18–19 December 2000).

43. These were the BIS, World Bank, European Corporate Governance Network, the International Corporate Governance Network, the International Federation of Stock Exchanges, the World Federation of Investors, the Institute of Internal Auditors of Thailand, and the European Commission.

44. Interview, Bank of Japan official, Tokyo, 18 June 2002.

45. FSF Press Release, "First Asia-Pacific Regional Meeting of the FSF," Ref. No. 32/2001E, 19 October 2001.

46. The dominance of the United States (and the United Kingdom) in this area of international standard setting contrasts with the greater importance of Europe in technical product standard setting (see Mattli and Büthe 2003).

2. *A Theory of Compliance*

1. Ho (2001) also argues that domestic factors are important in compliance, but unlike this study, he focuses only on formal implementation (of the Basle capital adequacy accord).

2. See, among others, Chayes and Chayes (1995); Checkel (1999, 2000, 2001); the June 2000 edition of International Organization on "Legalization and World

Politics"; Haas (1990); Raustiala and Slaughter (2002); Risse, Ropp, and Sikkink (1999); Simmons (2000a, 2000b); Weiss and Jacobsen (1998).

3. Compliance is a "state of conformity between an actor's behaviour and a specified rule" (Raustiala and Slaughter 2002, 539). This definition owes much to Young (1979, 3). See also Shelton (2003, 5).

4. That is, both are continuous rather than binary variables.

5. As we saw in chapter 1, for example, the OECD's PCG represent an ambiguous compromise between different traditions of corporate governance.

6. For a review, see Maskin and Tirole (1999).

7. The International Organization for Standardization, a non-governmental organization, is the most important forum for the agreement of technical standards. See Mattli and Büthe (2003).

8. FSF, "What are Standards?" http://www.fsforum.org/compendium/what_are_standards.html (accessed 22 April 2003).

9. Of course, to the extent that bureaucratic capacity is a matter of political choice, governments may be in part responsible for administrative failure, so that it may be difficult in practice to distinguish between regulatory forbearance and administrative failure.

10. See also Weiss and Jacobson (1998, 4).

11. For a good review of rationalist approaches to compliance, see Raustiala (2000, 400–405, 409–11).

12. An example is technical standards, where the elaboration of a particular standard (not necessarily technically optimal) enables private sector actors to undertake costly investments.

13. A more radical view also takes ideas seriously as fostering compliance via depoliticization, but sees them as coercive rather than legitimate (Gill 1995; Soederberg 2003).

14. Some authors argue that norm internalization can be important at a relatively early stage (e.g., Hall 2003).

15. These may include public goods such as greater regional or global financial stability, as well as the benefits that a more "level regulatory playing field" may provide to private sector actors.

16. As Hamilton-Hart (2000, 110) points out, financial deregulation by contrast is politically easier because benefits are concentrated and costs are diffuse, so that a perverse combination of financial deregulation and weak regulation is likely.

17. The floor on average (international) corporate borrowing rates is generally set by the sovereign borrowing rate (correspondence with London bankers, 11 January 2006).

18. Similarly, Johnson et al. (1999) argue that crises reduce the private sector incentives for compliance with stricter corporate governance and disclosure standards.

19. Note that gross compliance costs are often substantial even for the best managed global firms. For example, HSBC, the most profitable British bank, estimated its global regulatory compliance costs for 2003 to be $400 million. ("HSBC Says Red Tape Cost it $400m Last Year," *FT.com*, 1 March 2004).

20. The literature on corporate finance distinguishes between countries in which most firms are widely held by diverse shareholders, as (on average) in the United Kingdom and the United States, and countries in which firms are narrowly held, as in most other countries (Berglöf and von Thadden 1999; La Porta, Lopez-de-Silanes, and Shleifer 1998a). Across Asia, family ownership is predominant and "pyramid" ownership structures and cross-shareholdings often result in opaque

ownership and control (Capulong et al. 2000, 1:23–28; Claessens, Djankov, Fan, and Lang 1999; Claessens, Djankov, and Lang 1999). "Relationship" or "connected" lending by banks is therefore common and is associated with relatively high corporate debt to equity ratios.

21. Note that the relationship between ownership concentration and compliance incentives at the firm level is not linear. At very high levels of ownership concentration owner-managers will have incentives more closely aligned with minority shareholders, leading them to prefer higher quality corporate governance. At moderate levels, owner-managers can have incentives to exploit minority shareholders (Durnev and Kim 2003, 18; Jensen and Meckling 1976). At the opposite extreme in which there are no large shareholders, managers will have incentives to exploit all shareholders and the latter will find it difficult to monitor managers. For many Asian firms, there is a large gap between levels of ownership and control. For example, Shin (2001, 4) estimates that in Korea just prior to the crisis dominant families controlled the top 30 chaebol by holding only 8.5 percent of total shares on average: various complicated intra-group cross-shareholdings facilitated their control, giving them a powerful incentive to use their control to exploit other shareholders.

22. Note this is a form of hybrid market-regulator pressure.

23. As noted in chapter 1, market participants have been generally uninterested in the standards-compliance assessments conducted by the IFIs. Moreover, there appears to be no strong relationship between compliance with key international standards and the credit ratings of banks and other firms (Fitch Ratings 2003b).

24. Some Asian officials believed international banks would charge an extra interest premium when lending to banks in countries that were clearly Basle noncompliant (interviews, Bank of Thailand officials, March 2002; correspondence with Hyoung-kyu Chey, March 2005 re Taiwan). Singapore's and Hong Kong's strategy of marketing themselves as predictable places in which to invest in an otherwise uncertain region suggests there is a belief that regulatory quality can attract investors. One major U.S. institutional investor, CalPERS, took the unusual step of withdrawing its investments from some emerging market countries that it deemed had poor standards of transparency and corporate governance, including Indonesia, Malaysia, China, the Philippines, and Thailand.

25. For example, foreign listings on U.S. stock exchanges require compliance with the provisions of the U.S. Sarbanes-Oxley Act of 2002, including senior executive certifications of financial reports, the prohibition of loans to executives and directors, and other rules relating to audit committee independence.

26. Foreign firm lobbying on Sarbanes-Oxley has so far largely focused on obtaining diplomatic support from home authorities to pressure the American authorities to waive aspects of the 2002 Act, not upon asking home governments to raise domestic corporate governance requirements to American levels. The UK authorities have notably emphasized their intention to resist the adoption of U.S.-style listing standards.

27. For example, Depository Receipts traded on U.S. stock exchanges only trigger U.S. reporting requirements if they are sponsored by the company that issued the original securities.

28. Separately capitalized *subsidiaries* of foreign bank parents are regulated in the same way as domestic banks.

29. See, for example, the provisions in the December 1991 Foreign Bank Supervision Enhancement Act (U.S.).

30. Countries that do not meet the SDDS requirements are publicly listed on the IMF's Dissemination Standards Bulletin Board (DSBB), making private sector monitoring relatively easy. Although the IMF does not claim to monitor in detail the quality of the data placed by the country on the DSBB, various cross-checks embedded in the SDDS framework help to promote substantive compliance.

31. This literature is vast, but see Bird (1996); Gould (2003); Gould-Davies and Woods (1999); IEO (2003); Ivanova et al. (2003); Kahler (1993); Killick (1996); Polak (1990); Stallings (1992); Stone (2004).

32. For example, both Singapore and Hong Kong have adopted bank capitalization standards that are well in excess of international standards as well as international and regional norms.

33. Some individual firms may exceed both domestic and international standards, but this is unlikely to be true on average in developing countries.

34. It will also increase as private sector compliance costs and third party monitoring costs rise.

35. Note that in the empirical chapters I use the international standards that were in place at the time as the relevant benchmarks.

36. See the Deloitte-Touche IAS Plus website, http://www.iasplus.com/country/country.htm.

37. As noted earlier, FSSAs/ROSCs tend to have quantitative assessments of country compliance removed prior to publication. The eStandardsForum provides a six-point scale of compliance with all international standards by country over time, but the assessments are based on publicly available information, mainly published FSSAs/ROSCs, and even a quick perusal reveals that its quality is low. Standard & Poor's, the ratings agency, has provided a corporate governance ratings service for companies and governments in recent years, but few ratings have been undertaken. Since 2002, the World Economic Forum's *Global Competitiveness Report* has included in its annual survey of business executives the results of a question concerning the quality of national accounting and auditing standards, but it is unclear whether responses to this question reflect perceptions of formal standards or the quality of actual practice.

38. Assessing substantive compliance with the former would require detailed consideration of national laws relating to electoral processes, the media, police, employment, and education (among many other things), and investigation of the degree to which legal, political, and social institutions observed and protected the rights of individuals under such laws.

39. However, many individual IFRS often allow considerable flexibility in terms of application.

40. Outside of the core areas of financial regulation (banking, securities, accounting, auditing, and corporate governance), this generalization is less true. For example, London and New York currently share a relatively relaxed attitude to the regulation of hedge funds.

41. Arnold Schilder, "Banks and the Compliance Challenge," speech to the Asian Banker Summit, Bangkok, 16 March 2006, available at: http://www.bis.org/review/r060322d.pdf (accessed 23 March 2006). For example, the international credit rating agencies often compare Asian bank regulatory standards with more stringent U.S. standards (e.g., Fitch Ratings 2003a).

42. I.e., the limits placed on institutional capacity by the level of economic development and the supply of relevant skilled human resources.

43. Indonesia is a partial exception, and here exogenous capacity constraints are more substantial than in the other cases (see chapter 3).

44. The model also implies that compliance outcomes will be of an intermediate quality for the international standards identified in quadrant 3, but for reasons of space I leave the assessment of compliance in these areas aside.

3. Banking Supervision in Indonesia

1. For reviews of the key events, see Blustein (2001, 85–115); Djiwandono (2006); MacIntyre (2003, 91–100); Hamilton-Hart (2000).

2. Indonesia—Memorandum of Economic and Financial Policies, 31 October 1997. http://www.imf.org/external/np/loi/103197.htm#memo.

3. The government's economic team roughly corresponded to BI's Monetary Board, which consisted of the Minister of Finance (Mar'ie Muhammad), the Governor of BI (Soedradjad Djiwandono), the Coordinating Minister of the Economy and Finance (Saleh Afiff), the Coordinating Minister of Industry and Trade (Hartarto), the State Secretary (Moerdiono), and academic experts (Professors Widjojo Nitisastro and Ali Wardhana) (Boediono 2001).

4. Sadli (1998, 275); Blustein (2001, 101); IEO (2003, 28); interviews, Dr. Soedradjad Djiwandono (ex-Governor, Bank Indonesia), Singapore, 14 May 2002; Dr. Tubagus Feridhanusetyawan, Senior Economist, Centre for Strategic and International Studies (CSIS), Jakarta, 27 May 2002.

5. This story has been well summarized in IEO (2003, 29–33) and by MacIntyre (2003, 91–100).

6. Structural conditionality can be divided into short-term measures that must be met before the next review and long-term measures that should be completed by the end of the program (IEO 2003, 75). Commitments made to the IMF are of four main varieties (table 3.1). "Prior actions" are measures required before the Executive Board can consider a program request or review. "Performance criteria" govern disbursement; if they are not met disbursements are automatically interrupted. "Measures" or "targets" have no conditionality attached; many of the various governance reforms fell into this category. "Structural benchmarks" do not directly govern disbursement but trigger discussion on corrective action if not met.

7. Indonesia—Letter of Intent and Memorandum of Economic and Financial Policies, 14 May 1999. http://www.imf.org/external/np/loi/1999/051499.htm.

8. Interviews, Bank Indonesia, Jakarta, May 2002.

9. Indonesia had published only four ROSCs, on data dissemination, accounting/auditing, corporate governance, and fiscal transparency, by November 2006.

10. Confidential interview, IMF staff member, May 2002.

11. I use the Basle Committee's own *Core Principles Methodology* (BCBS 1999) to assess Indonesian compliance in these areas.

12. An IMF technical assistance mission in 1994 examined bank supervision data provided by BI and identified insolvencies in a number of private banks and their recapitalization by cheap loans from BI, to the benefit of well-connected corporations. These findings were not communicated to the Executive Board or even widely discussed within the IMF itself (IEO 2003, 107). The World Bank's independent Operations Evaluation Department (1999, 20) also criticized senior World Bank management for ignoring the conclusions of a staff mission to Jakarta in August 1996. Again, the staff found evidence of extensive and ongoing lending by state-owned and private sector banks to connected debtors and cronies of the regime, high levels of NPLs (over 25 percent of total loans), extensive creative

loan accounting, poor credit assessment standards, and evidence of corruption in the banks and within BI (partly facilitated by a large World Bank loan in the early 1990s for the recapitalization of state-owned banks). The Bank's senior management and executive board rejected the staff report's recommendation that the program be cancelled, on the grounds that this would lose it leverage over the government (Blustein 2001, 94–95; World Bank, Operations Evaluation Department 1999, 1, 56). In short, none of the major players, domestic or international, were willing to lend real support to the efforts of the few reformers within Indonesia to impose tighter financial sector supervision before the crisis.

13. Private banks, which grew rapidly from the 1980s, were often used to channel cheap finance to family firms, with the result that bank owners often became the banks' major debtors. One regulator recalled sending a letter to the largest bank, Bank Central Asia (BCA), in the early 1990s, asking that it observe the new single lending limit rule. However, a powerful crony of Suharto's and head of the Salim Group, Liem Sioe Liong, controlled BCA; the regulator was told to back down in a direct call from Suharto's own office (interview, bank regulator, Jakarta, May 2002).

14. Interview, Dr. Soedradjad Djiwandono, ex-Governor, Bank Indonesia, Singapore, 14 May 2002; Binhadi (1995, 240–41). The internationally recognized CAMELS bank rating system was introduced in February 1991, replacing the previous system. It stands for Capital adequacy, Asset quality, Management, Earnings, Liquidity, and Sensitivity to market risk.

15. LLLs are limits on the amounts bank may loan to single, group and related borrowers, usually expressed as a percentage of bank capital. Only in April 1997 was the CAMELS rating process improved to include compliance with the LLL and net open position limits. Net open positions are calculated as the sum of the absolute value of the net difference between balance sheet assets and liabilities in each currency, plus the net difference in claims and liabilities comprising off-balance sheet commitments and contingencies in each currency.

16. An IMF self-assessment (Lane et al. 1999, 26) subsequently admitted the IMF strategy was ill advised.

17. In late January 1998, with the banking system still hemorrhaging, the GOI was forced to adopt a blanket guarantee of all bank liabilities and assets (including banks' deposits in the liquidated banks). In the increasingly uncertain political environment, however, BLBI continued to expand. In all, 164 banks (two-thirds of the total) received Rp 183 trillion of BLBI from mid-1997 through 1999 (Djiwandono 2002).

18. A Supreme Audit Committee investigation later put the amount of misused funds at Rp 82 trillion (IEO 2003, 121).

19. Governor Syahril Sabirin argued that the case was politically motivated and relied on an ambiguous clause in the new Central Bank Act concerning the requirements for his removal. Here, the adoption of one international standard (legal central bank independence) may therefore have retarded compliance with others.

20. Even after the crisis, most brokerage business involved kickbacks between buyer and seller. Most large privatizations, mergers, and rights issues required participating banks, domestic and foreign, to offer bribes in order to win business (confidential interviews, private sector analysts, Jakarta, May 2002).

21. See IMF (2004b, 33); Robison and Hadiz (2004, 191–95). Both BI and IBRA employees are generally protected against most lawsuits, but they may still be tried if they are found to have acted with criminal negligence (interviews, IBRA, Jakarta, May 2002).

22. BI Regulation No. 1/1/PBI/1999, 18 May 1999.

23. However, note that BI only has the authority to supervise banks and hence does not possess the ability to supervise on a consolidated basis, though it does

require banks to provide consolidated statements that include any nonbank affiliates (interviews, Bank Indonesia, Jakarta, May 2002). The 1999 Central Bank Act assigned BI responsibility for bank supervision on a temporary basis, pending the establishment of an independent financial supervisory agency. Originally scheduled to be established by the end of 2002, it is now to be set up by the end of 2010, at which time all financial sector supervision will be consolidated into a single body.

24. Interview, Bank Indonesia, Jakarta, May 2002. IBRA was established in January 1998.

25. For a brief review of this political transformation, see MacIntyre (2003, 137–49), and Robison, Rodan, and Hewison (2002).

26. This was mainly due to Governor Syahril's refusal to resign in the wake of his indictment in the Bank Bali affair. In addition, BI rejected two of Wahid's appointees as heads of state banks. On the government's long and unsuccessful struggle to remove Syahril, see Robison and Hadiz (2004, chap. 9).

27. Interview, Dr Hadi Soesastro, Executive Director, Centre for Strategic and International Studies (CSIS), Jakarta, 31 May 2002.

28. About Rp 260 trillion of assets still unsold or under negotiation with debtors was transferred to the MOF, with an estimated recovery rate of only 10 percent (World Bank 2004c, 2).

29. Yoshitomi et al. (2003, 103); "Indonesian Banks: Friends and Family," *The Economist,* 18 October 2003; Robison and Hadiz (2004, 198–99).

30. Interviews, IBRA, Jakarta, May 2002.

31. "IBRA installs new management team for BII," *Jakarta Post,* 20 May 2002.

32. Interviews, Centre for Strategic and International Studies (CSIS), and IBRA Oversight Committee (KPPT), Jakarta, May 2002.

33. Loan loss provisioning is a major gap in the BCP and so I use U.S. and UK standards as an international benchmark in this area.

34. Connected lending occurs when a bank lends to a person or entity which can control or significantly influence a bank either directly or indirectly.

35. BI Circular Letter, "Appraisal of Earning Assets for Calculation of Risk-Weighted Assets," No. 2/12/DPNP, 12 June 2000.

36. U.S. bank loan accounting standards moved toward FLC in the early 1990s, followed by IFRS (in the form of IAS 39) and later the Basle Committee (BCBS 1999a). FLC approaches to valuing impaired loans are based upon discounted cash flow (DCF) methods, which require "expected loss provisioning." The relevant U.S. standards are Statements on Financial Accounting Standards [SFAS] 15, 114, and 118 (U.S. OCC 2001, 71; U.S. OCC 2003, 13). Under IAS 39's fair value accounting, gains or losses on loan portfolios may be recognized directly through the income statement, thereby dispensing with loan loss provisioning (see Jackson and Lodge 2000).

37. BI Regulation 7/2/PBI/2005, "Concerning Asset Quality Rating For Commercial Banks," 20 January 2005, 29–30.

38. Interviews, Bank Indonesia, Jakarta, May 2002.

39. Interviews, Bank Mandiri, Jakarta, May 2002.

40. About two-thirds of bank income in 2001–2 came from holdings of government securities and recapitalization bonds (interviews, IMF, May 2002).

41. Interviews, IMF staff, May 2002; IMF 2004b, 20.

42. "Bank Mandiri trial draws closer," *FT.com,* 28 September 2005.

43. Connected borrowers were defined as senior management, commissioners, relatives of these officers, and companies in which these officers hold at least a 25 percent interest (Binhadi 1995, 222–23).

44. "Group" borrowers were defined as companies at least 35 percent owned by another borrowing company or individual.

45. IBRA audits of banks taken over after 1997 showed that an average of about 50 percent of total bank lending was to related parties. Average connected lending was estimated to be nearly 20 times the legal limit (Pangestu and Habir 2002, 26).

46. Interviews, Bank Indonesia, Jakarta, May 2002.

47. "Ruling Allows Depositors to Assess Bank Record," *The Jakarta Post*, 28 December 2001.

48. PricewaterhouseCoopers 2001; "IAS Plus, Country Updates," January 2002. http://www.iasplus.com/country/country.htm (accessed 21 March 2006).

49. Interviews, IMF, Jakarta, May 2002.

50. Bank Indonesia, "Requirement for Commercial Banks to Apply the Standards for the Practice of the Bank Internal Audit Function," Jakarta, 1999.

51. Interview, Bank Indonesia, Jakarta, May 2002.

52. The former are unaudited, while the latter are audited, suggesting that auditors have in some cases forced more negative loan classifications upon banks.

53. See the relatively negative World Bank (2004d) ROSC on Indonesia's corporate governance.

54. Indonesia's institutional investor sector remains very underdeveloped and government-dominated.

55. "The Kiemas Political Agenda," *Laksamana.net*, 3 January 2004.

56. "Indonesia Wins One in War on Corruption," *Asia Times Online*, 31 January 2006; "Looming Large," *Time Asia*, 15 July 2002.

57. Regulation No. 7/2/PBI/2005 on the Valuation of Earning Assets Quality aimed to increase bank lending to SMEs in relatively underdeveloped regions by eliminating the requirement for banks to assess project viability and by extending the scope for use of collateral. BI Regulation No. 7/3/PBI/2005 also raised the maximum LLL for commercial banks to unaffiliated parties from 20 to 25 percent of bank capital for private projects and to 30 percent for government infrastructure projects implemented by SOEs.

58. "Probe launched into Bank Mandiri Loans," *FT.com*, 13 April 2005.

59. "Indonesia State Bank Arrests," *FT.com*, 18 July 2005.

60. Note that Hamilton-Hart's focus is largely upon the effectiveness of regulatory outcomes rather than compliance *per se*. She also explains why administrative capacity varied widely across different policy areas.

61. Interviewees generally concurred that capacity problems were not the main obstacle to improved regulation and supervision (Bank Indonesia, IBRA, CSIS, and Bank Mandiri, Jakarta, May 2002).

62. BI's relative financial independence compared to IBRA may have contributed to the apparently lower incidence of regulatory failures in the former.

63. Specific areas in which IMF pressure was important include the provision of monthly bank financial data on the BI website, permanent on-site bank supervisors, and consistent loan classification for group debtors.

4. Corporate Governance in Thailand

1. The PCG, including in their revised 2004 form, explicitly recognized both the "Anglo-Saxon" shareholder model and the "Continental" stakeholder model of corporate governance. This also makes them difficult to use for compliance

assessment purposes. The World Bank (2005a) "template" for country corporate governance assessments (ROSCs) raises virtually all of the issues that are prominent in contemporary corporate governance debates, but does relatively little benchmarking against specific international standards. Thailand's first ROSC, on corporate governance, was published in June 2005 (World Bank 2005b).

2. For example, on the central issue of ensuring board independence from management, the PCG tentatively state that "[b]oards should consider assigning a sufficient number of non-executive board members capable of exercising independent judgment to tasks where there is a potential for conflict of interest" (OECD 2004, 25). The New York Stock Exchange (NYSE), in contrast, required listed companies to have "independent" directors on their boards and provided detailed rules specifying the nature of such independence. Since 2003, NYSE required such independent directors to be in a majority. Most Asian countries still lag this U.S. standard, but most specified minimum numbers or proportions of independent directors on company boards and adopted U.S.-style language on independence (OECD 2003, 88). For NYSE rules, see "Section 303A: Corporate Governance Rules," 3 November 2004, 4–7. http://www.nyse.com/pdfs/section303A_final_rules.pdf (accessed 30 May 2005).

3. SET, "Qualifications of Independent Directors," Bor.Jor./Ror.01–05, 28 October 1993.

4. Major corporate families included Chearavanont (CP Group), Sophonpanich (Bangkok Bank), Lamsam (Thai Farmers Bank), Karnasutra (Italian-Thai), Shinawatra (telecommunications), Bhirombhakdi (Boon Rawd Brewery), Bodharamik (Jasmine International), Leophairatana (Thai Petrochemical Industries), Ratanarak (Siam City Cement, Bank of Ayudhya), Asavabhokin (Land & Houses), Kanjanapas (Bangkok Land). See "Crisis Wipes Out Thai Billionaires," *Bangkok Post*, 22 June 1998.

5. Interviews, Internal Auditors' Association of Thailand, and Thailand Development Research Institute (TDRI), Bangkok, March 2002.

6. Note that the "minority" term can be misleading, since outside shareholders are often in a numerical and ownership majority. Hence, I generally use the latter term, except when referring to real minorities.

7. Improvements to Thailand's corporate governance framework were stressed in the first and fourth Letters of Intent to the IMF of 14 August 1997 and 26 May 1998. http://www.imf.org/external/np/loi/081497.htm and http://www.imf.org/external/np/loi/052698.htm (accessed 16 June 2005).

8. Outside or independent directors are those with no managerial, financial, or personal linkages to a company's owners or managers.

9. Stricter Asian standards on shareholder rights are intended to redress the historical weakness of outside shareholders in Asian countries.

10. SET, "The Principles of Good Corporate Governance," 2002. http://www.set.or.th/en/education/infoserv/files/CG15-ENG.pdf (accessed 1 June 2005).

11. See KSE 2003, s.48–5(1).

12. Interviews, SEC, 7 March 2002.

13. Richard Moore, PricewaterhouseCoopers, "Good Corporate Governance: Is it a Realistic Ambition?," n.d. http://www.pwcglobal.com/extweb/manissue.nsf/DocID/5370299E1F7C269C85256922003428BF (accessed March 15, 2002).

14. Companies are also prohibited from making loans to directors and executives.

15. The SEC does require remuneration committees for listed companies with employee share ownership programs (ESOPs) that offer shares to managers at a discounted price (interviews, SEC, 7 March 2002).

16. "New Rule to Demand Nominee Disclosure," *Bangkok Post*, 18 July 2003.

17. Until 1999, inspection was the job of the SET (interviews, SEC, March 2002).

18. SET, "Rules and Procedures and Disclosure of Connected Transactions for Listed Companies," Bor.Jor./Por.22–00, 17 February 1993; DFAT (2002, 2:125).

19. SET, "Disclosure of Information and Act of Listed Companies Concerning the Connected Transactions," Bor.Jor./Por.22–01, 19 November 2003.

20. Under cumulative voting, shareholders may cast all of their votes for contested board seats for a single candidate. Compared to seat-by-seat voting, this system can allow minority shareholders to obtain board representation.

21. A class action is a lawsuit in which one representative sues a defendant(s) on behalf of others who have suffered a similar kind of harm.

22. A derivative action is a lawsuit brought by a shareholder on behalf of the corporation, generally to enforce action against senior management or directors in the event that the corporation fails to enforce its rights against such parties.

23. The Corporate Library, *News Brief* 4, no. 44 (4–10 December 2002).

24. "Minister Curbs Bank of Thailand Powers," *FT.com*, 2 June 2005.

25. The Banking Act of 1962 limits an individual's ownership of bank equity to 5 percent of the total, including shareholdings by companies controlled by that individual, spouse, or minor child. However, this limit does not apply to other family members. Various pyramiding and cross-ownership structures meant that families were able to control banks in practice.

26. In order to provide a picture of substantive compliance, CLSA analysts are asked to make some subjective judgments about the quality of a company's corporate governance (CLSA Emerging Markets 2003, 11–12).

27. Standard and Poor's (2004a, 7, 2004b, 3, 2004c, 7). The minimum individual company score was only 4 for Thailand compared to 16 for Singapore (in which 45 companies were studied).

28. The SEC noted the publication of the World Bank ROSC on its homepage for months, claiming that "the report has proven that Thailand is on its way to fully comply with international principles of corporate governance." This is a generous interpretation even by the World Bank's standards. http://www.sec.or.th/en/index.php (accessed 28 March 2006).

29. Certainly, there are exceptions to this generalization (see CLSA Emerging Markets 2005, 84–86). For example, Siam Cement and Siam Commercial Bank, in which the Thai royal family's Crown Property Bureau have large stakes, have very good reputations for corporate governance.

30. Interview, Dr. Pisit Leeahtam, Professor of Finance, ex-deputy finance minister, Chulalongkorn University, 6 March 2002.

31. The constitutional reforms of late 1997 played an important role, with changes in the electoral system strengthening political parties and reducing their number (MacIntyre 2003, 149–51).

32. This said, Thaksin's election strategy was to win sufficient votes from rural voters through a series of populist promises (Hewison 2005; Robison, Rodan, and Hewison 2002; Pasuk and Baker 2003).

33. For example, the government announced a new corporate governance committee in 2002 (designated the "Year of Corporate Governance"), chaired by the prime minister and including representatives from the SET, SEC, MOF, and accounting bodies. It had little impact.

34. "Thailand: Prime Minister Mixes Business and Politics," *Far Eastern Economic Review*, 11 December 2003; "The Deal of the Century," *The Nation* (Bangkok).

http://www.nationmultimedia.com/specials/shincorp/ (accessed 27 March 2006); "Ample Rich Transaction Raises Questions," *FT.com*, 1 February 2006.

35. There are grounds for doubting the verdicts of both the SEC and the Constitutional Court. Required by the electoral laws to disclose assets under his control, Thaksin and his wife had transferred most of their 35 percent stake in Shin Corp to their children and Thaksin's brother-in-law just before the election to meet a Thai law preventing cabinet members from holding stakes in companies that benefit from government policy. Thaksin also claimed no knowledge that his personal driver, maid, and security guard also held substantial shares in his family's companies.

36. "Disposal Would Give Thaksin Maximum Mileage," *FT.com*, 12 January 2006.

37. See http://capital.sec.or.th/webapp/webnews/news.php?id=&cboType=S&news_id=1774&sdate=2006-03-10 (accessed 24 March 2006).

38. Currently, the Minister of Finance is chairman of the SEC Board, on which the permanent secretaries of the Ministries of Finance and Commerce also sit. To pursue criminal violations of the code, the SEC must file a complaint with the police or the Department of Justice's Department of Special Investigation (World Bank 2005b, 4). The probability of such a complaint being filed against one of the prime minister's family in the Thaksin era was close to zero.

39. Due to the weak stock market incentives to improve corporate governance, the Thai SEC has worked with the SET and Thailand Rating and Information Services (TRIS) to provide administrative incentives to improve corporate governance. If listed companies obtain a high corporate governance rating from TRIS, the SEC and SET oblige with reduced listing fees, fast track approvals, tax benefits, etc. Needless to say, the effects of this initiative have been disappointing.

40. Adam Bryant, "A Plan for Foreign Corporate Accountability," *New York Times*, 2 April 1998, D4.

41. This was focused on Temasek's takeover of Shin Corp in 2006, though the military government that replaced Thaksin's announced that it would also seek to reduce foreign ownership levels in a range of sectors ("Thailand acts to reassure foreign investors," *FT.com*, 18 January 2007).

5. Banking Supervision and Corporate Governance in Malaysia

1. Dr. Mahathir made way for his successor, Abdullah Ahmad Badawi, in October 2003.

2. Prime Minister Mahathir Bin Mohamad, "Budget Speech 1999," 23 October 1998. http://www.treasury.gov.my/englishversionbaru/index.htm (accessed 1 October 2003).

3. See Ministry of Finance (Malaysia) (1999, 39–40).

4. Malaysian representatives were involved in the negotiation of the BCP over 1996–97 and in regional meetings of APEC finance ministers (interviews, Australian Embassy, Jakarta, May 2002).

5. Malaysia's corporate sector was mostly indebted to domestic banks, in contrast to Indonesia. In 1996, only 4 percent of net financing was from foreign banks. This meant that the relationship between exchange rate depreciation (the ringgit depreciated about 40 percent against the U.S. dollar from July 1997 to July 1998)

and the solidity of private sector balance sheets was much less toxic for Malaysia than for Indonesia, Thailand, and Korea.

6. The United Malays National Organisation was in turn dominated by Dr. Mahathir since he became prime minister in 1981 and UMNO President in 1982.

7. Bank Bumiputera's finance subsidiary, Bumiputera Malaysia Finance, lost large sums due to mismanagement and fraud in the early 1980s in a major scandal that severely weakened its parent bank and eventually brought to light the group's deep political connections (see Hamilton-Hart 2002, 119–21).

8. "IMF Concludes 2002 Article IV Consultation With Malaysia," *IMF Public Information Notice No. 02/135,* 10 December 2002. http://www.imf.org/external/np/sec/pn/2002/pn02135.htm (accessed 29 September 2003).

9. Remarks by Mr. Awang Adek Hussin, Assistant Governor, BNM, in ADBI (2000, 4).

10. Corporate governance in the banking sector is addressed in section 2.

11. Unusually, the issue is avoided on the BNM and MOF websites (though in various places BNM emphasizes the need for supervised banks to have independent boards).

12. Prime Minister Mahathir Bin Mohamad, "Budget Speech 1999," 23 October 1998. http://www.treasury.gov.my/englishversionbaru/index.htm (accessed 1 October 2003). The NEAC's blueprint for reform, released in July 1998, promoted a "balanced" reform agenda that aimed at improving transparency, recapitalizing weak banks, etc., as well as maintaining equity and socio-economic harmony.

13. Anwar himself had long been associated with the NEP and had his own links to the business sector (Case 2005, 288).

14. Danaharta (2003, Appendix 2). Note that the bulk of these NPLs were managed on behalf of the government rather than purchased outright by Danaharta.

15. Danaharta expected to achieve a total recovery rate (net of defaults) of 59 percent by the time it was wound up in 2005. See Danaharta, *Operations Report,* 31 December 2002. http://www.danaharta.com.my/default.html (accessed 10 March 2003); Danaharta, "Within Sight of the Finishing Line," press release, 11 March 2005; IMF (2004c, 35).

16. "Rebranding Mahathir," *Asiaweek,* 29 June 2001; Matthew Montagu-Pollock, "Change at Last in Malaysia," *Asiamoney: GIC Daily Bulletin,* 29 January 2002.

17. Estandards Forum, *Weekly Report* 2, no. 35 (29 April–3 May 2002): 7.

18. "Mahathir Is Hinting at Exceptions: Malaysia Uncertain on Bank Overhaul," *International Herald Tribune,* 7 October 1999.

19. "Malaysian Regulator Plays Crucial Role in Bank Merger," *FT.com,* 13 March 2006.

20. E.g., BNM does not allow the inclusion of deferred tax assets as capital for purposes of calculation of risk-weighted CARs, in marked contrast to Japan (BNM 2003, 124).

21. Prime Minister Mahathir Bin Mohamad, "Budget Speech 1999," 23 October 1998. http://www.treasury.gov.my/englishversionbaru/index.htm (accessed 1 October 2003).

22. From December 1997, BNM calculated the NPL to total loan ratio by subtracting interest in suspense and specific provisions from the gross NPL figure. This has the effect of reducing reported NPLs by 3–4 percentage points. The NPL figures reported in figure 5.1 are re-adjusted to take this into account.

23. The latter is generally recognized to have played a key role in promoting voluntary debt restructuring in Malaysia's corporate sector. See "Caught up in Court," *The Economist*, 4 January 2003.

24. BNM, "Banking Measures," 23 September 1998. http://www.bnm.gov.my/index.php?ch=8&pg=14&ac=497 (accessed 30 September 2003).

25. Public Bank Berhad, *2005 Annual Report*, 220.

26. For example, in October 2003 Moody's weighted average Bank Financial Strength Rating (BFSR) was D+ for Malaysian banks, compared to E+ in Indonesia, D– in Thailand and Korea, and B in Singapore and Australia (Moody's Investor Services 2004, 20). The scale is from A (strongest) to E (weakest).

27. BNM, "Stabilization Package for the Financial Sector," 25 March 1998. http://www.bnm.gov.my/index.php?ch=8&pg=14&ac=466 (accessed 13 October 2003).

28. In April 2004, KLSE changed its name to Bursa Malaysia. To avoid confusion I refer to KLSE throughout.

29. Unfortunately, these ROSCs, especially the most recent one, focus largely on assessing formal rather than substantive compliance.

30. Indeed, when UMNO moved later to promote inward FDI in the manufacturing sector, foreign firms were increasingly exempted from the bumiputera ownership provisions of the ICA. The absence of similar protection for the Chinese business community led many Chinese family firms to partner with bumiputera interests (Khoo 2001, 187–88).

31. http://www.sc.com.my/eng/html/cg/implementation.html#imp_rep_FI (accessed 31 March 2006); CLSA Emerging Markets (2005, 62).

32. The Malaysian Institute of Directors also provides training in corporate governance issues (World Bank 1999, s.2).

33. Also, under the Companies Act, interested parties are *not* required to abstain, creating a conflict and enforcement problem (World Bank 2005c, 6).

34. KLSE, "New Measures to Enhance Transparency," 31 August 1998. http://www.mir.com.my/lb/econ_plan/contents/press_release/klse.htm (accessed 6 April 2004).

35. "Behind Daim's Fall," *Far Eastern Economic Review*, 27 June 2002; Matthew Montagu-Pollock, "Change at Last in Malaysia," *GIC Daily Bulletin*, 29 January 2002.

36. eStandardsForum, *Weekly Report* 3, no. 17 (6–10 January 2003). However, note that data on fines, reprimands, etc., can point both ways: it could mean more effective enforcement or increased incidence of noncompliant corporate behavior.

37. http://www.sc.com.my/eng/html/cg/imp_rep_66–70.html (accessed 31 March 2006).

38. One possible indicator of this is the length of shareholder meetings, which tend to be largely perfunctory in most countries. A recent survey of major listed companies in four countries found that "[m]ore than 70% of shareholders' meetings in Malaysia run longer than an hour, while the percentage stands at 23% in Korea, 30% in Thailand, and 35% in Indonesia" (Nam and Nam 2004, 65).

39. Of 42 Malaysian companies surveyed, 7 were banks.

40. Standard and Poor's (2004a, 7; 2004b, 3; 2004c, 7). The minimum score was only 4 for Thailand compared to 44 for Malaysia and 16 for Singapore (in which 45 companies were studied). Another survey reflects the general opinion that corporate governance in Malaysia has been better than in the other crisis-hit countries, but still middling by international standards (Nam and Nam 2004, 97–101).

41. Some large family-owned companies have strong corporate governance reputations, including Public Bank Berhad and RBH (CLSA Emerging Markets 2005, 63).

42. Again, the exception was CalPERS, the U.S. institutional investor, which stated its intention in 1998 not to invest in Malaysian companies because of firm- and political-level governance failures.

6. *Banking Supervision, Corporate Governance, and Financial Disclosure in Korea*

1. MOFE, "Korea: A New Model Economy Beyond the Crisis," November 2002, 2–4. http://english.mofe.go.kr/publications/view.html?sn=2621&sub=01&page=2&q=&flag= (accessed 22 June 2005). As Lee et al. (2005, 24) point out, the delegitimation of the pre-crisis Korean model was made easier by the fact that it lacked a clear theoretical economic foundation, in contrast to the neoliberal alternative.

2. Interview, Dr. Buhm-soo Choi, Advisor to the Director, Financial Supervisory Commission (FSC), Seoul, Korea, 20 September 2000.

3. Ibid.

4. "Korea—Letter of Intent to the IMF," 3 December 1997. http://www.imf.org/external/country/KOR/index.htm?pn=11.

5. Interview, Dr. Kap-soo Oh, Assistant Governor, Financial Supervisory Service, 20 September 2000.

6. The views of western critics of the IMF packages, such as Jeffrey Sachs, Martin Feldstein, and Robert Wade also received much attention in the local press, itself heavily dependent upon chaebol advertising revenue (Yoon 2000).

7. The latter was Jeffrey Jones, formerly the head of American Chamber of Commerce in Seoul and a senior partner of Kim & Chang, the largest law firm in Korea.

8. Interviews, MOFE, Seoul, September 2000.

9. E.g., see the claims by the FSS Governor in "Foreword" to FSS (2002b).

10. Korean rules did not distinguish between general and special provisions until 1994 (Chey 2006, chap. 6).

11. This paragraph draws on interviews with current and former regulators, Seoul, September 2000.

12. Helpfully, the IMF published an FSSA report on Korea in March 2003 (IMF 2003a). Financial disclosure in the banking sector is discussed in section 4.

13. "Act on the Establishment of Financial Supervisory Organizations," chap. 4, sec. 1, articles 61, 62.

14. Interview, Dr. Kap-soo Oh, Assistant Governor, Financial Supervisory Service, 20 September 2000.

15. The FSS argues that it covers legal expenses for criminal and civil lawsuits against their staff for work-related actions (IMF 2003a, 38). However, this may not provide sufficient reassurance for such staff.

16. Interviews, FSC, Seoul, September 2000.

17. Ibid.

18. Concerns were also raised that the proposed sale of two nationalized Daewoo creditor banks, Korea First and Seoul Bank, to foreign investors would reduce the government's ability to manage the Daewoo crisis (Haggard 2000, 150; Noland 2000b, 235–36).

19. On the Big Deal, see "Agreement for the Restructuring of the Top 5 Chaebol," 7 December 1998. http://wfile.fss.or.kr/data1/en/nws/981208-1.html (accessed September 7, 2004).

20. An intra-family dispute led to Hyundai group's partial breakup in August 2001.

21. This evidence was part of a U.S. countervailing duty investigation that found in favor of Micron Technologies, who petitioned that Hynix received unfair government subsidies over this period (U.S. ITA 2003, 7).

22. Pirie (2005, 34) claims that the regulatory authorities imposed "hard budget constraints" on Daewoo and Hyundai, ignoring that the authorities tried hard to avoid their collapse.

23. U.S. ITA (2003, 34).

24. Banks with CARs of at least 10 percent were designated as "first class" and subject to lighter supervision (interviews, FSC, Seoul, September 2000).

25. Initially, Won 64 trillion was injected into the financial sector over 1998–99. Further public funds were employed in a second round of financial restructuring after the Daewoo bankruptcy. In total, Won 168 trillion in public funds were used by May 2005, of which Won 76 trillion was recouped (MOFE, "Public Fund Operations as of End May 2005," 27 June 2005).

26. Korean Financial Supervisory Service, *Weekly Newsletter* 1, no. 24 (16 September 2000): 2–4.

27. FSS, "Strengthening of Loan Classification and Provisioning," 1 July 1998, *FSS Press Release*, no. 10.

28. However, the weaker nonbank financial institution (NBFI) sector was permitted to delay the implementation of FLC until June 2000, due to fears of its impact on growth (FSC interviews, Seoul, September 2000).

29. Banks are required to identify all customers whose capacity to repay interest and principal is potentially impaired and then to decide the amount of each loan that is likely to be collected. These expected repayments are then placed in the Substandard category. The net difference between estimated repayments and the loan's face value is placed in Doubtful or Estimated Loss categories, with the latter reserved for assets that are unlikely to be collected. Banks are expected to make provisions in excess of the minimum required ratio for each category.

30. However, the value and liquidity of collateral in Korea and the United States is taken into account in the classification of loans (since it can affect the DCF value of the loan). The FSS requires banks to set clear criteria for establishing the market value of collateral, taking into account recovery fees, the illiquidity of real estate collateral, etc. Korean collateral valuation practices are relatively conservative and the bankruptcy and legal regimes relatively efficient (Song 2002, 14).

31. Interviews, MOFE, September 2000.

32. The BOK defines the interest coverage ratio as: operating income/interest expenses x 100.

33. The gap ratio is (foreign currency assets—foreign currency liabilities)/ total foreign assets. The minimum is 0 percent for maturities of up to 7 days and –10 percent for maturities of up to one month.

34. KDB and Export-Import Bank still exceeded the 25 percent large exposure limit as of December 2005. See http://efisis.fss.or.kr/index.html (accessed 3 April 2006). The development banks were exempted from many of the most important of Korea's prudential rules (FSS 2002a, chap. 9).

35. FSS Press Release, "Findings of General Examination on Kookmin Bank," 10 September 2004, FSC/FSS, Seoul.

36. For an exception, see Jun and Gong (1995).

37. In 1997, 87 percent of total financing by the top 11–30 chaebol, the largest borrowers, consisted of short-term debt (Capulong et al. 2000, 2:125).

38. Cash flow rights are the claims on cash payouts that accrue proportionally to all shareholders; control rights derive from the ability of some shareholders to control the election of directors and other major corporate decisions in excess of their direct share ownership.

39. "Korea—Letter of Intent," 3 December 1997. http://www.imf.org/external/np/loi/120397.htm#memo (accessed 12 August 2003).

40. Notably in the 7 February 1998 LOI: "Korea—Letter of Intent and Memorandum of Economic Policies, 7 February 1998." http://www.imf.org/external/np/loi/020798.htm (accessed 12 August 2003).

41. Dr. Kap-Soo Oh, "Increasing Transparency and Corporate Governance," speech to the American Chamber of Commerce in Seoul, 11 December 2002.

42. Hahn-koo Lee, President, FKI, "Fallacies of the IMF Era," *Korean Focus*, May/June 1998.

43. "Large" companies were defined as those with assets greater than 2 trillion won (KSE 2003, s.48–5[1]).

44. Interviews, MOFE, Seoul, September 2000.

45. "Outside Directors Poor in Monitoring Management," *The Korea Herald*, 30 November 2000.

46. Against strong chaebol opposition, the government also moved in October 2000 to restrict large shareholders to a 3 percent maximum share when voting on cumulative voting. This limit now also applies to voting on the election of an auditor or audit committee member.

47. Cho Young-sam, "Seoul to Work Out Corporate Governance Bill," *The Korea Herald*, 22 October 2000.

48. "Samsung Best in Corporate Governance," *The Korea Herald*, 4 February 2002.

49. "Shareholder Activists Call for Tougher Steps to Monitor Chaebol Owners," *The Korea Herald*, 31 March 2000.

50. "Seoul Decides to Phase in Class-Action Suit System," *The Korea Herald*, 28 October 2000.

51. "Compromise clears way to class-action suits in '04," *Joong Ang Daily*, 3 June 2003; IMF (2003a, 63–64, 65).

52. For a description of PSPD's major activities and actions in this area, see http://eng.peoplepower21.org/contents/actionbody_economy.html (accessed 8 July 2005).

53. "Sovereign Asset Sells Entire Stake in SK Corp," *FT.com*, 17 July 2005.

54. "Korean Report Hails Foreign Influence," *FT.com*, 26 March 2004.

55. The chaebol mouthpiece, the FKI, continued to criticize the government's "blind acceptance" of Western corporate governance standards ("Hostile Reform," *Korea Times*, 19 May 2004).

56. The limit on intra-group voting rights of financial subsidiaries is to be reduced from 30 percent to 15 percent by 2008. Chaebol with more than Won 6 trillion in assets will also be prohibited from investing more than 25 percent of net assets in other companies, including intra-group companies ("Regulator Hits Back at Samsung Group," *FT.com*, 1 July 2005).

57. Dr. Kap-Soo Oh, "Increasing Transparency and Corporate Governance," speech to the American Chamber of Commerce in Seoul, 11 December 2002.

58. As noted in chapter 1, IAS/IFRS and U.S. GAAP standards have competed for some time for international best-practice status, though there has been recent

convergence between the two. I focus primarily on convergence upon the former, but note that the Korean authorities themselves have explicitly used U.S. GAAP as a joint convergence benchmark.

59. Dr. Kap-Soo Oh, "Increasing Transparency and Corporate Governance," speech to the American Chamber of Commerce in Seoul, 11 December 2002.

60. Korea—Letter of Intent, 2 May 1998. http://www.imf.org/external/np/loi/050298.htm (accessed 12 August 2003).

61. FSC/SFC, "Reform of Accounting Standards in Korea," 11 December 1998. http://wfile.fss.or.kr/data1/en/nws/reform1.html (accessed 27 September 2004).

62. See http://www.iasplus.com/country/korea.htm (accessed 18 June 2007).

63. The list of new accounting articles, issued April 1 1998, is available at http://www.kasb.or.kr/enghome.nsf (accessed 4 April 4, 2006).

64. FSC, "Standards for the Combined Financial Statements." http://wfile.fss.or.kr/data1/en/nws/enbodo17.htm (accessed 7 April 2004).

65. The companies were ranked by market capitalization in September 2004. The sixth largest company, Korea Telecom, was discarded because of the poor quality of its English financial reports.

66. See World Economic Forum (2003, 610), and later issues through 2006.

67. eStandardsForum, *Weekly Report* 3, no. 28 (24–28 March 2003).

68. "The Securities and Futures Commission Takes Disciplinary Measures Against Kookmin Bank for Accounting Irregularities," FSS Press Release, 30 August 2004; FSS, "Weekly Newsletter" 5, no. 37 (24 September 2004).

69. Korean auditing standards are set by KICPA and are essentially translations of International Standards on Auditing.

70. The second-largest bank, Shinhan, was omitted because it did not provide full annual reports in English.

71. From January 2001, such information was required for specific risks.

72. Recognizing these shortcomings, KASB drafted a new accounting standard for financial institutions, SKAS 24, effective from end-2006 (see IMF 2003a, 35).

73. "S. Korea Steps up its Efforts to Become a Hub," *FT.com*, 11 April 2006.

74. Chul-kyu Kang, Chairman, Korea Fair Trade Commission, "How to Overcome the Korea Discount?," speech to the Asia Society, 13 May 2004. http://ftc.go.kr/data/hwp/asia%20society_written%20remark%20by%20chul-kyu%20kang.doc (accessed 4 April 2006); IIF (2003, 5).

7. *Practical and Theoretical Implications*

1. At the time, Moody's stand-alone financial strength ratings for Thai banks ranged from E+ to D, that is, at the very weak end of the spectrum, but their standard credit ratings were much higher. Similarly, in February 2005 Moody's assigned long-term senior debt ratings of A1 to most major Japanese banks ("investment grade"), but gave these same banks stand-alone ratings of E+ to D (Moody's Investor Services 2005).

2. As of 6 February 2005, only 25 companies had been rated, 14 of which were from Russia.

3. After the demise of Suharto in May 1998.

4. For the Thai case, see "Economic Nationalism Grips Thailand," *FT.com*, 27 February 2007. Recent Korean examples include the regulatory suspension of Deutsche Bank by the Korean authorities in June 2005 for selling complex

derivatives to SOEs that went bad ("S Korea Set to Suspend Deutsche," *FT.com*, 25 June 2005), and the pressure on the government to take action against perceived profiteering by foreign investors in Korea ("Seoul raids Lone Star on Tax Evasion Charges," *FT.com*, 30 March 2006).

5. Note that the regime literature commonly distinguishes compliance from "regime effectiveness," the latter being the extent to which an international regime achieves its main goals. See Shelton (2003, 5); Keohane, Haas, and Levy (1993); Young (1994, 142–52); Young and Levy (1999).

6. For an application to the Japanese case in recent years, see Walter (2006).

7. As noted previously, family and state corporate ownership and relatively bank-based financial systems are shared characteristics of most developing countries, not just Asian ones.

8. Interviews, Asian regulators, 2002.

9. Arnold Schilder, "Banks and the compliance challenge," speech to the Asian Banker Summit, Bangkok, 16 March 2006. http://www.bis.org/review/r060322d.pdf (accessed 23 March 2006).

References

ADBI (Asian Development Bank Institute). 2000. "High-Level Dialogue on Banking Regulation and Financial Market Development: New Issues in the Post-Crisis Recovery Phase." *ADBI Executive Summary Series,* No. S36/01, 8–9 June.

Amsden, Alice. 1989. *Asia's Next Giant: South Korea and Late Industrialization.* New York: Oxford University Press.

Amyx, Jennifer A. 2004. *Japan's Financial Crisis: Institutional Rigidity and Reluctant Change.* Princeton: Princeton University Press.

APEC Economic Committee. 1999. "APEC Economies beyond the Asian Crisis." APEC Secretariat, Singapore.

Asian Policy Forum. 2001. *Designing New and Balanced Financial Market Structures in Post-Crisis Asia.* Tokyo: APF/ADB Institute, October.

Aviram, Amitai. 2003. "Regulation by Networks." *John M. Olin Law & Economics Working Paper,* No. 181. University of Chicago Law School, March.

Ayers, Ian, and John Braithwaite. 1992. *Responsive Regulation: Transcending the Deregulation Debate.* New York: Oxford University Press.

Baliño, Tomàs Jose, and Angel Ubide. 1999. "The Korean Financial Crisis of 1997: A Strategy of Financial Sector Reform." *IMF Working Paper,* No. 99/28, March.

Barth, James R., Gerard Caprio, Jr., and Ross Levine. 2002. "Bank Regulation and Supervision Database." World Bank.

——. 2006. *Rethinking Bank Regulation: Till Angels Govern.* New York: Cambridge University Press.

Barton, Dominic, Paul Coombes, and Simon Chiu-Yin Wong. 2004. "Transparency: Asia's Governance Challenge." *McKinsey Quarterly* 2:54–61.

BCBS (Basle Committee on Banking Supervision). 1988. *International Convergence of Capital Measurement and Capital Standards.* Basle: BCBS, July.

——. 1991a. *Measuring and Controlling Large Credit Exposures.* Basle: BCBS, January.

——. 1991b. *Amendment of the Basle Capital Accord in Respect of the Inclusion of General Provisions/General Loan-Loss Reserves in Capital.* Basle: BCBS, November.

——. 1997. *Core Principles for Banking Supervision.* Basle: BCBS, September.

——. 1998. *Enhancing Bank Transparency.* Basle: BCBS, September.

BCBS (Basle Committee on Banking Supervision). 1999a. *Sound Practices for Loan Accounting and Disclosure.* Basle: BCBS, July.

——. 1999b. *Best Practices for Credit Risk Disclosures.* Basle: BCBS, July.

——. 1999c. *Enhancing Corporate Governance for Banking Organizations.* Basle: BCBS, September.

——. 1999d. *Core Principles Methodology.* Basle: BCBS, October.

——. 1999e. *Recommendations for Public Disclosure of Trading and Derivatives Activities of Banks and Securities Firms.* Basle: BCBS/IOSCO Technical Committee Joint Paper, October.

——. 2002. *Supervisory Guidance on Dealing with Weak Banks.* Basle: BCBS, March.

——. 2005. *International Convergence of Capital Measurement and Capital Standards: A Revised Framework.* Basle: BCBS, November).

Bebchuk, Lucian A., and Mark J. Roe. 1999. "A Theory of Path Dependence in Corporate Governance and Ownership." *Columbia Center for Law and Economic Studies,* Working Paper No. 131, November.

Beck, Thorsten, Asli Demirgüç-Kunt, and Ross Levine. 1999. "A New Database on Financial Development and Structure." *World Bank,* June.

——. 2003. "Bank Supervision and Corporate Finance." *World Bank Policy Research Working Paper,* No. 3042, May.

Beeson, Mark, and Iyanatul Islam. 2005. "Neo-liberalism and East Asia: Resisting the Washington Consensus." *Journal of Development Studies* 41 (2): 197–219.

Bennett, Colin J. 1991. "Review Article: What Is Policy Convergence and What Causes It?" *British Journal of Political Science* 21 (2): 215–33.

Berger, Peter L., and H. H. Michael Hsaio, eds. 1987. *In Search of an East Asian Developmental Model.* New Brunswick, NJ: Transaction Books.

Berglöf, Erik, and Ernst-Ludwig von Thadden. 1999. "The Changing Corporate Governance Paradigm: Implications for Transition and Developing Countries." *SITE Working Paper,* June.

BI (Bank Indonesia). 2000. *Annual Report 2000.* Jakarta: BI.

——. 2002. *Annual Report 2002.* Jakarta: BI.

——. 2004. *Financial Stability Review.* Jakarta: BI. No. 1, June.

——. 2005. *Banking Supervision Report, December 2004.* Jakarta: BI, March.

Binhadi. 1995. *Financial Sector Deregulation, Banking Development and Monetary Policy: The Indonesian Experience 1983–1993.* Jakarta: Institut Bankir Indonesia.

Bird, Graham. 1996. "The International Monetary Fund and Developing Countries: A Review of the Evidence and Policy Options." *International Organization* 50 (3): 477–511.

Black, Bernard S., Barry Metzger, Timothy O'Brien, and Young Moo Shin. 2001. "Corporate Governance in Korea at the Millennium: Enhancing International Competitiveness, Final Report and Legal Reform Recommendations to the Ministry of Justice of the Republic of Korea," *Journal of Corporation Law* 26 (2001): 537–608.

Blue Ribbon Committee. 1999. *Improving the Effectiveness of Corporate Audit Committees.* New York: New York Stock Exchange and National Association of Securities Dealers, February.

Blustein, Paul. 2001. *The Chastening: Inside the Crisis that Rocked the Global Financial System and Humbled the IMF.* New York: Public Affairs.

Blyth, Mark. 2002. *Great Transformations: Economic Ideas and Institutional Change in the Twentieth Century.* Cambridge, UK: Cambridge University Press.

BNM (Bank Negara Malaysia). 2000. *Annual Report 2000.* Kuala Lumpur: BNM.

——. 2001. *Annual Report 2001.* Kuala Lumpur: BNM.

——. 2002. *Annual Report 2002.* Kuala Lumpur: BNM.

——. 2003. *Annual Report 2003.* Kuala Lumpur: BNM.

BNM (Bank Negara Malaysia). 2005. *Annual Report 2005*. Kuala Lumpur: BNM.

Boediono. 2001. "The Fund-Supported Program in Indonesia: Comparing its Implementation Under Three Regimes." Remarks at a seminar on IMF conditionality, Tokyo, 10 July.

BOK (Bank of Korea). 2004. *Financial Statement Analysis for 2003*. Seoul: Bank of Korea, August.

Boorman, Jack, Timothy D. Lane, Marianne Schulze-Gattas, Aleš Bulir, Atish R. Ghosh, A. Javier Hamann, Alex Mourmouras, and Steven Phillips. 2000. "Managing Financial Crises—The Experience in East Asia." *IMF Working Paper*, No. 00/107, June.

Boorman, Jack, and Andrea Richter Hume. 2003. "Life with the IMF: Indonesia's Choices for the Future." Paper presented at the 15th Congress of the Indonesian Economists Association, Malang, Indonesia, July 15.

BOT (Bank of Thailand). 2000. *Supervision Report*. Bangkok: BOT.

——. 2002. "Draft Guidelines on Corporate Governance for Financial Institutions." February, mimeo.

Boughton, James M., and Alex Mourmouras. 2002. "Is Policy Ownership an Operational Concept?" *IMF Working Paper*, WP/02/72, April.

Cady, John. 2005. "Does SDDS Subscription Reduce Borrowing Costs for Emerging Market Economies?" *IMF Staff Papers* 52, no. 3 (December).

Calomiris, Charles W., and Robert E. Litan. 2000. "Financial Regulation in a Global Marketplace." *Brookings-Wharton Papers on Financial Services* 1:283–339.

Calomiris, Charles W., and Andrew Powell. 2000. "Can Emerging Market Bank Regulators Establish Credible Discipline? The Case of Argentina, 1992–1999." *NBER Working Paper*, No. 7715, May.

Caprio, Gerard, and Daniela Klingebiel. 2003. "Episodes of Systemic and Borderline Financial Crises." World Bank, January.

Capulong, Ma. Virginita, David Edwards, David Webb, and Juzhong Zhuang, eds. 2000. *Corporate Governance and Finance in East Asia: A Study of Indonesia, Republic of Korea, Malaysia, Philippines, and Thailand*. 2 vols. Manila: Asian Development Bank.

Case, William. 2005. "Malaysia: New Reforms, Old Continuities, Tense Ambiguities." *Journal of Development Studies* 41 (2): 284–309.

CESR (Committee of European Securities Regulators). 2005. "Concept Paper on Equivalence of Certain Third Country GAAP and on Description of Certain Third Countries' Mechanisms of Enforcement of Certain Financial Information: Feedback Statement." CESR/05/001, February.

Chang, Ha-Joon. 1999. "The Economic Theory of the Developmental State." In *The Developmental State*, edited by Meredith Woo-Cumings, 182–99. Ithaca: Cornell University Press.

Chayes, Abram, and Antonia Handler Chayes. 1993. "On Compliance." *International Organization* 47 (2): 175–205.

——. 1995. *The New Sovereignty: Compliance with International Regulatory Agreements*. Cambridge, MA: Harvard University Press.

Checkel, Jeffrey T. 1999. "Sanctions, Social Learning, and Institutions: Explaining State Compliance with the Norms of the European Human Rights Regime." *ARENA Working Paper*, WP 99/11, University of Oslo.

——. 2000. "Compliance and Conditionality." *ARENA Working Paper*, WP 00/18, University of Oslo.

——. 2001. "Why Comply? Social Learning and European Identity Change." *International Organization* 55 (3): 553–88.

Chey, Hyoung-kyu. 2006. *The Implementation of the Basle Accord in Japan, Korea, and Taiwan*. London: Unpublished Ph.D. thesis, London School of Economics and Political Science.

Cho, Yoon Je. 2001. "The Role of Poorly Phased Liberalization in Korea's Financial Crisis." In *Financial Liberalization: How Far, How Fast?*, edited by Gerard Caprio, Patrick Honohan, and Joseph E. Stiglitz, 159–87. Cambridge: Cambridge University Press.

Choi, Daeyong (Office of the Prime Minister). 2001. "A Radical Approach to Regulatory Reform in Korea." Paper presented to the Annual 2001 Conference of the American Society for Public Administration at Rutgers University, NJ, March.

Chopra, Ajai, Kenneth Kang, Meral Karasulu, Hong Liang, Henry Ma, and Anthony J. Richards. 2001. "From Crisis to Recovery in Korea: Strategy, Achievements, and Lessons." *IMF Working Paper*, WP/01/154, October.

Christofides, Charis, Christian Mulder, and Andrew Tiffin. 2003. "The Link between Adherence to International Standards of Good Practice, Foreign Exchange Spreads, and Ratings." *IMF Working Paper*, WP/03/74, April.

Claessens, Stijn, Simeon Djankov, Joseph Fan, and Larry Lang. 1999. "Expropriation of Minority Shareholders: Evidence from East Asia." *World Bank Working Paper*, February.

Claessens, Stijn, Simeon Djankov, and Larry Lang. 1999. "The Separation of Ownership and Control in East Asian Corporations." *World Bank Working Paper*, November.

Clark, Alastair. 2000. "International Standards and Codes." *Financial Stability Review*, December, 162–68.

CLSA Emerging Markets. 2001. *CG Watch: Corporate Governance in Emerging Markets*. CLSA Emerging Markets, April.

——. 2003. *CG Watch: Corporate Governance in Asia—Fakin' It: Board Games in Asia*. CLSA Emerging Markets, in collaboration with the Asian Corporate Governance Association, April.

——. 2005. *CG Watch 2005: Corporate Governance in Asia*. CLSA Emerging Markets, in collaboration with the Asian Corporate Governance Association, October.

Cole, David C., and Betty F. Slade. 1996. *Building a Modern Financial System: The Indonesian Experience*. Cambridge: Cambridge University Press.

——. 1998. "Why has Indonesia's Financial Crisis Been so Bad?" *Bulletin of Indonesian Economic Studies* 34 (2): 61–66.

Corsetti, Giancarlo, Paolo Pesenti, and Nouriel Roubini. 1998. "Paper Tigers? A Model of the Asian Crisis." Working paper, December.

Danaharta. 1998. *Annual Report 1998*. Kuala Lumpur: Danaharta.

——. 2003. *Operations Report, Six Months Ended 30 June 2003*. Kuala Lumpur: Danaharta.

Das, Udaibir S., Marc Quintyn, and Michael W. Taylor. 2002. "Financial Regulators Need Independence." *Finance and Development* 39, no. 4 (December).

Das, Udaibir S., Marc Quintyn, and Kina Chenard. 2004. "Does Regulatory Governance Matter for Financial System Stability?" *IMF Working Paper*, No. WP/04/89, May.

Demirgüç-Kunt, Asli, and Ross Levine. 1999. "Bank-Based and Market-Based Financial Systems: Cross-Country Comparisons." *World Bank Working Paper*, No. 2143, July.

DFAT (Department of Foreign Affairs and Trade, Australia). 1999. *Asia's Financial Markets: Capitalizing on Reform*. Canberra: East Asia Analytical Unit.

——. 2002. *Changing Corporate Asia: What Business Needs to Know*. 2 vols. Canberra: Economic Analytical Unit.

Diaz-Alejandro, Carlos F. 1985. "Good-bye Financial Repression, Hello Financial Crash." *Journal of Development Economics* 19 (1/2): 1–24.

Dobson, Wendy, and Gary C. Hufbauer. 2001. *World Capital Markets: Challenge to the G-10*. Washington, DC: Institute for International Economics.

Downs, George W., David M. Rocke, and Peter N. Barsoom. 1996. "Is the Good News about Compliance Good News about Cooperation?" *International Organization* 50 (3): 379–406.

Durnev, Art, and E. Han Kim. 2003. "To Steal or Not to Steal: Firm Attributes, Legal Environment, and Valuation." Unpublished paper, April.

Eichengreen, Barry. 2000. "The International Monetary Fund in the Wake of the Asian Crisis." In *The Asian Financial Crisis and the Architecture of Global Finance*, edited by Gregory Noble and John Ravenhill, 170–91. Melbourne: Cambridge University Press.

Eichengreen, Barry, and Michael Mussa. 1998. *Capital Account Liberalization*. Washington, DC: IMF.

EMEPG. 2001. *Seoul Report: Rebuilding the International Financial Architecture*. Seoul: EMEPG.

Enoch, Charles, Olivier Frécaut, and Arto Kovanen. 2003. "Indonesia's Banking Crisis: What Happened and What Did We Learn?" *Bulletin of Indonesian Economic Studies* 39, no. 1: 75–92.

Ernst & Young. 2006. *Global Nonperforming Loan Report*. Ernst & Young, Global Real Estate Center.

Evans, Peter. 1992. "The State as Problem and Solution: Predation, Embedded Autonomy, and Structural Change." In *The Politics of Economic Adjustment*, edited by Stephan Haggard and Robert R. Kaufman, 139–81. Princeton: Princeton University Press.

Finance Committee on Corporate Governance (Malaysia). 1999. *Report on Corporate Governance*. Kuala Lumpur: Securities Commission, February.

——. 2000. *Malaysian Code on Corporate Governance*. Kuala Lumpur: Securities Commission, March.

Finnemore, Martha, and Kathryn Sikkink. 1998. "International Norm Dynamics and Political Change." *International Organization* 52 (4): 887–917.

Fitch Ratings. 2001. "Asian Sovereign and Bank Rating Outlook." October.

——. 2002. "Korean Banks' Asset Quality—Fact or Fiction?" March.

——. 2003a. "Japanese Banks: Results for 2002/2003—Where's the Way Out?" 25 June.

——. 2003b. "Are Credit Ratings Correlated with Regulatory Capital?" 26 November.

——. 2003c. "Bank Rating Methodology." 20 March.

——. 2004. "Korean Banks in 2004: A Better Year Ahead?" 26 February.

——. 2005. "Indonesian Banks: Ownership Developments, 1H05 Results, and Outlook," October.

——. 2006. "Korean Banks—H106 Results." 19 September.

FSF (Financial Stability Forum). 2000a. *Issues Paper of the Task Force on Implementation of Standards*. Basle: 15 March.

——. 2000b. *Report of the Follow-Up Group on Incentives to Foster Implementation of Standards*. Basle: 31 August.

——. 2001. *Final Report of the Follow-Up Group on Incentives to Foster Implementation of Standards*. Basle: FSF, 21 August.

FSS (Financial Supervisory Service, Korea). 2000. *Financial Supervisory System in Korea*. Seoul: FSS, December.

——. 2001. *Financial Supervisory System in Korea*. Seoul: FSS, December.

——. 2002a. *Regulation on Supervision of Banking Business*. Seoul: FSS, amended 1 May 2002.

——. 2002b. *Financial Supervisory System in Korea*. Seoul: FSS, December.

——. 2003a. *Financial Supervision in Korea*. Seoul: FSS.

——. 2003b. *Financial Supervisory System in Korea*. Seoul: FSS, December.

——. 2003c. *Annual Report*. Seoul: FSS, December.

G7 Finance Ministers. 1999. "Strengthening the International Financial Architecture." *Report of G7 Finance Ministers to the Cologne Economic Summit*, June.

G22. 1998a. *Report of the Working Group on Transparency and Accountability*, October.
——. 1998b. *Report of the Working Group on Strengthening Financial Systems*, October.
——. 1998c. *Report of the Working Group on International Financial Crises*, October.
Garrett, Geoffrey. 1998. *Partisan Politics in the Global Economy*. Cambridge: Cambridge University Press.
Garrett, Geoffrey, and Barry Weingast. 1993. "Ideas, Interests, and Institutions: Constructing the European Community's Internal Market." In *Ideas and Foreign Policy: Beliefs, Institutions, and Political Change*, edited by Judith M. Goldstein and Robert O. Keohane, 173–206. Ithaca: Cornell University Press.
Gill, Stephen. 1995. "Globalisation, Market Civilisation, and Disciplinary Neoliberalism." *Millennium* 24 (3): 399–423.
Glennerster, Rachel, and Yongseok Shin. 2003. "Is Transparency Good for You, and Can the IMF Help?" *IMF Working Paper*, WP/03/132.
Goldstein, Morris. 2001. "IMF Structural Conditionality: How Much Is Too Much?" *Institute for International Economics Working Paper.*
Gomez, Edmund T., and Jomo K.S., eds. 1999. *Malaysia's Political Economy*. Cambridge: Cambridge University Press.
Gomez, Edmund T. 2004. "Paradoxes of Governance: Ownership and Control of Corporate Malaysia." In *The Governance of East Asian Corporations: Post Asian Financial Crisis*, edited by Ferdinand A. Gul and Judy S.L. Tsui, 117–37. Houndmills and New York: Palgrave Macmillan.
Graham, Edward M. 2003. *Reforming Korea's Industrial Conglomerates*. Washington, DC: Institute for International Economics.
Haas, Peter M. 1992. "Introduction: Epistemic Communities and International Policy Coordination." *International Organization* 46 (1): 1–35.
Haas, Peter M., ed. 1997. *Knowledge, Power, and International Policy Coordination*. Columbia: University of South Carolina Press.
Hadiz, Vedi R., and Richard Robison. 2005. "Neo-liberal Reforms and Illiberal Consolidations: The Indonesian Paradox." *Journal of Development Studies* 41 (2): 220–41.
Haggard, Stephan. 1990. *Pathways from the Periphery*. Ithaca: Cornell University Press.
——. 2000. *The Political Economy of the Asian Financial Crisis*. Washington, DC: Institute for International Economics.
Haggard, Stephan, and Robert R. Kaufman. 1992. "Institutions and Economic Adjustment." In *The Politics of Economic Adjustment*, edited by Stephan Haggard and Robert R. Kaufman, 3–40. Princeton: Princeton University Press.
——. 1995. *The Political Economy of Democratic Transitions*. Princeton: Princeton University Press.
Haggard, Stephan, and Sylvia Maxfield. 1996. "Financial Internationalization and the Developing World." *International Organization* 50 (1): 35–68.
Hahm, Joon-Ho, and Frederick S. Mishkin. 2000. "The Korean Financial Crisis: An Asymmetric Information Perspective." *Emerging Markets Review* 1 (1): 21–52.
Hall, Peter A., and David Soskice, eds. 2001. *Varieties of Capitalism: The Institutional Foundations of Comparative Advantage*. Oxford: Oxford University Press.
Hall, Rodney Bruce. 2003. "The Discursive Demolition of the Asian Development Model." *International Studies Quarterly*, 47: 71–99.
Hamilton-Hart, Natasha. 2000. "Indonesia: Reforming the Institutions of Financial Governance." In *The Asian Financial Crisis and the Architecture of Global Finance*, edited by Gregory Noble and John Ravenhill, 108–31. Melbourne: Cambridge University Press.
——. 2002. *Asian States, Asian Bankers: Central Banking in Southeast Asia*. Ithaca: Cornell University Press.

Hamilton-Hart, Natasha, and Jomo K.S. 2003. "Financial Capacity and Governance in Southeast Asia." In *Southeast Asian Paper Tigers? From Miracle to Debacle and Beyond,* edited by Jomo K.S., 220–79. Abingdon: RoutledgeCurzon.

Hansmann, Henry, and Reinier Kraakman. 2000. "The End of History for Corporate Law." *Yale Law and Economics Working Paper,* No. 235, January.

Hardy, Daniel C. 2006. "Regulatory Capture in Banking." *IMF Working Paper,* No. WP/06/34, January.

Havrylyshyn, Oleh, and John Odling-Smee. 2000. "Political Economy of Stalled Reforms." *Finance and Development* 37, no. 3.

Hay, Colin. 2004. "The Normalizing Role of Rationalist Assumptions in the Institutional Embedding of Neoliberalism." *Economy and Society* 33 (4): 500–527.

Hegarty, John, Frédéric Gielen, and Ana Cristina Hirata Barros. 2004. "Implementation of International Accounting and Auditing Standards: Lessons Learned from the World Bank's Accounting and Auditing ROSC Program." World Bank, September.

Henning, C. Randall. 1994. *Currencies and Politics in the U.S., Germany, and Japan.* Washington, DC: Institute for International Economics.

Hewison, Kevin. 2000. "Thailand's Capitalism Before and After the Economic Crisis." In *Politics and Markets in the Wake of the Asian Crisis,* edited by Richard Robison, Mark Beeson, Kanishka Jayasuriya, and Hyuk-Rae Kim, 192–211. London: Routledge.

——. 2005. "Neo-liberalism and Domestic Capital: The Political Outcomes of the Economic Crisis in Thailand." *Journal of Development Studies* 41 (2): 310–30.

Ho, Daniel E. 2002. "Compliance and International Soft Law: Why do Countries Implement the Basle Accord?" *Journal of International Economic Law* 5 (3): 647–88.

Holloway, Richard, ed. 2002. *Stealing from the People: 16 Studies on Corruption in Indonesia.* 4 vols. Jakarta: Aksara Foundation.

Honohan, Patrick, and Daniela Klingebiel. 2000. "Controlling Fiscal Costs of Banking Crises." World Bank.

Huang, Haizhou, and S. Kal Wajid. 2002. "Financial Stability in the World of Global Finance." *Finance and Development* 39, no. 1.

Hundt, David. 2005. "A Legitimate Paradox: Neo-liberal Reform and the Return of the State in Korea." *Journal of Development Studies* 41 (2): 242–60.

IEO (Independent Evaluation Office, IMF). 2002. *Evaluation of the Prolonged Use of IMF Resources.* Washington, DC: IMF, August.

——. 2003. *The IMF and Recent Capital Account Crises: Indonesia, Korea, Brazil.* Washington, DC: IMF, July.

——. 2005. *Report on the Evaluation of the IMF's Approach to Capital Account Liberalization.* Washington, DC: IMF, April.

——. 2006. *Report on the Evaluation of the Financial Sector Assessment Program.* Washington, DC: IMF, January.

IIF (Institute of International Finance). 2002. *Report of the Working Group on Crisis Prevention.* Washington, DC: IIF.

——. 2003. *Corporate Governance in Korea: An Investor Perspective.* Washington, DC: IIF Equity Advisory Group, Task Force Report, July.

——. 2006. *Investor Relations: An Approach to Effective Communication and Enhanced Transparency—Update of Key Borrowing Countries.* Washington, DC: IIF, September.

Ikenberry, G. John. 1992. "A World Economy Restored: Expert Consensus and the Anglo-American Postwar Settlement." *International Organization* 46 (1): 289–321.

IMF. 1999a. *External Evaluation of IMF Surveillance: Report by a Group of Independent Experts.* Washington, DC: IMF.

——. 1999b. *Malaysia: Selected Issues.* Washington, DC: IMF Staff Country Report No. 99/86, September, IMF.

IMF. 2001a. *Emerging Market Financing.* Washington, DC: IMF.
——. 2001b. *Korea: Selected Issues.* Washington, DC: IMF.
——. 2002. *Indonesia: Selected Issues.* Washington, DC: July, IMF.
——. 2003a. *Republic of Korea: Financial System Stability Assessment.* Washington, DC: IMF Country Report No. 03/81, March.
——. 2003b. *Japan: Financial System Stability Assessment and Supplementary Information.* Washington, DC: IMF Country Report No. 03/287, September.
——. 2003c. *International Standards: Background Paper on Strengthening Surveillance, Domestic Institutions, and International Markets.* Washington, DC: IMF, 5 March.
——. 2004a. *Singapore: Financial System Stability Assessment.* Washington, DC: IMF Country Report No. 04/104, April.
——. 2004b. *Indonesia: Selected Issues.* Washington, DC: IMF Country Report No. 04/189, July.
——. 2004c. *Indonesia: 2004 Article IV Consultation and Post-Program Monitoring Discussions—Staff Report; Staff Statement; and Public Information Notice on the Executive Board Discussion.* Washington, DC: IMF Country Report No. 04/188, June.
——. 2004d. *Financial Sector Regulation: Issues and Gaps—Background Paper.* Washington, DC: Prepared by Staff of the Monetary and Financial Systems Department, August 17.
——. 2006. *Indonesia: Fourth Post-Program Monitoring Discussions.* Washington, DC: IMF Country Report No. 06/85, February.
Ito, Takatoshi, and Kimie Harada. 2003. "Market Evaluations of Banking Fragility in Japan: Japan Premium, Stock Prices, and Credit Derivatives." *NBER Working Paper,* No. 9589, March.
Ivanova, Anna, Wolfgang Mayer, Alex Mourmouras, and George Anayiotos. 2003. "What Determines the Implementation of IMF-Supported Programs?" *IMF Working Paper,* WP/03/8, January.
Jackson, Patricia, and David Lodge. 2000. "Fair Value Accounting, Capital Standards, Expected Loss Provisioning, and Financial Stability." *Financial Stability Review,* June.
Jang, Hasung. 2001. "The Case of Korea." Paper presented to 3rd Asian Roundtable on Corporate Governance, Singapore, 4–6 April 2001.
Jang, Hasung, and Joongi Kim. 2001. "Korea Country Paper: The Role of Boards and Stakeholders in Corporate Governance." Paper presented to 3rd Asian Roundtable on Corporate Governance, Singapore, 4–6 April 2001.
Jayasuriya, Kanishka. 2000. "Authoritarian Liberalism, Governance and the Emergence of the Regulatory State in Post-Crisis East Asia." In *Politics and Markets in the Wake of the Asian Crisis,* edited by Richard Robison, Mark Beeson, Kanishka Jayasuriya, and Hyuk-Rae Kim, 315–30. London: Routledge.
——. 2005. "Beyond Institutional Fetishism: From the Developmental to the Regulatory State." *New Political Economy* 10 (3): 381–87.
Jensen, Michael C., and William H. Meckling. 1976. "Theory of the Firm: Managerial Behavior, Agency Costs, and Ownership Structure." *Journal of Financial Economics* 3 (4): 305–60.
Jo, Sung-Wook. 2001. "Corporate Governance and Firm Profitability: Evidence from Korea before the Economic Crisis." December, mimeo.
Johnson, Chalmers. 1982. *MITI and the Japanese Miracle.* Stanford: Stanford University Press.
Johnson, Simon, Peter Boone, Alasdair Breach, and Eric Friedman. 1999. "Corporate Governance in the Asian Financial Crisis." Unpublished paper, November.
Jordan, Cally, and Giovanni Majnone. 2002. "Financial Regulatory Harmonization and the Globalization of Finance." *World Bank Policy Research Working Paper,* No. 2919, October.

Jomo K.S., and Natasha Hamilton-Hart. 2001. "Financial Regulation, Crisis, and Policy Response." In *Malaysian Eclipse: Economic Crisis and Recovery*, edited by Jomo K.S., 67–89. London: Zed Books.

Jun, I., and Gong, B. 1995. "Corporate Governance in Korea." Korea Economic Research Institute, Seoul.

Kahler, Miles. 1990. "Orthodoxy and Its Alternatives: Explaining Approaches to Stabilization and Adjustment." In *Economic Crisis and Policy Choice*, edited by Joan Nelson, 33–61. Princeton: Princeton University Press.

——. 1992. "External Influence, Conditionality, and the Politics of Adjustment." In *The Politics of Economic Adjustment*, edited by Stephan Haggard and Robert R. Kaufman, 89–138. Princeton: Princeton University Press.

——. 1993. "Bargaining with the IMF: Two-Level Strategies and Developing Countries." In *Double-Edged Diplomacy*, edited by Peter B. Evans, Harold K. Jacobson, and Robert D. Putnam, 363–94. Berkeley: University of California Press.

——. 2000. "Conclusion: The Causes and Consequences of Legalization." *International Organization* 54 (3): 661–84.

KAI-KASB (Korea Accounting Institute-Korea Accounting Standards Board). 2000. "Preface to the Statements of Korea Accounting Standards." 25 August.

——. 2001. *KAI-KASB Report 1999–2000*. Seoul: KAI-KASB.

Kaminsky, Graciela. 1999. "Currency and Banking Crises: The Early Warnings of Distress." *IMF Working Paper*, WP/99/178, December.

Kapstein, Ethan B. 1994. *Governing the Global Economy*. Cambridge: Harvard University Press.

KCCG (Korean Committee on Corporate Governance). 1999. "Code of Best Practice for Corporate Governance." Seoul: KCCG, September.

Keck, Margaret E., and Kathryn Sikkink. 1998. *Activists Beyond Borders: Advocacy Networks in International Politics*. Ithaca: Cornell University Press.

Keefer, Philip. 2001. "When Do Special Interests Run Rampant? Disentangling the Role of Elections, Incomplete Information, and Checks and Balances in Banking Crises." Development Research Group, World Bank, January.

Keefer, Philip, and David Stasavage. 2003. "The Limits of Delegation, Veto Players, Central Bank Independence, and the Credibility of Monetary Policy." *American Political Science Review* 93 (3): 407–23.

Keohane, Robert O. 1984. *After Hegemony*. Princeton: Princeton University Press.

Khoo, Boo Teik. 2001. "The State and the Market in Malaysian Political Economy." In *The Political Economy of South-East Asia: Conflicts, Crises, and Change*, edited by Garry Rodan, Kevin Hewison, and Richard Robison, 178–205. Melbourne: Oxford University Press.

Killick, Tony. 1996. "Principals, Agents, and the Limitations on BWI Conditionality." *World Economy* 19 (2): 211–29.

Kim, Il-Sup. 2000. "Financial Crisis and its Impact on the Accounting System in Korea." Chairman, Korea Accounting Standards Board, October 20, 2000.

Kim, Kyeong-won, ed. 2001. *Three Years after the IMF Bailout: A Review of the Korean Economy's Transformation since 1998*. Seoul: Samsung Economic Research Institute.

KLSE (Kuala Lumpur Stock Exchange). 1998. *Corporate Governance: 1998 Survey of Institutional Groups*. Kuala Lumpur: KLSE/PWC.

——. 2005. *Listing Requirements for Main Board and Second Board*. Kuala Lumpur: KLSE, January.

Koh, Phillip T. N., and Lum Chee Soon. 2004. "Corporate Governance of Banks in Asia: Country Paper Malaysia." ADBI, June.

Korea Accounting Standards Board. 2001. "Standard for the Disclosure of Transactions between Related Parties." *Discussion Paper*, 12, February.

Krugman, Paul. 1994. "The Myth of Asia's Miracle." *Foreign Affairs* 73: 2–78.

——. 1998. "What Happened to Asia?" Unpublished paper. MIT, January.

KSE (Korea Stock Exchange). 2003. *Listing Regulations.* Seoul: KSE, updated 23 December 2003.

Kydland, Finn, and Edward S. Prescott. 1977. "Rules Rather than Discretion: The Inconsistency of Optimal Plans." *Journal of Political Economy* 85 (3): 473–92.

Lane, Timothy, Atish Ghosh, Javier Hamann, Steven Phillips, Marianne Schulze-Ghattas, and Tsidi Tsikata. 1999. "IMF-Supported Programs in Indonesia, Korea, and Thailand: A Preliminary Assessment." *IMF Occasional Paper,* no. 178, June.

La Porta, Rafael, Florencio Lopez-de-Silanes, and Andrei Shleifer. 1998a. "Corporate Ownership Around the World." *Harvard Institute of Economic Research Paper,* no. 1840, August.

——. 1998b. "Law and Finance." *Journal of Political Economy* 106 (6): 1113–55.

La Porta, Rafael, Florencio Lopez-de-Silanes, Andrei Shleifer, and Robert Vishny. 1999. "The Quality of Government." *Journal of Law and Economic Organization* 15 (1): 222–79.

Lee, Keun, Byung-Kook Kim, Chung H. Lee, and Jaeyeol Yee. 2005. "Visible Success and Invisible Failure in Post-Crisis Reform in the Republic of Korea: Interplay of Global Standards, Agents, and Local Specificity." *World Bank Policy Research Working Paper,* 3651, June.

Lindblom, Charles E. 1977. *Politics and Markets: The World's Political and Economic Systems.* New York: Basic Books.

Lindgren, Carl-Johan, Tomás J. T. Baliño, Charles Enoch, Anne-Marie Gulde, Marc Quintyn, and Leslie Teo. 1999. "Financial Sector Crisis and Restructuring: Lessons from Asia." *IMF Occasional Paper,* 188.

MacIntyre, Andrew. 1993. "The Politics of Finance in Indonesia: Command, Confusion, and Competition." In *The Politics of Finance in Developing Countries,* edited by Stephan Haggard, Chung H. Lee, and Sylvia Maxfield, 123–64. Ithaca: Cornell University Press.

——. 2003. *The Power of Institutions: Political Architecture and Governance.* Ithaca: Cornell University Press.

Majone, Giandomenico. 2005. "Strategy and Structure: The Political Economy of Agency Independence and Accountability." In OECD, Working Party on Regulatory Management and Reform, *Designing Independent and Accountable Regulatory Authorities for High Quality Regulation,* 126–55. Paris: OECD, proceedings of an Expert Meeting in London, United Kingdom, 10–11 January 2005.

Maskin, Eric, and Jean Tirole. 1999. "Unforeseen Contingencies and Incomplete Contracts." *Review of Economic Studies* 66 (1): 83–114.

Mattli, Walter, and Tim Büthe. 2003. "Setting International Standards: Technological Rationality or Primacy of Power?" *World Politics* 56 (1): 1–42.

Maxfield, Sylvia. 1998. "Understanding the Political Implications of Financial Internationalization in Emerging Market Countries." *World Development* 26 (7): 1201–19.

Mayer, Wolfgang, and Alex Mourmouras. 2002. "Vested Interests in a Positive Theory of IFI Conditionality." *IMF Working Paper,* WP/02/73.

McKinnon, Ronald I. 1973. *Money and Capital in Economic Development.* Washington, DC: Brookings Institution.

——. 1993. *The Order of Economic Liberalization: Financial Control in the Transition to a Market Economy.* 2nd ed. Baltimore: Johns Hopkins University Press.

Meesook, Kanitta, Il Houng Lee, Olin Liu, Yougesh Khatri, Natalia Tamirisa, Michael Moore, and Mark H. Krysl. 2001. *Malaysia: From Crisis to Recovery.* Washington, DC: IMF, Occasional Paper No. 207.

Ministry of Finance (Malaysia). 1999. *Economic Report 1998–1999.* Kuala Lumpur: MOF.

Mishkin, Frederic S. 2001. "Financial Policies and the Prevention of Financial Crises in Emerging Market Countries." *NBER Working Paper,* No. 8087, January.

Mitchell, Ronald B. 1998. "Sources of Transparency: Information Systems in International Regimes." *International Studies Quarterly* 42: 109–30.

Moody's Investor Services. 1999. *Rating Methodology: Bank Credit Risk—An Analytical Framework for Banks in Developed Markets.* April.

——. 2003a. *Bank Risk Monitor, March 2003.* Issue 3.

——. 2003b. *Moody's Rating Symbols and Definitions.* August.

——. 2004. *Bank Risk Monitor, February 2004.* Issue 6.

——. 2005. *Bank Credit Research: Monthly Ratings List.* February.

Naim, Moises. 1999. "Fads and Fashion in Economic Reforms: Washington Consensus or Washington Confusion?" Paper prepared for the IMF Conference on Second Generation Reforms, Washington, DC, October 26.

Nam, Sang-Woo, and Il Chong Nam. 2004. *Corporate Governance in Asia: Recent Evidence from Indonesia, Republic of Korea, Malaysia, and Thailand.* Tokyo: Asian Development Bank Institute, October.

Nathan, Rabindra S. 2001. "Malaysia Country Paper." Paper prepared for 3rd OECD/World Bank Asian Roundtable on Corporate Governance, 26–27 April, Singapore.

Nathan, Rabindra S., Chiew Sow Lin, and Soo Wai Fong. 2000. "Country Paper for Malaysia." Paper prepared for 2nd ADB/OECD/World Bank Asian Roundtable on Corporate Governance, 31 May–2 June, Hong Kong.

Nikomborirak, Deunden. 2000. "Building Better Corporate Governance: The Challenge Facing Thai Companies." Mimeo, TDRI.

——. 2004. "Problems of Corporate Governance Reform in Thailand." In *The Governance of East Asian Corporations: Post Asian Financial Crisis,* edited by Ferdinand A. Gul and Judy S. L. Tsui, 216–35. Houndmills and New York: Palgrave Macmillan.

Nobes, Christopher, ed. 2001. *GAAP 2001: A Survey of National Accounting Standards Benchmarked against International Accounting Standards.* Anderson, BDO, Deloitte Touche Tohmatsu, Ernst & Young, Grant Thornton, KPMG, PricewaterhouseCoopers.

Noland, Marcus. 2000a. "Japan and the International Economic Institutions." Paper presented to the Fifth Biennial Conference of the Centre for Japanese Economic Studies, Macquarie University, 6–7 July.

——. 2000b. *Avoiding the Apocalypse: The Future of the Two Koreas.* Washington DC: Institute for International Economics.

North, Douglass. 1990. *Institutions, Institutional Change, and Economic Performance.* New York: Cambridge University Press.

Oatley, Thomas, and R. Nabors. 1998. "Redistributive Cooperation, Market Failure, Wealth Transfers, and the Basle Accord." *International Organization* 52 (1): 35–54.

OECD. 1999a. *OECD Principles of Corporate Governance.* Paris: OECD, Ad Hoc Task Force on Corporate Governance, SG/CG(99)5.

——. 1999b. *Economic Surveys: Korea 1998–1999.* Paris: OECD.

——. 2003. *White Paper on Corporate Governance in East Asia.* Paris: OECD, July.

——. 2004. *OECD Principles of Corporate Governance.* Paris: OECD.

Olson, Mancur. 2000. *Power and Prosperity.* New York: Basic Books.

Pangestu, Mari, and Manggi Habir. 2002. "The Boom, Bust, and Restructuring of Indonesian Banks." *IMF Working Paper,* WP/02/66, April.

Park, Jae-Ha. 2004. "Corporate Governance of Banks in Republic of Korea." Asian Development Bank Institute conference, June 10–11.

Pasuk, Phongpaichit, and Chris Baker. 2003. "Pluto-Populism in Thailand: Business Remaking Politics." Unpublished paper.

Peek, Joe, and Eric S. Rosengren. 2000. "Determinants of the Japan Premium: Actions Speak Louder than Words." *Journal of International Economics* 53: 283–305.

Pempel, T. J. 1999. "The Developmental Regime in a Changing World Economy." In *The Developmental State*, edited by Meredith Woo-Cumings, 137–81. Ithaca: Cornell University Press.

Pike, Christopher J., and James B. Thomson. 1992. "FDICIA's Prompt Corrective Action Provisions." *Economic Commentary*, Federal Reserve Bank of Cleveland, September, 1–6.

Pirie, Iain. 2005. "The New Korean State." *New Political Economy* 10 (March): 25–42.

Pistor, Katharina. 2000a. "The Standardization of Law and Its Effect on Developing Economies." *G-24 Discussion Paper*, No. 4, June.

——. 2000b. "Patterns of Legal Change: Shareholder and Creditor Rights in Transition Economies." *EBRD Working Paper*, No. 49.

Podpiera, Richard. 2004. "Does Compliance with Basel Core Principles Bring Any Measurable Benefits?" *IMF Working Paper*, PW/04/204, November.

Polak, J. 1991. "The Changing Nature of the IMF Conditionality." *Princeton Essays in International Finance*, No. 184.

Polsiri, Piruna, and Yupana Wiwattanakantang. 2004a. "Business Groups in Thailand: Before and After the East Asian Financial Crisis." *Center for Economic Institutions Working Paper*, No. 2004–13, Hitotsubashi University, April.

——. 2004b. "Corporate Governance of Banks in Thailand." Asian Development Bank Institute, June 2004.

Porter, Michael E. 1992. "Capital Choices: Changing the Way America Invests in Industry." *Journal of Applied Corporate Finance* 5 (Summer): 4–16.

PricewaterhouseCoopers. 2001. *Indonesian GAAP: Similarities and Differences among IAS, Indonesian GAAP, U.S. GAAP and UK GAAP*. PwC, August.

——. 2002. "Malaysian Corporate Governance Survey 2002: Executive Summary." In conjunction with the Kuala Lumpur Stock Exchange.

Quintyn, Marc, Silvia Ramirez, and Michael W. Taylor. 2007. "The Fear of Freedom: Politicians and the Independence and Accountability of Financial Sector Supervisors." *IMF Working Paper*, No. WP/07/25, February.

Rajan, Raghuram G., and Luigi Zingales. 1998. "Which Capitalism? Lessons from the East Asian Crisis." *Journal of Applied Corporate Finance* 11 (3): 40–48.

Raustiala, Kal, and David G. Victor. 1998. "Conclusions." In *The Implementation and Effectiveness of International Environmental Commitments*, edited by David G. Victor, Kal Raustiala, and Eugene B. Skolnikoff, 659–707. Cambridge: MIT Press.

Raustiala, Kal. 2000. "Compliance & Effectiveness in International Regulatory Cooperation." *Case Western Reserve Journal of International Law* 32: 387–440.

Raustiala, Kal, and Anne-Marie Slaughter. 2002. "International Law, International Relations, and Compliance." In *The Handbook of International Relations*, edited by Walter Carlsnaes, Thomas Risse, and Beth A. Simmons, 538–58. Thousand Oaks, CA: Sage.

Risse, Thomas, Stephen C. Ropp, and Kathryn Sikkink, eds. 1999. *The Power of Human Rights: International Norms and Domestic Change*. Cambridge: Cambridge University Press.

Risse, Thomas. 2000. "'Let's Argue!': Communicative Action in World Politics." *International Organization* 54 (1): 1–39.

Robison, Richard. 2005. "How to Build Market Societies: The Paradoxes of Neoliberal Revolution." *New Political Economy* 10 (2): 247–57.

Robison, Richard, and Kevin Hewison. 2005. "Introduction: East Asia and the Trials of Neo-liberalism." *Journal of Development Studies* 41 (2): 183–96.

Robison, Richard, Gary Rodan, and Kevin Hewison. 2002. "Transplanting the Regulatory State in Southeast Asia: A Pathology of Rejection." *City University of Hong Kong Working Paper Series*, no. 33, September.

Robison, Richard, and Vedi R. Hadiz. 2004. *Reorganising Power in Indonesia: The Politics of Oligarchy in an Age of Markets.* Abingdon/New York: RoutledgeCurzon.

Rodrik, Dani. 1989. "Promises, Promises: Credible Policy Reform via Signalling." *Economic Journal* 99 (September): 756–72.

——. 2000. "Institutions for High-Quality Growth: What They Are and How to Acquire Them." *NBER Working Paper*, No. 7540, February.

Rojas-Suarez, Liliana. 2001a. "Rating Banks in Emerging Markets: What Credit Rating Agencies Should Learn From Financial Indicators." *Institute for International Economics Working Paper*, 01–6.

——. 2001b. "Can International Capital Standards Strengthen Banks in Emerging Markets?" *Institute for International Economics Working Paper*, 01–10.

Rosenbluth, Frances, and Ross Schaap. 2002. "The Domestic Politics of Banking Regulation." Working paper, Yale/UCLA, February.

Rosser, Andrew. 2002. *The Politics of Economic Liberalisation in Indonesia: State, Market, and Power.* Richmond: Curzon.

Ruggie, John G. 1998. "What Makes the World Hang Together? Neo-Utilitarianism and the Social Constructivist Challenge." *International Organization* 52 (4): 855–85.

Sally, Razeen. 1998. *Classical Liberalism and International Economic Order.* London: Routledge.

Schamis, Hector E. 2002. *Re-Forming the State: The Politics of Privatization in Latin America and Europe.* Michigan: University of Michigan Press.

Schneider, Benu, and Sacha Silva. 2002. "Conference Report on International Standards and Codes: The Developing Country Perspective." Conference held at the Commonwealth Secretariat, 21 June. Overseas Development Institute, London.

Skocpol, Theda. 1985. "Bringing the State Back In: Strategies of Analysis in Current Research." In *Bringing the State Back In*, edited by Peter B. Evans, Dietrich Rueschemeyer, and Theda Skocpol, 3–43. Cambridge: Cambridge University Press.

Searle, Peter. 1999. *The Riddle of Malaysian Capitalism.* St. Leonard's: Allen and Unwin.

SEC Thailand (Securities and Exchange Commission). 2002. "Agenda for Enhancing Corporate Governance of Thai Listed Companies." Mimeo, 7 March.

SET (Stock Exchange of Thailand). 1998. "Policy Statement: The SET Code of Best Practice for Directors of Listed Companies." Bangkok: SET Listing Department, Bor. Jor./.Ror.26–00, 19 January.

——. 1999. "Best Practice Guidelines for Audit Committee." Bangkok: SET Listing Department, Bor.Jor./Ror.25–00, June 23.

Shaw, Edward S. 1973. *Financing Deepening in Economic Development.* New York: Oxford University Press.

Shelton, Dinah, ed. 2003. *Commitment and Compliance: The Role of Non-Binding Norms in the International Legal System.* New York: Oxford University Press.

Shin, Kwang-Shik. 2001. "Competition Policy and Corporate Restructuring in Korea." *KDI Working Paper*, 2001–4, June.

Shirai, Sayuri. 2001a. "Searching for New Regulatory Frameworks for the Intermediate Financial Market Structure in Post-Crisis Asia." *ADB Institute Research Paper*, 24, September.

——. 2001b. "Overview of Financial Structures in Asia: Cases of the Republic of Korea, Malaysia, Thailand, and Indonesia." *ADB Institute Research Paper*, 25, September.

Shleifer, Andrei, and Robert W. Vishny. 1997. "A Survey of Corporate Governance." *Journal of Finance*, 52: 737–83.

Shleifer, Andrei, and Daniel Wolfenson. 2000. "Investor Protection and Equity Markets." *NBER Working Paper*, No. 7974, October.

Siamwalla, Ammar. 1998. "Can a Developing Democracy Manage Its Macroeconomy? The Case of Thailand." Mimeo, Thailand Development Research Institute, revised 21 May.

Simmons, Beth A. 2000a. "International Law and State Behaviour: Commitment and Compliance in International Monetary Affairs." *American Political Science Review* 94 (4): 819–35.

——. 2000b. "The Legalization of International Monetary Affairs." *International Organization* 54 (3): 573–602.

——. 2000c. "Money and the Law: Why Comply with the Public International Law of Money?" *Yale Journal of International Law* 25 (2): 323–62.

——. 2001. "The International Politics of Harmonization: The Case of Capital Market Regulation." *International Organization* 55 (3): 589–620.

Simmons, Beth A., and Zachary Elkins. 2004. "The Globalization of Liberalization: Policy Diffusion in the International Political Economy." *American Political Science Review* 98 (1): 171–89.

Soederberg, Susanne. 2003. "The Promotion of 'Anglo-American' Corporate Governance in the South: Who Benefits from the New International Standard?" *Third World Quarterly* 24 (1): 7–27.

Soederberg, Susanne, Georg Menz, and Philip G. Cerny, eds. 2005. *Internalizing Globalization: The Rise of Neoliberalism and the Decline of National Varieties of Capitalism.* London: Palgrave Macmillan.

Song, Inwon. 2002. "Collateral in Loan Classification and Provisioning." *IMF Working Paper*, WP/02/122, July.

Stallings, B. 1992. "International Influence on Economic Policy: Debt, Stabilization, and Structural Reform." In *The Politics of Economic Adjustment: International Constraints, Distributive Conflicts, and the State*, edited by Stephan Haggard and Robert R. Kaufman, 41–88. Princeton: Princeton University Press.

Standard & Poor's. 2002. "Corporate Governance Scores: Criteria, Methodology, and Definitions."

——. 2004a. "Corporate Governance Disclosures in Thailand: A Study of SET50 Companies." Joint report by S&P and Corporate Governance and Financial Reporting Centre, NUS Business School, Singapore.

——. 2004b. "Corporate Governance Disclosures in Malaysia." Joint report by S&P and Corporate Governance and Financial Reporting Centre, NUS Business School, Singapore.

——. 2004c. "Corporate Governance Disclosures in Singapore." Joint report by S&P and Corporate Governance and Financial Reporting Centre, NUS Business School, Singapore.

——. 2004d. "Country Governance Study: Korea." March.

Stigler, George. 1971. "The Economic Theory of Regulation." *Bell Journal of Economics* 2: 3–21.

Stone, R. W. 2004. "The Political Economy of IMF Lending in Africa." *American Political Science Review* 98 (4): 577–92.

Sundararajan, V. 2001. "Financial System Standards and Financial Stability." *IMF Working Paper*, WP/01/62, May.

Thatcher, Mark, and Alex Stone Sweet. 2002. "Theory and Practice of Delegation to Non-Majoritarian Institutions." *West European Politics* 25 (1): 1–22.

Thurbon, Elizabeth. 2003. "Ideational Inconsistency and Institutional Incapacity: Why Financial Liberalisation in South Korea Went Horribly Wrong." *New Political Economy* 8 (3): 341–61.

Tietmeyer Report. 1999. *International Cooperation and Coordination in the Area of Financial Market Supervision and Surveillance.* Basle, 1999.

Underdal, Arild. 1998. "Explaining Compliance and Defection: Three Models." *European Journal of International Relations* 4 (1): 5–30.

Underhill, Geoffrey R. D., and Xiaoke Zhang. 2005. "The Changing State-Market Condominium in East Asia: Rethinking the Political Underpinnings of Development." *New Political Economy* 10 (1): 3–26.

U.S. Council of Economic Advisors. 1999. *Annual Report, 1999.* Washington, DC: U.S. Government Printing Office.

U.S. GAO (General Accounting Office). 2003. *International Financial Crises: Challenges Remain in IMF's Ability to Anticipate, Prevent, and Resolve Financial Crises.* Report to the Chairman, Committee on Financial Services, and to the Vice Chairman, Joint Economic Committee, House of Representatives. Washington, DC: GAO-03–734, 16 June.

U.S. ITA (International Trade Administration). 2003. "Issue and Decision Memorandum for the Final Determination in the Countervailing Duty Investigation of Dynamic Random Access Memory Semiconductors from the Republic of Korea." C580–851, 16 June.

U.S. OCC (Comptroller of the Currency), Administrator of National Banks. 2001. *An Examiner's Guide to Problem Bank Identification, Rehabilitation, and Resolution.* Washington, DC: OCC, January.

——. 2003. "Bank Accounting Advisory Series." Washington, DC, September.

U.S. Treasury. 2000. *Report on IMF Reforms.* Washington, DC: U.S. Treasury.

van de Walle, Nicholas. 2001. *African Economies and the Politics of Permanent Crisis, 1979–1999.* Cambridge: Cambridge University Press.

Wade, Robert. 1990. *Governing the Market.* Princeton: Princeton University Press.

Wade, Robert, and Frank Veneroso. 1998. "The Asian Crisis: The High Debt Model Versus the Wall Street—Treasury—IMF Complex." *New Left Review,* 288, March/April: 3–23.

Walter, Andrew. 2006. "The Discretionary Regulatory State: Japan's New Financial Regulatory System." *Pacific Review* 19 (4): 405–28.

Weiss, Edith Brown, and Harold K. Jacobson, eds. 1998. *Engaging Countries: Strengthening Compliance with International Accords.* Cambridge: MIT Press.

Weiss, Linda, and John M. Hobson. 2000. "State Power and Economic Strength Revisited: What's So Special about the Asian Crisis?" In *Politics and Markets in the Wake of the Asian Crisis,* edited by Richard Robison, Mark Beeson, Kanishka Jayasuriya, and Hyuk-Rae Kim, 53–74. London: Routledge.

Weiss, Linda. 2003. "Guiding Globalisation in East Asia: New Roles for Old Developmental States." In *States in the Global Economy: Bringing Domestic Institutions Back In,* edited by Linda Weiss, 245–70. Cambridge: Cambridge University Press.

Weyland, Kurt. 2002. *Politics of Market Reform in Fragile Democracies: Argentina, Brazil, Peru, and Venezuela.* Princeton: Princeton University Press.

Williamson, John. 1990. "What Washington Means by Policy Reform." In *Latin American Adjustment: How Much Has Happened?* edited by John Williamson, 7–38. Washington, DC: Institute for International Economics.

——. 1994. "In Search of a Manual for Technopols." In *The Political Economy of Policy Reform,* edited by J. Williamson, 11–28. Washington, DC: Institute for International Economics.

Williamson, Oliver E. 1999. *The Mechanisms of Governance.* Oxford: Oxford University Press.

Woo-Cumings, Meredith [Woo, Jung-en]. 1991. *Race to the Swift: State and Finance in Korean Industrialization.* New York: Columbia University Press.

——, ed. 1999a. *The Developmental State.* Ithaca: Cornell University Press.

Woo-Cumings, Meredith [Woo, Jung-en]. 1999b. "Introduction: Chalmers Johnson and the Politics of Nationalism and Development." In *The Developmental State*, edited by Meredith Woo-Cumings, 1–31. Ithaca: Cornell University Press, 1999.

——. 2003. "Diverse Paths towards 'The Right Institutions': Law, the State, and Economic Reform in Asia." In *States in the Global Economy: Bringing Domestic Institutions Back In*, edited by Linda Weiss, 200–224. Cambridge: Cambridge University Press.

Woo Yun Kang Jeong & Han. 2004. *Corporate Governance in Korea*. Seoul: Woo Yun Kang Jeong & Han.

World Bank. 1993. *The East Asian Miracle: Economic Growth and Public Policy*. Washington, DC: World Bank.

——. 1999. *Malaysia: Corporate Governance Assessment and ROSC Module*. Washington, DC: World Bank.

——. 2001. *World Development Report 2002: Building Institutions for Markets*. Washington, DC: World Bank/Oxford University Press.

——. 2003. *Thailand Economic Monitor*. Bangkok: World Bank, May.

——. 2004a. *East Asia Update: Strong Fundamentals to the Fore*. Washington, DC: Regional Overview, April.

——. 2004b. "Report on the Observance of Standards and Codes: Republic of Korea." *Accounting and Auditing*, Washington, DC: World Bank, 30 June.

——. 2004c. *Indonesia Financial Sector Monthly Report*, No. 42. Washington, DC: World Bank, February.

——. 2004d. *Report on the Observance of Standards and Codes (ROSC): Corporate Governance Country Assessment, Republic of Indonesia*. Washington, DC: World Bank, August.

——. 2005a. *Template for Country Assessment of Corporate Governance*. Washington, DC: World Bank, Revision 4.1, March.

——. 2005b. *Report on the Observance of Standards and Codes (ROSC): Corporate Governance Country Assessment, Thailand*. Washington, DC: World Bank, June.

——. 2005c. *Report on the Observance of Standards and Codes (ROSC): Corporate Governance Country Assessment, Malaysia*. Washington, DC: World Bank, June.

World Bank Operations Evaluation Department. 1999. "Indonesia Country Assistance Note." Report No. 19100, Washington, DC: World Bank, 4 February.

World Economic Forum. 2003. *The Global Competitiveness Report 2002–2003*, ed. Peter K. Cornelius. New York: Oxford University Press.

Yoon, Young-Kwan. 2000. "Globalization and Institutional Reform: The Case of the Korean Economic Crisis in the Late 1990s." Paper prepared for 18th World Congress of the International Political Science Association, Quebec City, August 1–5, 2000.

Yoshitomi, Masuru, and ADBI Staff. 2003. *Post-Crisis Development Paradigms in Asia*. Tokyo: Asian Development Bank Institute.

Young, Oran R. 1979. *Compliance and Public Authority: A Theory with International Applications*. Baltimore: Johns Hopkins University Press.

——. 1994. *International Governance: Protecting the Environment in a Stateless Society*. Ithaca: Cornell University Press.

Young, Oran R., and Marc Levy. 1999. "The Effectiveness of International Environmental Regimes." In *The Effectiveness of International Environmental Regimes: Causal Connections and Behavioral Mechanisms*, edited by Young, 1–32. Cambridge: MIT Press.

Index